THEIR BROTHERS' KEEPERS

Their Brothers' Keepers

By PHILIP FRIEDMAN

Foreword by Rev. John A. O'Brien, S.J., Ph.D.

HOLOCAUST LIBRARY

NEW YORK

Copyright © 1978, by Ada Friedman
First published in 1957 by Crown Publishers, Inc.
Library of Congress Catalog Card No. 57-8773
Publication of this book was made possible by a grant
from Benjamin and Stefa Wald.

Cover design by Eric Gluckman
Printed in the United States of America
by Waldon Press, Inc., New York

TABLE OF CONTENTS

ACKNOWLEDGMENT

The author wishes to express his gratitude to the many friends who were helpful to him in his research and in the preparation of this book. I wish to express my gratitude to the Anti-Defamation League of B'nai B'rith, whose invaluable encouragement and guidance from the very inception of this book and whose faith in its meaning were a constant inspiration. I am particularly indebted to Dr. Joseph L. Lichten, to Mr. Louis Falstein, and to my wife, Dr. Ada Friedman, for their assistance and devoted cooperation while I was working on this volume. My sincere thanks go also to Mr. Oscar Cohen, Mr. Oscar Tarcov; and to Mr. Herbert Michelman of Crown Publishers for their efforts and competent advice.

P. F.

FOREWORD

The story of Hitler's efforts to solve the "Jewish problem" in Germany and in all the countries which fell under the yoke of the Nazis, by the simple expedient of exterminating them, has often been told. It is a ghastly and shocking tale of brutality, torture, and murder, which in deliberate, systematic savagery on a grand scale is probably unsurpassed in all the annals of human history. From such a rehearsal readers instinctively recoil, for it does not make pleasant reading.

Alongside of this depressing chronicle there is another which has been related only in fragments, and too seldom: it is the story of the compassion, sympathy, bravery, and heroism of the thousands of men and women who shielded and befriended the victims at the risk of imprisonment, torture, and death. This is a story which needs to be told if we are to get a true picture of the moral caliber of the people whose homelands were used for the liquidation of the Jewish population. It is needed to balance the degradation and baseness of the Jew-baiters with the gallantry and heroism of the Jew-aiders.

This is the report which Philip Friedman presents. It is timely, reassuring, and inspiring. It shows that nineteen centuries of Christian teaching were not without results. So deeply had the fundamental law of the Christian religion, the duty to love one's neighbor, been woven into the warp and woof of the Christian conscience that thousands in all lands defied the sternest edicts and threats of the Gestapo and sheltered Jews in their homes, in monasteries, churches, convents, orphanages, and rectories. They proved that they *were* their brothers' keepers and that not

7

in vain had Jesus of Nazareth related the parable of the Good Samaritan.

This was the faith which prompted Jozefek, the cattle dealer in Lwów, to shelter thirty-five Jews even though it led to his being hanged in the public square. Such, too, was the belief which motivated the Mother Superior and the nuns of the Benedictine convent at Vilna to hide imperiled Jews in their convent, and to clothe them in their own garb in order to hide them more effectively; it prompted them to scour the countryside for food for them and to offer to die with them in their ghetto. This was the creed which nerved the Protestant minister, Pastor Vergara, to rescue at the risk of his life seventy Jewish children who were in danger of being killed. Such, too, were the ideals which buttressed Edoardo Focherini, editor of the Bologna Catholic daily *Avvenire d' Italia*, to rescue Jews even though it cost him the lives of his seven children in a concentration camp.

How inspiring it is to see Archbishop Saliège of Toulouse defy the Nazi occupation authorities with the fearless ultimatum: "There is a Christian morality ... that confers rights and imposes duties. These duties and these rights come from God. One can violate them. But no mortal has the power to suppress them ... The Jews are our brethren ... No Christian dare forget that ... France, which cherishes in the conscience of all its children the tradition of respect for the individual ... is not responsible for these horrors."

In that brave utterance the Archbishop was but echoing the words of Pope Pius XI, spoken to a great gathering when Hitler was seeking to press his anti-Semitic measures upon Italy. Pointing out the close kinship between the Hebrew tradition and Christian culture, the Pontiff stressed our spiritual descendence from Abraham: "Anti-Semitism is a repugnant movement in which we Christians can have no part ... We are the spiritual offspring of Abraham." So stirred was the venerable prelate as he pleaded for the protection of Jews from the cruel measures of the Nazis that tears came into his eyes, and he ended his address with the memorable statement: "Anti-Semitism is inadmissible. *Spiritually we are Semites.*" In using the term "Semites," he wished to identify himself with the persecuted victims of the anti-Semitic campaign then darkening the skies of Europe.

That the pronouncements of church authorities were no idle utterances but found lodgment in the minds, hearts, and actions of their members is evident from the accusation hurled at the Church by the pro-Nazi journalist, Jacques Marcy: "Every Catholic family shelters a Jew . . . Priests help them across the Swiss frontier . . . Jewish children have been concealed in Catholic schools; the civilian Catholic officials receive intelligence of a scheduled deportation of Jews, advise a great number of refugee Jews about it, and the result is that about 50 per cent of the undesirables escape."

How inspiring it is to see Protestant, Greek Orthodox, and Catholic clergymen and members of their respective flocks thunder their protests against the anti-Semitic measures of the Nazis and risk their lives in the attempt to rescue Jews from the claws of the prowling Gestapo!

Alas! all too often the Christian people of the countries under the Nazi heel were compelled to undergo the horror of watching in stunned silence and agonizing impotence as their Jewish neighbors were seized and shipped to the gas ovens of Auschwitz, Buchenwald, and Dachau. Why? Because they could not fight armored tanks and machine guns with bare hands. Such was the predicament of millions who loathed the Nazi creed and all its works.

It is not the least of the merits of this book that the author not only refrains from any sweeping indictment of the captor peoples, but is eager to point out numerous typical instances of high heroism on the part of the population in rescuing Jews from the terrible fate which the Nazis had in store for them. The work shows clearly that they were more sinned against than sinning. This verdict is confirmed by the horror and revulsion experienced by most Europeans in learning only after the war of the extent of the Nazi success in liquidating approximately six million of the eight million Jews in the countries groaning under Hitler's domination.

This is a work not of heat, but of light. It seeks not to inflame the passions of vengeance but to throw the spotlight upon the mercy, compassion, decency, and honor which flowered in the action of so many people in all walks of life. They were peasants, housewives, factory workers, teachers, professional men, and clergy of all faiths, who fought with bare hands against the mightiest military juggernaut in modern times; they fought for the despised and persecuted Jew, and by their sacrifices and heroism they have enriched all humanity and strengthened the solidarity of human brotherhood. They make us proud of our common humanity and give ground for the hope that the ultimate victory will rest on the side of decency and honor. These are the true heroes of our time and they will be enshrined in the hearts and minds of men as long as memory endures.

While the work is narrative in character, and rarely wanders into the detours of reflection, some conclusions of peculiar timeliness and relevance can scarcely fail to make their impact upon the reader. Foremost among these is the enormous hazard inherent in the very nature of the totalitarian state. How else can one explain the immeasurable destruction, suffering, and death inflicted upon the world by the ascent to power of a Hitler or of a Stalin? The whole gigantic machinery of government is perverted into the execution of their sadistic urges, blood-lusts, and irrational hatreds. What a silent but eloquent plea for the principles of democracy with its system of checks and balances, and its widespread distribution of power, rooted in the franchises of its citizens!

Another truth which emerges from this narrative in an impressive manner is this: racial and religious hatred is a luxury in which no nation or group can indulge without the danger of setting its own house on fire. It is like playing with dynamite or—even worse!—with hydrogen bombs. The insensate fury which such hatred releases comes back to plague and bestialize the hater: it degrades, demoralizes, and dehumanizes him as no external enemy can possibly do.

It affords a striking illustration of the inescapable fact that we are all traveling in the same boat. The occupant who drives a hole under the part where his neighbor is seated, finds that the water engulfs him as well and carries him to destruction. This little book teaches us to purge our hearts of all the hatreds which blight our common humanity: such is an altruism which pays rich dividends; it is good patriotism, good Judaism, good Christianity and plain common sense.

The mills of God grind slowly, but they grind exceedingly fine. The Third Reich which Hitler boasted was to last for a thousand years went down into the rubble under the shells of Russian guns and bombs from American planes. It has faded from the earth like an ugly memory, a poisonous gas, a hideous nightmare. Out of the holocaust arose the remaining persecuted, decimated Jews who were to have been exterminated forever; with them arose the Republic of Israel and nationhood for the outcast children of Israel in their ancestral homeland. Here is retribution on a cosmic scale for Nazi hatred, oppression and cruelty: the unwritten final chapter in *Mein Kampf*.

The cannons of war are silenced now. Subdued, if not altogether banished, is the hatred of the Jews which the Nazis whipped into a frenzy never witnessed before. Auschwitz, Dachau, and Buchenwald live only as symbols of horror and infamy. Can such an outrage happen again? Civilization must build up its defenses—social, cultural and spiritual—so that the massacre of any people will never again be attempted. The struggle will not be an easy one. It must be waged with courage, determination, and with all the light which science and religion can throw upon man's groping efforts to emancipate himself from the strait jacket of racial and religious hatreds in order to see in every man his brother.

This book encourages, guides, and helps us in that enterprise.

Although the author personally experienced the lash of Nazi cruelty, he writes in a calm, objective manner, and seeks with surprising magnanimity to focus attention chiefly upon the humane, noble, and heroic deeds of mercy, self-sacrifice, and love which relieve the horror of the Nazi nightmare. He thus sets an example for each of us. I commend this work to all who are interested in seeing how people reached up gentle hands and took Christ's law of love out of the sky and, even in the fiery ordeal of war, put it into practice; how, in fact, they became *their brothers' keepers*. It is a stimulating and inspiring story and I hope it is read by millions.

Father John A. O'Brien
University of Notre Dame

INTRODUCTION

The vast area of Europe seized and held by the Nazis and their accomplices during World War II contained approximately 8,300,000 Jews. It is estimated that 6,000,000 perished by Nazi lethal devices, disease, or starvation. Considering that Hitler mobilized all of Germany's resources for the avowed purpose of annihilating the Jews, and that in this work he found helpers and collaborators among the native population in almost all Nazi-occupied countries, it is indeed a miracle that more than 2,000,-000 remained alive. Those surviving were saved by flight, emigration, or evacuation before the arrival of the Germans and the changeable fortunes of war. But at least a million Jews survived in the very crucible of the Nazi hell, the occupied areas.

How this million survived is the theme of our story. These candidates for the Nazi crematoria could not have lived to witness the collapse of the Reich that was to endure a thousand years if they had relied on their own resources. The miracle could not have been accomplished without the active assistance of the Christian population.

We will never know how many of the approximately 300,-000,000 Europeans who lived briefly under the Nazi heel helped Jews. It is not the number that matters. What matters is that a small army of valorous men and women opened their hearts and their homes to a people marked for extinction, defying the invader and death itself. In the words of the Jewish writer, Sholem Asch:

"It is of the highest importance not only to record and recount, both for ourselves and for the future, the evidences

of human degradation, but side by side with them to set
forth the evidences of human exaltation and nobility. Let
the epic of heroic deeds of love, as opposed by those of
hatred, of rescue as opposed to destruction, bear equal
witness to unborn generations.

"On the flood of sin, hatred and blood let loose by Hitler
upon the world, there swam a small ark which preserved
intact the common heritage of a Judeo-Christian outlook,
that outlook which is founded on the double principle of
love of God and love of one's fellow men. The demonism
of Hitler had sought to overturn and overwhelm it in the
floods of hate. It was saved by the heroism of a handful of
saints."

In European countries occupied or dominated by Germany,
the reaction to anti-Semitic laws and the policy of extermination varied considerably. Many factors were responsible for this.
First, there were the conditions prevailing in the individual countries before the Nazi assault. Some countries—the Western and
Scandinavian—had a long history of liberal and democratic
traditions so that the general population tended to be sympathetic to countrymen of Jewish origin. Similarly, the Greeks, the
Bulgarians, and the Czechs tried to help the Jews. In other
countries, particularly in Eastern Europe, where centuries of
serfdom, drudgery, and oppression by foreign occupying powers
gave root to exaggerated nationalistic feeling, xenophobia, and
hatred, the general population was least likely to risk Nazi dis-
pleasure. Here only a small, though significant, minority dared
to help the Jews or even to manifest feelings of sympathy for
the persecuted. In all countries, large groups of people were
neutral or just indifferent to the sufferings of their fellow citizens
of Jewish origin. In some countries, passive humanitarians—
those who were sympathetic but too afraid to dare to express
their opinions or to help the Jews—constituted a large group of
the population. Considering this background, one must regard

the gallant few whose bravery rescued so many of the doomed as even greater heroes.

Hiding a Jew was not an easy matter. It required more than willingness, courage, and readiness to imperil the lives of one's family; a proper place was necessary, an ability to camouflage the hide-out, contact with like-minded individuals who would risk taking the Jew in the event of an imminent raid. Experience had taught the host as well as the one in hiding that movement of and frequent changes in hiding places were essential for survival. Thus, the saving of one Jew or a whole family often involved the co-operation of many Christians. Frequently a Jewish family was divided among several hosts. Hiding a large family or a group of Jews in a private home, particularly in urban areas, almost inevitably ended in disaster. Sizable groups found shelter in monasteries, convents, mountain hide-outs, or bunkers in the woods; they fared less well in cities or even small towns. It was difficult to buy provisions for those in hiding; tongues would begin to wag, neighbors grow suspicious. In the large cities it was possible to buy small quantities of food in scattered black-market centers and thus avoid arousing suspicion, but in smaller localities this technique was difficult to apply. Many homes did not have inside toilets, and so there was the problem of disposing of refuse. A great deal of ingenuity was required when a "guest" became ill or died, or when a pregnant woman was about to give birth. The presence of small children increased the danger of being found out. Sleeping pills were used liberally to keep children from crying excessively.

The building and arrangement of hiding places became an art. People built double walls and hanging ceilings behind which Jews sometimes lived for years. Attics and cellars were camouflaged. Used also were annexes in old office buildings, as was done in the case of the Franks in Amsterdam. Jews were hidden in pigsties, cowsheds, stables, haystacks, or cemetery graves. Emanuel Ringelblum, martyred historian and archivisit of Warsaw, his family, and a score of Jews who had escaped the last agonizing moments of the burning ghetto were accommodated in a specially prepared underground bunker of a Polish gardener, Pan Wolski. On top of this ingenious hide-out a sprouting greenhouse was planted as a disguise. Had not an informer carried word to the Gestapo, the eminent Ringelblum and the saintly Polish gardener, Wolski, might be alive today.

Hiding places were often so cramped that the Jews inside took turns lying down. Some places were so crowded those in hiding were forced to stand immobile for hours, and were permitted to exercise their limbs only in the dark of night when their host let them out for a brief period. A Jewish woman hiding in Warsaw lived for eighteen months in a standing position. After the Nazis were driven out, she required hospitalization to cure her legs. There are two recorded cases of pigeon houses being used as places to hide. Meir Stein of Warsaw lived in a pigeon house located near a forest. The Polish Underground supplied him with food and water. Stein, who was named "The Eagle" by his friends, survived the Nazis; his inspiring story was put into verse by a Jewish poet in Brazil. Gusia Obler of Halicz, who escaped the pogroms of September, 1942, found shelter in a pigeon house in a suburb of Lwów. Her host, a Polish brush-maker, eventually became fearful of reprisals and induced her to leave. But she survived and now lives in Israel.

There are known cases of hospital personnel hiding Jewish women. On occasion, even a Jewish male desperate for shelter was accommodated in a hospital bed, although the presence of a circumcised patient imperiled the whole staff. During the Nazi reign of terror in Cracow, a Jewish mother brought her small boy to St. Lazarus Hospital. The boy had a broken leg. Both mother and child had "Aryan" documents, but Dr. Lachowicz, the chief physician, and the admitting nurse both took note of the fact that the prospective patient was circumcised. His presence at the hospital would be deemed by the Germans a crime punishable by death. However, the doctor and nurse admitted the boy but sent the mother away. The boy's leg was treated, and his belly bandaged as a precaution against Gestapo visits. During one such raid, Dr. Lachowicz refused to remove his young patient's bandages, pleading with the Gestapo that the boy was a Christian, assuring the Germans that on their next visit he would show them proof. Two weeks later the Gestapo returned, but the boy was no longer on the premises. The staff had removed him to a convent in the neighborhood of Miechow. The Germans, who did not neglect making periodic searches among the nuns also, found the boy and threatened to execute him. The nuns insisted the boy was a Christian. They presented an official statement, signed by Dr. Lachowicz, explaining that a bad fall had so injured the boy's foreskin and his leg that an operation was later performed to save his life.

Jewish children were hidden by their mothers or by Gentiles in baking stoves, garbage bins, and boxes. In Warsaw this writer saw a child who had been kept in a box concealed in a dark cabin. The child was almost totally blind; the muscles of his limbs were atrophied, and he could not walk. His speech was a series of inarticulate sounds. This six-year-old Jewish boy, reared in a world of darkness, was not undernourished; his foster mother had simply taken all necessary precautions for their mutual safety.

The Gestapo was constantly on the alert for the thousands of Jews who seemed to burrow into the ground like moles. Among their allies were collaborationists, professional informers, anti-Semites, drunks, and prattlers. To anyone turning in a Jew, the Gestapo usually paid one quart of brandy, four pounds of sugar, and a carton of cigarettes, or a small amount of money. Incidentally, the prices varied at different places and times. The host was usually executed on the spot, or hanged in a public place as an object lesson to "Aryans" who entertained the notion of hiding a Jew.

In 1942, when the Germans ran amuck slaughtering the Jews of Tarnopol, several desperate men and women pleaded with a Ukrainian doorkeeper to let them hide in the large, abandoned attic of an office building. They were aware that the ground floor of the building was occupied by the Gestapo, but they were surrounded; all avenues of escape were closed. The old doorkeeper agreed and led them upstairs. He did not reveal the terrible secret even to his wife. He bought food for his "tenants" from his own money and took it to them after office hours, when the ground floor was empty. One day, unable to sustain the burden of his secret, the doorkeeper revealed it to his wife. At a party, after several drinks, she whispered the intelligence to her brother, who hated Jews. The brother threatened to go to the Gestapo, and the doorkeeper tried dissuading him. They quarreled, fought, and as the brother-in-law started for the door to summon the Gestapo, the doorkeeper grabbed an ax and killed him. After the German retreat and the return of the Russians, the doorkeeper helped his twenty-one Jewish "guests" to settle in Zbaraż. One day he came to his friends and pleaded with them to hide him because his wife and her family were seeking to avenge the man he had slain. When the Jews made preparations to emigrate, the old doorkeeper joined them.

The Lwów cattle dealer, Józefek, met a different fate. He was hanged in a public square for concealing thirty-five Jews. His body was left dangling for several days as a warning to others. In Athens twelve Greeks were publicly hanged for helping a group of Jews to escape.

On occasion, Jewish guests, fearful of the consequences to their hosts if they were caught, left the places of safety of their own free will, often to commit suicide. "We are trailed and hunted," wrote Francisca Rubinlicht of Warsaw. "We can no longer find a place to hide. Our money is gone. We cannot stay here any longer because we have been threatened with being reported to the Gestapo. If this happens, our protectors will suffer as well. We cannot commit suicide in this place because our protector will be victimized. So we have decided," the note goes on to say, "to surrender, in the knowledge that we can swallow the [suicide] pills that now constitute our only, our priceless possession."

The good, generous, and godly people who hid Jews feared not only the wrath of the Nazis; they also had to contend with anti-Semites among the local population, and terror organizations that preached the gospel of hatred even after the war. There are numerous recorded instances concerning Poles who gave protection to their Jewish countrymen and later were shot by terrorist groups. Andrzej Kowalski of Parczew, Poland, who had concealed six Jewish families without remuneration during the war, was forced by anti-Semites to leave his home and settle elsewhere. Two Polish families of Bialystok who had put their lives in peril by helping Jews during the Occupation were forced by their neighbors to look elsewhere for home and sustenance. They left for West Germany, and then were helped by the Jewish Labor Committee to emigrate to the United States. In 1946 the Jewish Committee of Bialystok was aiding 180 Christian families who were being persecuted by illegal Rightist groups for their generosity to Jews during the evil time of Hitler. In bidding good-by to two Jewish women he had hidden in his place until the Nazis were driven out, the Polish beggar, Karol Kicinski, pleaded, "Please don't tell anyone I saved you; I fear for my life."

CHAPTER ONE

THE HEART OF WOMAN

Emanuel Ringelblum on more than one occasion recorded the valorous deeds of Jewish women whose capacity to love, endure, sacrifice, and fight during the years of the Nazi Locust will inspire poets and historians alike for many years to come. The hymn to the heroic non-Jewish women who risked their lives for the victims of Nazi barbarism is yet to be written and the song is yet to be sung. It would require more than can be told in the pages of one book to call the roll of the women of many nations, political persuasions, and varying social strata who gave their time, their wealth, even their lives for those who had been marked by Hitler for extermination. Behind each proud name cited in these chapters stand the nameless, anonymous legions of women whose inspiring acts will live as long as the conscience of mankind is disturbed by the remembrance of the murderous Hitler era.

Anna Simaite was a Lithuanian, rather on the stout side, with a broad peasant face, and flaxen hair which she parted in the middle and braided into a coil to crown her head. In her early childhood Anna had many Jewish friends and classmates. Among her favorite authors was the famous Polish writer Eliza Orzesz-kowa, who wrote a number of stories about Jews and whose distinguished novel *Meir Ezofowicz* treated the Jew with compassion and love. Her grandfather, a liberal, broad-minded man, taught the girl to consider the Jews objectively and not through the distorted vision of bigotry and anti-Semitism. When Anna entered high school in Riga, she joined a Social Revolutionary underground organization aimed at destroying the tsarist regime that spread its tentacles from faraway St. Petersburg. Later, she studied at the Teachers' Seminary in Moscow, and after graduation became completely absorbed by the plight of the underprivileged, choosing to devote her life to the children of the poor.

But soon after the outbreak of World War II, we find Anna Simaite in charge if the cataloguing department of the old and famed Vilna University. She was counted among the best literary critics in Lithuania; her position and reputation were secure if she chose to remain silent. But Anna Simaite chose to fight. Ten years later, after the guns had been stilled and weeds had grown high over the shattered brick and mortar of the walled-in ghettos, Anna explained her compulsion to act. "When the Germans forced Jews of Vilna into a ghetto, I could no longer go on with my work. I could not remain in my study. I could not eat. I was ashamed that I was not Jewish myself. I had to do something. I realized the danger involved, but it could not be helped. A force much stronger than myself was at work."

Obsessed with the notion that only by helping the Jews could she fulfill herself as a human being, Anna Simaite turned toward the ghetto. Non-Jews were prohibited from entering this reservation where the Jews of Vilna had been immured to suffer briefly before they were exterminated. Anna, the non-Jew, was determined to breach the ghetto walls, to offer her services, to declare her oneness with the sufferers. She appeared before the German authorities and presented them with a singularly innocent plan. In the ghetto were books that had been borrowed from the University library some time before by Jewish students. Would the Germans permit her, a conscientious librarian, to go behind the barbed wires and high walls in order to rescue the priceless volumes? The Germans granted her request, and for a few weeks Anna enjoyed a limited immunity. She prowled among the crowded hovels of the ghetto, which had been the slum area of Vilna before the war, offering her aid to the hapless Jews. When the Germans declared that she was taking too much time reclaiming her valuable books, Anna contrived new schemes. As time went on, she became completely absorbed by the feverish life of the ghetto. She visited friends, ran to amateur theatricals and concerts, attended lectures, art exhibits, and teas. She could not get over the fact that the Jews, whom the occupying power had sentenced to death by starvation, torture, and deportation, spent all their waking hours celebrating life.

As Anna went back and forth, she got in touch with people in the Aryan part of the city, people who might risk taking in an old friend languishing in the ghetto. There were those who nodded quick assent, and others who wavered while Anna pleaded with them and tried to infuse them with the courage she possessed in such abundance. And there were those who spat in her face. But she was not to be insulted, intimidated, or diverted from her mission. She sought out hiding places for Jewish children whom she later helped spirit out of the ghetto. She obtained forged Aryan papers for Jews who determined to scale the ghetto walls. She proudly enlisted as a courier, smuggling letters from leaders of the ghetto Underground to their compatriots outside, letters that could not under any circumstances be sent through the mails. Assisted by a small, valiant group of friends, among them the well-known Lithuanian poet Baruta, Anna carried food to the starving Jews. For those among the decimated ghetto-dwellers who resolved to make a last stand against the enemy, she brought small arms and ammunition. It goes without saying that each article Anna smuggled inside the reservation, she carried at the risk of her life, were it a small gun hidden on her person, or a bouquet of roses for some beauty-starved woman of the desolate ghetto. She came always laden with things and thus did she leave, carrying precious archives, rare books, documents, and scraps of diaries of the martyrdom of the walled-in people to be preserved for another time. She hid the precious objects in the vaults of the Seminar for Lithuanistics at the University.

In April of 1942, Jacob Gens, the commander of the Vilna ghetto, cautioned Anna Simaite that the Gestapo was becoming suspicious of her activities. This warning came at the time when

the Germans were launching their campaign for total extermination of the ghetto-dwellers. Anna scorned the commander's
warning; her own fate seemed inconsequential in the face of the
disaster threatening the Jews. She organized a rescue group in
the Aryan sector of the city, determined to save as many Jewish
children as possible. She worked tirelessly, bribing guards,
wheedling, cajoling, her life as much in danger as the lives of the
skeleton children she snatched from the ghetto to hide among
non-Jews. For a short time she evaded the Gestapo net by taking
shelter among members of the Underground, but in the summer
of 1944 the inevitable happened: Anna was seized by the Gestapo. Threatened, beaten, starved, still she betrayed no secrets.
Finally she was sentenced to death.

Without Anna's knowledge, the University interceded on her
behalf, bribing a high Nazi official. The death sentence was
commuted, and Anna was deported to the notorious Dachau
concentration camp and later transferred to a camp in Southern
France, where the Allied armies found her barely clinging to
life. Following the Liberation, she went to Toulouse, penniless,
her health shattered. After a period of convalescence in a hospital, Anna found a job as dishwasher in a small restaurant.
Despite the fact that she lived the withdrawn life of a refugee,
word mysteriously got around that Anna Simaite was in France
and in need of help. Messages with offers of aid began to arrive
at her flat. The offers came from organizations like the Union
of Lithuanian Jews of America, and from individuals to whom
her name had become a legend. Determined to earn her own
livelihood, Anna Simaite declined the aid. When the job as
dishwasher came to an abrupt end, she went to Paris and found
employment first in a laundry, then as a doll seamstress, and
finally as a librarian.

Anna might have remained in Paris to live out the rest of her
days if the news of her survival had not reached some of her
former "children." Letters began to arrive from many parts of
the world. All of her "children" implored her to come and live

with them. One of the most persistent of correspondents was Tania Wachsman, a mother of two children, who lived in a *kibbutz* in Israel. "My dear Mother," Tania began each letter, "when will you finally come to us?" Anna hesitated—she did not want to be a burden—but in the end yielded to Tania's pleas.

She arrived in Israel in the spring of 1953. Everywhere in the new republic she was received with flowers and applause. She was feted by the Association of Lithuanian Jews and by the editorial staff of the largest Hebrew daily newspaper, *Davar.* The government of Israel granted her a pension, an honor she refused but eventually agreed to accept. What impressed Anna more than the receptions, flowers, and emoluments was the welcome accorded her by the "children" whom she had helped to survive the ghetto. "It is not possible for me to tell you how much I appreciate this warmhearted reception," she said. "I have not the words. I am here . . . among my kin."

And there she lives, among her "children," in a place called Petah Tikvah—the woman with the peasant face, her gray hair parted smoothly in the center—writing essays, memoirs and articles.

"For me, as a Lithuanian," she says, "it is a very sad thing to admit that not all of my co-nationals, during the years of the Jewish ordeal, showed compassion for the victims. To my great sorrow, it must be admitted that some elements among the Lithuanians even collaborated in the extermination of the Jews." As for the Vilna ghetto where she virtually lived in those terrible days, she has this to say: "How the Jews stood it, I do not know. The Jews of the Vilna ghetto and all other ghettos were great heroes, even if they themselves did not realize it."

It is not possible to call to memory the Vilna ghetto without also invoking the name of Anna Simaite, who stormed its walls, clutching a gun for resistance and a crushed flower for the comfort of some beauty-starved soul.

*   *   *   *   *

The small nunnery was located not far from the Vilna Colony railroad station. During the German occupation there were only seven sisters in this Benedictine convent, all from Cracow. The Mother Superior, a graduate of Cracow University, was a comparatively young woman of thirty-five at the time when the Jews were driven from their homes. Although the convent was too far removed from the ghetto for her to hear the cries of a tortured people, the Mother Superior seemed always to be gazing in that direction, as though she were waiting for a summons. She found it hard to keep her mind on the work which had previously claimed all her time and love, the ministering to the poor and the miserable.

One day she decided that the time had come to act. She summoned the other nuns and, after prayer, they discussed the subject of the ghetto. Not long afterward, as a result of this conversation, a few of the sisters appeared before the gate of the ghetto. The guards did not suspect the nuns of any conspiratorial designs. Eventually contact was established between the convent and the Vilna ghetto, and an underground railroad was formed. The seven nuns became experts in getting Jews out of the ghetto and hiding them at the convent and in other places. At one period it seemed as if the small nunnery were bulging with nuns, some with features unmistakably masculine.

Among those hidden in the convent were several Jewish writers and leaders of the ghetto Underground: Abraham Sutzkever, Abba Kovner, Edek Boraks, and Arie Wilner. Some stayed a long time, others returned to the ghetto to fight and die. When, in the winter of 1941, the Jewish Fighters' Organization was formed, the Mother Superior became an indispensable ally. The Fighters needed arms, and the Mother Superior undertook to supply them. Assisted by the other nuns, she roamed the countryside in search of knives, daggers, bayonets, pistols, guns, grenades. The hands accustomed to the touch of rosary beads became expert with explosives. The first four grenades received gratefully by the Fighters were the gift of the Mother Superior, who instructed Abba Kovner in their proper use, as they were of a special brand unfamiliar to him. She later supplied other weapons. Although she worked selflessly, tirelessly, she felt not enough was being done. "I wish to come to the ghetto," she said to Abba Kovner, "to fight by your side, to die, if necessary. Your fight is a holy one. You are a noble people. Despite the fact that you are a Marxist [Kovner was a member of *Hashomer Hatzair*] and have no religion, you are closer to God than I."

Her ardent wish to enter the ghetto to fight and, in the end, to die the martyred death of the Jews was not realized. She was too valuable an ally, and was prevailed upon to remain on the Aryan side. In addition to supplying arms, she also acted as a liaison between the Jewish Fighters' Organization inside the ghetto and the Polish Underground with which they were desperately trying to establish a military partnership. The partnership was never achieved, but this failure was not her fault. And although the battle was lost, she was not the loser. Her heroism was enshrined in the hearts of those who would remember.

* * * * *

Janina Bucholc-Bukolska was employed in the small firm of Rybczynski on Miodowa Street in Warsaw. The tiny office, which specialized in translations, was always overcrowded. Papers and documents were piled on desks, shelves, and cabinets. The papers were not even remotely connected with translations; they were, in fact, birth certificates, marriage records, school diplomas, food ration cards, letters of recommendation from employers, and all manner of documents and forms. Mrs. Bukolska was a large woman, awkward in movement. Wearing the thick glasses she depended on, she sat calmly in the midst of this chaos of papers and attended busily to her work. Her work, among other things, consisted of supplying false identification cards to Jews. A German policeman would sometimes pass outside the window and gaze curiously at the picture of industry and prosperity inside. Customers were always coming and going.

The males among Bukolska's clients invariably wore bushy mustaches and the women displayed peroxide-blonde hair. In fact, not one person entered the office who did not have a Nordic appearance save Mrs. Bukolska herself, and she was the only Gentile in the crowd. All the others had been Aryanized, in appearance at least, before they came to her. They brought with them photographs, fingerprints, and other pertinent information, most of it spurious. Janina Bukolska then had the Aryan identity papers known as *Kennkarten* made up by an expert.

The customers entered her office as Jews and left as Gentiles. But they seldom went out without consulting with Bukolska about a possible place to hide in the Aryan sector. She took down their names. Finding places for the new Aryans to live was one of Bukolska's occupations. This was far from easy, as the Germans offered ten pounds of sugar and a pint of vodka as a reward for surrendering a Jew hiding in the Aryan sector of the city. The punishment for hiding a Jew or helping one to find a place to hide was death.

Mrs. Bukolska shrugged off all obstacles placed in her way. After a busy day at the overcrowded office, she spent her evenings visiting around, ringing doorbells, inquiring whether the good people of Warsaw would consider giving shelter to one of her new Aryans. On occasion she met with a bit of good luck, as she did when Dr. Jan Zabinski, director of the Warsaw zoo, offered her clients some cages vacated by animals that had perished for lack of food. But in most instances she met with reticence, refusal, and abuse; often she was threatened with the Gestapo. Her labors continued, however, and her "business" prospered until the last ghetto hovel had been put to the torch by the Nazis and the last Jew murdered. And even then Pani Janina carried on, for her work was not finished. It came to an end only when the Hitler hordes were driven out of her beloved country.

* * * * *

A roll call of heroic women who risked their lives to help a cause that appeared lost would not be complete without the mention of Sophia Debicka, Jadzia Duniec, Irena Adamowicz, Janina Plawczynska, and Rena Laterner. Sophia Debicka came from a family of Polish intellectuals and was related to the veteran Socialist leader, Stephanie Sempolowska. She hid several Jewish women in her house, camouflaging them as nurse, seamstress, cook, and maid. She seized a little Jewish girl from a transport, declaring the child was her daughter. Her home became an operational base for the Jewish Fighters' Organization of Warsaw. She alerted her friends in the Postmaster's office who examined letters addressed to the Gestapo, to intercept those containing tips from informers about Jews hiding in the Christian sector.

Jadzia Duniec, a Catholic girl of Vilna, did not leave behind a long record of deeds which would memorialize her. She died too young. But for a brief period before the Gestapo captured and executed her, Jadzia served as a courier and liaison between Jewish underground organizations and the outer world. She supplied weapons to the Szeinbaum fighting group in Vilna, and she was often sent to Kaunas and Shavli on errands for the Fighters. She died as she lived, courageously. Her name deserves to be remembered, for she was one of a small, valiant group.

Irena Adamowicz belonged to the same small group. Irena was not so young as Jadzia. She came of a pious, aristocratic Polish family, and before the war she was an executive of the Polish Girl Scouts. During the German occupation she became a courier between the ghettos of Warsaw, Vilna, Kaunas, Shavli, Bialystok, and other cities. Along with several other Christian women, she volunteered for this work that meant certain death if she were captured. Among her co-workers, though Irena probably never met them, were two wrinkled old ladies, Janina Plawczynska and Rena Laterner. Both these venerable ladies were in their seventies. They carried messages between the Fighters and the Polish Underground in Warsaw. After the collapse of the ghetto uprising, they sheltered ten Fighters in a bunker they erected. They perished with the ten Jews.

* * * * *

Mother Maria of Paris was a Russian woman, born Elizabeth Pilenko. Her grandfather was a Don Cossack general; her grandmother a descendant of a French officer in Napoleon's army. The first woman to be graduated from the Theological Seminary in Russia, Elizabeth became a distinguished poetess and an active Socialist. Soon after her graduation she married, but her married life was tragic. A little daughter died at the age of four, and later the marriage ended in divorce. Elizabeth's second husband was D. E. Skobtzoff, a writer, by whom she had a son, Yuri. After the Bolshevik Revolution the Skobtzoffs left their native Russia and went to live in Paris. In 1932 Elizabeth divorced her second husband and became a nun, taking the name Maria.

She was no longer a young woman when the Nazis overwhelmed France. She was fifty, past the age when one joins with conspirators and those who imperil their lives for one cause or another. But she enlisted readily, out of a strong inner need to help those in greatest jeopardy, the Jews. The reflective poetess, the nun who not long before had withdrawn from the storms and stresses of the world, was in a short time transformed into an exalted partisan of a cause. As she joined the battle, she was certain beyond any doubt that the path she now chose would eventually bring her closer to her God. She took command of a clandestine organization of Greek Orthodox priests for rescuing Jews, particularly children. A small convent in Paris became the headquarters of the group. Liasion was established with the Catholic Underground headed by the Jesuit Father Pierre Chaillet. Food and clothing were collected at the convent and sent to the Jews in the Drancy concentration camp. A hidden mill inside the convent turned out identification papers and German documents for Jews who were still at large. Scores of Jews were given temporary shelter in the Little Cloister until more secure

and permanent hiding places could be found for them. In the midst of these feverish activities Mother Maria, who was in full charge, found time to indulge an old passion, the writing of verse. After the Germans had foisted the Jewish badge on the French, Mother Maria wrote a poem brimming with anger and defiance; the Jewish badge intended by the Nazis as a symbol of humiliation, she cried, was in fact a mark of distinction. Widely circulated among those who read Russian, the poem stirred the Nazis no less than it did its Russian-speaking readers, though for different reasons.

In the early morning of February 7, 1943, a Gestapo man by the name of Hofman came with several guards to the convent on Rue de Lourmel. He demanded to see Mother Maria, and was told he would have to come another time—Mother Maria was out, in the country. The Germans left, but not without taking along Mother Maria's young son Yuri as a hostage. Alarmed by the arrest, Mother Maria returned, and was immediately summoned to Gestapo headquarters. She demanded the release of her son, who was in no way involved in any of her activities.

During the angry interrogation, Hofman turned to the nun's mother, who accompanied her: "You educated your daughter very stupidly," he shouted. "She helps Jews only."

"This is not true," the old woman replied. "She is a Christian who helps those in need. She would even help *you*, if you were in trouble."

"You will never see your daughter again," the Nazi said, by way of concluding the interview.

Mother Maria was arrested and taken to Romainville. Yuri was sent to the Compiègne concentration camp and later to Buchenwald where he was tortured to death. On April 24, 1943, Mother Maria was transferred to the notorious Ravensbrueck camp. There were 2,500 women in the cell block where she lived, most of them infested with vermin and suffering from dysentery and typhus. She helped where she could, with a morsel of food, a

kind word, a prayer. Weakened as her body was by the ravages
of hunger, disease, and torture, she continued to minister to the
women, moving about in the filthy, tightly packed barracks like
a disembodied shadow. She was a tight-lipped, grim witness to
Nazi barbarism. Daily she watched the guards come to fetch
Jewish women, whom they dragged to the crematoria for the
greater glory of the Reich. And she waited for her turn to take
the final walk. But the Gestapo seemed to be in no hurry.
Mother Maria, "criminal" though she was, possessed Aryan
papers; there were a great many Jewish women still to be exterminated.

Her turn finally came. She was last seen alive on March 31,
1945, one month and a few days before the collapse of the
Thousand-Year Reich. It is said that she committed one last
saintly act—exchanging, with a Jewish woman chosen for the
gas chamber, her precious Aryan card. But she was not quite
strong enough to walk to her execution upright; the guards
carried her.

BATTLE OF THE BADGE

In 1939, in Occupied Poland, the Nazis for the first time ordered the use of the Jewish badge. This distinctive marking isolating the Jew from the rest of the populace was not uniform in all areas occupied by the Germans. Often the emblem, shape, and size were left to the whim and the imagination of the local commander. In some areas the Jews were ordered to sew a yellow Star of David on their outer garments, yellow having been designated by the Thousand-Year Reich as the "Jew-color" (*Judenfarbe*). In certain other regions, a white and blue armband was prescribed. But most of the badges, whatever their over-all size and shape, employed the six-pointed Star of David.

A German scholar, Dr. Herbert Morgen, who had drunk deeply of the Nazi cup of wisdom, made the following observation after a journey through the "New German Eastern Area" (Occupied Poland): "As an external sign of belonging to their tribe, the Jews wore, depending on the directive of the Landrat, a yellow Star of David, a yellow triangle or something like it, on their breasts or back. The general impression one receives of this human mass is appalling. One inevitably arrives at the conclusion that he is confronted here with a completely degenerate, inferior segment of humanity."

The local commander at Ozorkow, near Lodz, implemented the orders of his superiors by branding his victims as though they were cattle. The Jews who were deemed fit for work found themselves marked with the letter *A*; the unfit were stamped *B*. In view of the fact that the imaginative commander had the Jews branded on the buttocks, one's fitness to work could not be fully determined until he dropped his trousers and turned his back on a fully accredited representative of the Third Reich. Those unfit were killed.

In due time a uniform badge was devised. On November 23, 1939, Hans Frank, Nazi governor of Poland, ordered all Jews aged ten and over to wear a white armband with a blue Star of David embossed on it. In other occupied territories in the East, local designs prevailed until the Reichminister of Interior, on September 1, 1941, decreed for all Jews in Germany, the "Protectorate of Bohemia and Moravia," and all other territories occupied by the Nazis, with the exception of Poland, the wearing of a yellow hexagram (Star of David), with the inscription *Jude* in black, to be sewn or pinned on the left breast. For some obscure reason the age of the wearer was lowered from ten to six.

The reaction of the non-Jewish population to this sweeping decree varied. A German-Jewish teacher who lived in Berlin at the time made the following observation in his memoirs: "On the morning following the order, I went out early to *slichaus* [Hebrew prayer before the Day of Atonement] and observed how the passers-by reacted to the Jewish badge." He was struck by the embarrassment of most people, coupled, no doubt, with a sense of guilt. "People looked away," he noted, "and behaved as if they did not notice the Star. The Hitler Youth apparently received orders not to take notice of the Star, and the apprehension that Jews would be molested in the streets [by the young rowdies] proved baseless." In another entry the chronicler described the following episode: A Jew emerged from his office wearing the new badge. A little Christian girl approached him, shook his hand, and said: "Heil Hitler, Herr Jude!" Taken aback, the Jew asked her the meaning of such a strange greeting. The girl's answer was swift and to the point; the teacher in school, she explained to the Jew, had instructed all the children to be particularly cordial to people wearing the Star.

Expressions of sympathy for the wearers of the Star took

varied forms. People put candy or fruit in their pockets, offered them seats in crowded trolleys and subways.

Siegmund Weltlinger, a Jewish communal official in Berlin, was approached one morning by a high German officer, a total stranger, who opened his cigarette case, bowed stiffly, and said: "Please help yourself, comrade."

General Helmuth Stieff, after a brief furlough in Berlin, wrote to his relatives from headquarters in Minsk: "This [Star] is unworthy of an allegedly cultured nation. . . . Someday we shall pay for this!"

An entry in Emanuel Ringelblum's Warsaw ghetto diary is pertinent: "A Jew riding in a crowded trolley car dropped his badge. A German officer warned the man: 'You, Jew, you just lost the Twentieth Century.' "

A Berlin correspondent of the London *Times* wrote in a September, 1941, issue of his newspaper: "Many German Aryans felt such a resentment at the . . . stigmatization of Jews that on the day the regulations came into force, they were seen in the streets openly shaking hands, at the risk of punishment, with Jewish acquaintances."

The risks involved were many, as illustrated by the incident recorded by a German writer, Joseph Radermacher. A man wearing the Jewish Star entered a trolley car, walked to a vacant seat, and sat down. The motorman ordered the Jew to vacate the seat and move to the platform, a place designated for Jews. As the cowed passenger rose to comply with the order, the motorman whispered to him, "Don't fret; a time will come when you'll regain your rights." The passenger, a disguised police agent, arrested the motorman.

A small, courageous minority of Germans made an effort to oppose the Hitler decrees, which were as humiliating to them as they were to the people who were the direct victims. An even smaller minority spat on the victims and reviled them. But most Germans hid behind a mask of indifference.

"Most people [Gentiles] pretend not to see the badge," a Jewish woman of Munich, Else Behrend-Rosenthal, observed. "Occasionally someone on the trolley will express satisfaction at the 'Jewish gang' now being exposed. But we also hear many expressions of disgust at these . . . measures, and much sympathy is shown to us."

Although the terror regime was still firmly entrenched, the Nazi hierarchy viewed with concern the friendly attitude shown toward the Jews by a tiny segment of the population. One of the most powerful and evil men in Nazidom, Propaganda Minister Joseph Goebbels, made the following entry in his diary: "I gave orders to investigate all Jews still left in Berlin. I do not want to see Jews with the Star of David running about in the capital. Either the Star must be taken from them and they be classed as 'privileged,' or they must be evacuated altogether from the capital of the Reich."

In addition to professing Jews, who were hardest hit by the decree, the badge was forced upon baptized Jews and descendants of mixed marriages, *Mischlinge*. Many of the former Jews and half-Jews who had long ago assumed they were Christians showed their deep humiliation at the badge by discontinuing church attendance and curtailing their social activities. Some of them hid the badge and thus courted death. Eventually, after many church protests, the *Mischlinge* were exempted from wearing the Star.

In most countries occupied by the Germans, the Gentile population did not hide its contempt for the badge. In Czechoslovakia the wearers of the badge were treated as heroes. Hubert Ripka, member of the Czechoslovak National Committee in London, addressed the Jews of his country over the BBC in the following words: "Jews of Czechoslovakia, we think of you with profound sympathy. . . . Today the Germans have designated you publicly by a mark of shame. The yellow Star is a mark of honor which all decent people will respect. . . . Jewish friends, do not hide your identity; be proud of it!"

In Poland, where Nazi savagery exceeded all bounds, the introduction of the badge aroused hardly any protest. The Hebrew Underground newspaper *Min ha'metzar* noted that several members of the Polish Socialist party (PPS) planned to wear the badge as a token of solidarity with the Jews, an action that never materialized. In Warsaw, the underground press of the Polish Socialist party printed an editorial attacking the badge. Expressions of protest came from other sources, but they were small, feeble voices.

It is a matter of record that the Germans were unable to create a quisling government in Poland. The activities of the Polish Underground were widespread and effective, and the Germans retaliated with raids on the civilian population, deporting many thousands of Poles to slave-labor camps and staging public executions. Poles of the Resistance trying to escape the Nazi wrath discovered an odd ally: the Jewish badge.

"A terrible day," Emanuel Ringelblum noted in his diary of May 8, 1940. "Everywhere the Germans are rounding up Poles. Jews are screened to make certain they are not camouflaged Poles. . . . I've heard that during the raid Jews of Aryan appearance were ordered to speak Yiddish to identify themselves."

A brisk trade developed, Poles buying or borrowing badges from Jews. The new enterprise, which was not without risks, flourished in candy stores, cafés, and on the streets of the ghetto. The ten or fifteen zlotys that changed hands enabled the Jew to buy a morsel of food; the badge gave the Aryan access to the ghetto, where he might transact some business or get in touch with the Jewish Underground.

* * * * *

While opposition to the badge was almost nonexistent in the Eastern European countries occupied by the Nazis, the West fought savagely against it.

On November 8, 1940, the German authorities in France issued a number of travel restrictions concerning Jews and Negroes. A small hitch developed almost from the start. According to the Prefect of Police in the Seine district, the regulations could be enforced only with respect to Negroes, who might be distinguished by the pigmentation of their skin. But how was a Jew to be told apart from another Frenchman?

Partly as an answer to the puzzled prefect, Adolph Eichmann, Chief of the Jewish Department of the Gestapo in Berlin, proposed at a conference with experts on Jewish affairs held in the capital on March 4, 1942, that the Jewish badge be introduced in *all* occupied countries. In accord with this suggestion and upon direct instructions of Himmler, Helmuth Knochen, Chief of German Security Police in the Occupied Zone of France (Northern France) and in Belgium, sent invitations to experts on Jews in France, Belgium, and Holland to convene in Paris on the fourteenth of March. Knochen intended to proceed without delay, but obstacles developed virtually from the start and in the most unforeseen places. Vichy, upon whom the Germans could rely on any number of issues, appeared completely unco-operative. Xavier Vallat, Commissioner on Jewish Affairs, balked at the notion of the Jewish badge. To the SS representative, Captain Dannecker, who reproached him for his vacillating stand, Vallat said: "I am an anti-Semite of a much older vintage than you! On that score, I could be your father!" It was with considerable relief, therefore, that the German Ambassador to Vichy, Otto Abetz, reported to Berlin on March 31 that the unco-operative Vallat had been removed from his post. However, the new commissioner, Darquier de Pellepoix, proved hardly more tractable.

Even as the battle of the badge raged in France, opposition reared its head in Belgium, where two German generals who were in charge of military administration in that country announced they would not enforce the decree. Obviously something had to be done about Brigadier General Eggert Reder and General von Falkenhausen.

While the procedure in France and Belgium bogged down in recriminations and negotiations, the German authorities decided to go ahead with the introduction of the badge in Holland, where the decree was published on April 27, 1942.

On June 3, 1942, the German military commander in France finally issued the long-disputed order directing all Jews six years of age and over to wear, on the left side of the chest, the yellow hexagram the size of a man's palm with the inscription *Juif* (Jew). Belgium reluctantly fell into line. In the Free Zone of France, however, the badge was not enforced until November 11 of that year, when the area was occupied by the Germans.

On the day it was introduced in France, according to eye-witness reports, people exchanged kisses with wearers of the badge, offered them seats in public vehicles; priests uncovered their heads before them. A large number of Frenchmen appeared in public displaying yellow handkerchiefs in their breast pockets, carrying bouquets of yellow flowers, or toying with small yellow stars. Students devised ways of ridiculing the German decree. The Nazis struck back, arresting a large number of "saboteurs" and exiling them to concentration camps, where they wore white armbands with the inscription "Jew-Friend" (*Ami de Juifs*). German police reports from various French cities confirmed the fact that the attitude of the Gentile population toward the badge was no less hostile elsewhere than in Paris.

On June 7, 1942, Jewish war veterans pinned on their Stars, in addition to their military decorations, and paraded along Paris boulevards to the applause and cheers of large crowds. Groups of non-Jews promenaded in the streets, displaying the badge on their buttocks. A high dignitary of the Catholic church, Monsignor Chaptal, Auxiliary Bishop of Paris, whose mother was Jewish, put on a Star and led a public procession to the police station, where he planned to register as a Star-bearer. Priests and nuns of Jewish descent, exempted from wearing the badge in France, appeared on the streets displaying the yellow Star. Everywhere the people of France greeted and applauded the Star-bearers.

In order to divide the Jewish populace and the opposition,

the Nazis decided to make small concessions. They exempted 10,000 Jews who were citizens of neutral countries from wearing the badge. Exemptions were also granted to distinguished French citizens of Jewish descent, among them the famous writer Madame Colette, the widow of Henri Bergson, the wife of the Vichy Ambassador, Madame de Brinon, and others. This still left 100,000 Jews who were ordered to put on the Star.

With the sweeping decree published, several textile firms were engaged to prepare 400,000 badges. The large number ordered was not due to any desire on the part of the Germans to give the moribund French textile industry the stimulus it badly needed; the round figures were come by as a result of thorough study carried on in Berlin, where it was concluded that each French Jew possessed at least three garments, in addition to an overcoat. When the time came for distribution, the Germans found to their dismay that the supply exceeded the demand. Only 83,000 Stars were claimed. The rest remained in the warehouses.

In the Low Countries, Holland and Belgium, opposition to the badge was instantaneous and strong. In Holland, many non-Jews appeared in public wearing the Star. Clergymen denounced it from pulpits. In Belgium, a Rexist newspaper in Brussels bemoaned the opposition to the badge. According to the pro-Nazi paper, Belgian teachers were carrying on an insidious campaign in the classrooms, informing their pupils that the Star was a mark of distinction. Shopkeepers in Antwerp sold Stars in the Belgian national colors. College students everywhere pinned them on their clothing. In Brussels, on the first Sunday after the introduction of the badge, the streets were filled with a be-Starred populace.

In Denmark, King Christian X voiced the attitude of his people when he declared: "The Jews are a part of the Danish nation. We have no Jewish problem in our country because we never had an inferiority complex in relation to the Jews. If the Jews are forced to wear the yellow Star, I and my whole family shall wear it as a badge of honor." The badge was not introduced in Denmark.

In the satellite country of Croatia, the Germans encountered strong opposition from the clergy, particularly from Archbishop Alois Stepinac, who in other respects failed to show any opposition to German-Croatian collaboration. The bishop's ire was aroused when the Nazis ordered two priests and six nuns in his archdiocese to wear the Star of David because they were of Jewish descent. Even after the Germans had rescinded the order, Archbishop Stepinac declared from the pulpit: "I have ordered the priests and nuns to continue wearing this sign belonging to the people from whom the Savior came."

The Nazis fared no better in Bulgaria, where the government opposed introduction of anti-Jewish legislation. In August of 1942, the Germans finally prevailed. The publication of the decree resulted in mass protests and several public demonstrations. Minister of Justice Partoff maintained his opposition even after the law had been enacted; he asked the Commissioner for Jewish Affairs, Alexander Beleff, not to enforce the wearing of the Star.

According to a report of a German official stationed in that country, Bulgarian authorities were completely remiss in carrying out anti-Jewish laws. It appears that in October, 1942, only 20 per cent of Sofia's Jews wore the insignia. Moreover, the manufacture of the Star was abruptly suspended by the government under the pretext that electric current was in short supply.

In the other Axis satellite countries the badge was introduced much later than envisioned by the planners in Berlin, because of the vigorous opposition of the population. In some countries the wearing of the badge could not be enforced until the semi-independent governments were replaced by local Nazis or taken over by the Germans. The North-Italian government decreed the use of the badge in October, 1943; it appeared in Hungary after March of 1944. Romania, despite its long record of anti-Semitism, did not fall in line until 1943–44, when *Festung Europa* was beginning to show fissures. The badge was never worn in Finland.

In view of the many disasters visited upon the Jews, the vigorous opposition shown in some countries to the Jewish badge and the victories won as a result of that opposition may appear insignificant. But there is a lesson to be drawn from this, one that transcends the issue involved. Where a government and a people fought Nazi encroachments, first on a relatively minor issue such as the Star of David, and later on matters of life and death, many Jews were saved from extermination. Such were the experiences in Denmark, Finland, Bulgaria, and Italy. In France, almost 75 per cent of the Jews were saved, and a substantial percentage of the Jewish population survived in Hungary and Romania also.

CHAPTER THREE

FRANCE

The words *Liberté, Égalité, Fraternité*, proclaimed by the French Revolution, served in the nineteenth and twentieth centuries as inspiration to many countries seeking a free and just life. Understandably, those words and the principles they embodied came under the most savage attacks by Nazi philosophers, political leaders, and educators.

In 1939, there lived in France approximately 300,000 Jews. Between 40,000 and 50,000 Jewish refugees from Holland and Belgium arrived in the country by 1940. After the collapse of the French Army, the country was divided into two zones: the northern, under German military occupation, and the southern, so-called Free Zone, the latter enjoying the fiction of possessing independent status under Marshall Petain in Vichy. In November, 1942, the Germans, together with their Italian allies, occupied the Free Zone.

The attitude of the French population toward the invaders could not be anything but hostile. Nevertheless, soon after the Occupation, small groups of collaborationists and long-repressed quislings sprouted like weeds all over the land. A Nazi-sponsored press declared itself the true voice of the French people, and a subservient administration in Vichy tried ingratiating itself with the conquerors by reactionary and fascist gestures and a virulent anti-Jewish policy. A Statute of Laws aimed at the Jews was promulgated, and a Commission on Jewish Affairs was created under the notorious anti-Semite, Xavier Vallat.

From the point of view of the Nazi masters, everything was coming along well. The collaborationists in France, as elsewhere, were apt, and often eager, pupils. The "final solution" to the

Jewish "question" appeared imminent. The local Fascists did not scruple to help in the solution; they demurred only when the Germans mentioned *extermination* as a way of solving the Jewish problem once and for all. Shocked at the naked brutality of the Nazis, the native Fascists balked. Couldn't the Germans settle for less than total extermination of the Jews? Would they agree to a "partial solution," if, let us say, the *foreign* Jews living in France were turned over to their tender mercies?

The Germans readily agreed. The unappeasable seemed content. They did not molest the French Jews until they had disposed of the foreign-born.

Of the 350,000 Jews living in France in 1940, from 75,000 to 90,000, according to varying estimates, were deported and killed. Thus, the number of Jews saved (about 75 per cent) was larger than in any other Nazi-controlled or satellite countries, except Finland, Bulgaria, Italy, and Denmark. Was this due to the policies of the Vichy government, the attitude of the French population, or the changeable fortunes of war? Was it because neutral Spain, Switzerland, and philo-Semitic Italy bordered France and its not easily accessible mountainous regions, where Jews could hide? Undoubtedly each of these factors played its part in the saving of Jews. If one were forced to settle on the most influential factor, however, he would have to choose the attitude of the French population.

Although most Frenchmen, like the majority of the Christians in other lands occupied by the Nazis, remained silent witnesses to the ordeal suffered by the Jews, a militant, articulate minority soon became the voice and conscience of France.

The Germans were quick to express their disappointment at the meager accomplishments of the French anti-Semites and collaborationists. The strident anti-Jewish propaganda carried on in France, even prior to World War II, by corrupt, venal politicians and journalists, the hysterical Jew-hatred of writers like Ferdinand Céline, Charles Maurras, the brothers Tharaud, and others, apparently did not impress most Frenchmen. In any case, the German Security Police Commander for Northern France and Belgium, Helmuth Knochen, stated petulantly in a report he submitted to his superiors in January, 1941: "It is almost impossible to cultivate in Frenchmen anti-Jewish feeling based on ideological grounds." He recommended outright bribes and other "economic advantages" that would "more easily create sympathy for the anti-Jewish struggle." As a result, informers were recruited to point out Jews in the streets and find them in hiding places. The reward ranged from 100 to 500 francs per Jew, depending on the importance of the victim.

But even economic incentives failed to produce the desired results. Heinz Roethke, Chief of the Jewish Section of the Gestapo, no longer could hide his disappointment. "It is necessary," declared Roethke, "to associate French anti-Semites in our drive to flush out the camouflaged Jews. Money," he said, attacking the economic incentive theory, "should play no part in this."

Home-grown Fascists complained as loudly as the Germans themselves at the failure of the anti-Jewish drive. The Chief of the Special Police of the Commission on Jewish Affairs reported in March, 1942, that his henchmen met with "incomprehension and even hostility. . . . The French population," he complained, "considers the anti-Jewish acts as something foreign, imposed upon us by German authorities."

A year passed without any appreciable gains being made in the anti-Jewish drive. "The large majority of Aryans continues to demonstrate an exaggerated philo-Semitism," a police report stated. "Our control, so far as the movement of Jews is concerned, is nonexistent. They [the Jews] change their dwellings constantly and camouflage themselves with the complicity of almost the total Aryan population."

In many instances, the Police for Jewish Affairs obtained only the most grudging co-operation from the regular police, the *gendarmerie*, and the civilian administration. Numerous reports from headquarters and from the regional offices of the PJA in

Paris, Marseilles, Bordeaux, Limoges, Clermont-Ferrand, Lyons, Nice, and Toulouse complained about a total disregard of their orders and requests on the part of the regional prefects. "They do not apply the [legal] sanctions we ask for [against the Jews]. . . . Many Jews [after their detention] escape from precints and offices of prefects, or even from offices of the central administration in Vichy. . . . In many instances, Jews are warned of imminent arrest, house searches, and raids which we are required to carry out [against them]." That these complaints had some basis in fact is illustrated by the following: A Jew with forged Aryan papers was caught in the streets of Lyons and brought to the police station. There he was abandoned by the arresting officer, who left abruptly without making any charges. The head of the police precinct, instead of imprisoning the man, inquired: "Why didn't you come directly to me with your problem? I would have helped you."

In 1942, the Nazis, impatient at their lack of progress toward their cherished final solution, planned a massive raid in Paris for the purpose of rounding up the 22,000 Jews still at large in the city. With characteristic lack of taste they chose July 14— Bastille Day, a holiday revered by all Frenchmen—for their action. On the advice of a high Nazi officer the raid was postponed two days. Members of the French police and administration who got wind of the plans warned the Jews of the coming raid. Jewish passers-by were approached by policemen and advised to hide. But despite the warnings and the help extended by many well-meaning and courageous Frenchmen, approximately 11,000 Jews were seized, among them 4,000 children. The brutality displayed by the Germans shocked all France, and numerous French officials began to voice open defiance.

According to a cable to the London *Times* in September of 1942, the military commander of Lyons, General de St. Vincent, refused flatly to obey an order from Vichy for mass arrests of Jews in the Free Zone. The general was summarily dismissed. Another *Times* cable of February, 1943, reported the arrest of

400 policemen and the execution of a score of them; the charge against them was refusal to round up and arrest foreign Jews. In Nice, occupied by the Italians, André Chaigneau, newly appointed Prefect of Police, invited to his offices representatives of the Jewish community for the purpose of expressing his regret at the anti-Jewish laws. "I will not allow any arbitrary acts against the Jews in my department," he declared, "nor will I leave the privilege of defending Jews to the Italians."

A French-Jewish historian, Léon Poliakov, himself a survivor of the Nazi holocaust in France, tells of the aid given Jews by thousands of Frenchmen, Dutch, and Belgians: "The *camouflés* in France and the *onderduikers* in Holland ran into the tens of thousands. Numerous clandestine organizations in these countries helped supply funds to the *camouflés*. Jews and non-Jews cooperated in this effort. Veritable factories for the manufacture of false identification papers operated in the large cities. Hiding Jews became a subsidiary activity of the Resistance movements. Across the Alps and the Pyrenees, along the hazardous routes, Dutch, Belgian, and French Jews were convoyed by the thousands to Switzerland or to Spain." Peasants, workmen, and professionals were part of the great network created for the purpose of rescuing the Jews. There were as well, among those who helped the humble and obscure, many men whose names are illustrious throughout the world. And famous French writers, both at home and abroad, cried out their sympathy for the persecuted Jews—Jacques Maritain, Paul Claudel, Francois Mauriac; the Leftist writers Paul Elouard and Louis Aragon; the existentialist, Jean-Paul Sartre; the eminent and venerable Romain Rolland; Andre Malraux, Antoine de Saint-Exupery; the survivor of Nazi concentration camps, David Rousset, and others.

Nor was the French Underground remiss in its role as a rescuer of Jews. The popular Resistance periodical *Combat* gave voice to French indignation in its issue of April 24, 1943: "At a time when France stands sickened with horror as a result of the monstrous treatment accorded the Jews whom Vichy is delivering like cattle to the Germans . . . when innocent men go to their death . . . their children abandoned . . . when the cream of the French people are opening their doors to these unfortunate children who will never again see their parents . . . when priests are flung into prisons for protecting from German bestiality those children whose only crime is being Jewish, *Combat* raises its voice in vehement protest. . . . Foreign Jews are suffering and enduring martyrdom. . . . We warn their tormentors, German or French! One day you will be brought to account!"

The Jews of France, eager to strike back, turned to the Underground in large numbers and were accepted on an equal basis in the French Resistance movement. Separate, exclusively Jewish Resistance groups or partisan units were rather few in France. The French-Jewish writer David Knout, himself a member of the Resistance, estimates Jewish participation in French fighting units during the early stages of the Occupation at about 33 per cent, and in groups such as *Combat* and *Liberté* at about 20 per cent.

Non-Jewish Resistance leaders were completely objective in their treatment of the Jewish members of their group, particularly when it came to assigning tasks to them. One of the first to be parachuted into France, in October, 1941, was a Jew named Riviere, known in the Resistance by the names "Rambert" or "Ronsard." Another Jew, Tayar, an expert in news transmission, was assigned to organize the clandestine radio center in Lyons. Jews who were qualified were permitted to reach positions of leadership. One of the leaders in the organization of the entire information network of the French Underground was a Jew, Colonel Manuel. The writer Marc Bloch was head of the information network for the region of Clermont-Ferrand and Limoges. Denise Mitrani, author of the book *Réseau d'évasion*, was one of the chief agents of VIC, an English organization that aided people who desired to escape France. The talented French poet, Francois Vernet, chief of the United

Resistance Movement (MUR) laboratory for forging documents, was a Salonikan Jew whose real name was Albert Sciaky. Among the followers of General de Gaulle were George Boris (Goldenberg) and Lt. Jacques Bingen, who organized the Free French merchant marine in North Africa. Pierre Mendes-France, arrested by the Germans in North Africa, escaped in time to become a bomber pilot with the Free French forces. The Underground group *Franc Tireur* was founded by Jean-Pierre Levy (Lenoir). Among the half dozen founders of *Liberation*, three were Jews. The secretary general of *Combat* was a Jew, Bernard, junior. After he was seized and deported, his sister Jacqueline took his place. Two Jews of world renown, Leon Blum and Daniel Mayer, actively fought the Germans. The aging Blum, several times premier of his country, was flung into a concentration camp after a mock trial by the Nazis. Daniel Mayer eluded the Germans and served with the Underground until the end of the war.

A story that well illustrates the important role of Jews in the French Resistance and the excellent relations between all those comprising the many groups is told by Léon Poliakov: a French duke came to London to join the Free French volunteers. The duke was advised to change his name in order to protect his family at home from German reprisals. The titled Frenchman agreed, and selected for himself the name of Levy as a gesture of solidarity with the Levys, Cohens, Blocks, and Greenbergs who in turn had adopted such Underground names as Durand, Martine, and Vernet.

*   *   *   *   *

The clergy of France, Catholic and Protestant alike, played a role second to none in their opposition to the anti-Jewish decrees and in their rescue activities on behalf of the persecuted. The highest dignitaries of the Catholic church in France early condemned the Nazi war of extermination against the Jews. The Archbishop of Toulouse, later elevated to Cardinal, Monsignor

Jules Gerard Saliege, stated in his famous letter of August 23, 1942: "There is a Christian morality . . . that confers rights and imposes duties. These duties and these rights come from God. One can violate them. But no mortal has the power to suppress them. Alas, it has been destined for us to witness the dreadful spectacle of children, women, and old men being treated like vile beasts; of families being torn apart and deported to unknown destinations . . . In our diocese, frightful things take place in the camps Noe and Recebedou . . . The Jews are our brethren. They belong to mankind. No Christian dare forget that! . . . France, my beloved land; France, which cherishes in the conscience of all its children the tradition of respect for the individual; France, the generous and chivalrous—France is not responsible for these horrors!"

The Bishop of Montauban, Monsignor Pierre-Marie Theas instructed the priests in his diocese to read the following urgent message: "My dear brethren: Scenes of indescribable suffering and horror are abroad in our land . . . In Paris, by tens of thousands, Jews are being subjected to the most barbarous treatment. In our district we are witnessing wretched spectacles of families being uprooted, of men and women being treated like beasts and later deported . . . to face the gravest perils. I indignantly protest in the name of Christian conscience and proclaim that all men . . . are brothers, created by the same God . . . The current anti-Semitic measures are a violation of human dignity and the sacred rights of the individual and the family. May God comfort and strengthen those who are persecuted."

The Bishop of Montauban was eventually deported, but other churchmen rose in their pulpits to voice the indignation of an outraged people. The Primate of France and Archbishop of Lyons, Cardinal Gerlier, defied the authorities with his letter of sympathy to the Grand Rabbi of France, after the crude Nazi attempt to burn the synagogues of Paris in October, 1941. Subsequently, in pastoral letters to the Catholics of France, Cardinal Gerlier called upon them to refuse to surrender to the authorities the hidden children of deported Jews. Moreover, he violently protested against the anti-Jewish atrocities and deportations, and enjoined French Catholics to give the victims every assistance.

Similar letters of protest were issued by bishops Delay of Marseilles, Moussaron of Albi, and Remond of Nice. A joint declaration, initiated by Cardinal [Suhard], Archbishop of Paris, in July of 1942 and submitted to Marshal Petain, stated: "We are profoundly shocked by the mass arrests and the inhuman treatment of the Jews at the Velodrome d'Hiver [in Paris]."

The Protestant church, though smaller than the Catholic, was no less active in its expressions of indignation and offers of aid. Marc Boegner, President of the National Council of the Reformed Church in France, wrote to the Grand Rabbi on March 26, 1941: "The National Council . . . has authorized me to express to you . . . our feelings of indignation at the racial laws introduced in our country . . . Our Church feels a deep sympathy with your communities . . . and for your faithful followers . . . Our Church has undertaken certain courses of action. It will not be diverted in its endeavors to have the anti-Jewish laws reexamined."

German authorities and officials in Vichy appeared unmoved by protests from the churchmen. The population of France, on the other hand, took them to heart. How effective the appeals of the clergy were may be gauged by the venomous attack against the Catholic Church published by a pro-Nazi journalist, Jacques Marcy. "Every Catholic family shelters a Jew," Marcy declared in a quisling newspaper published in Lyons. "The French authorities provide Jews with false identification papers and passports. Priests help them across the Swiss frontier. In Toulouse, Jewish children have been concealed in Catholic schools; the civilian Catholic officials receive intelligence of a scheduled deportation of Jews, advise a great number of the refugee Jews about it, and the result is that about 50 per cent of the undesirables escape." Moreover, protested the collaborationist newsman, "Catholic teachers distributed copies of a pastoral letter of Archbishop Saliege against the deportation."

The fulminations of this writer exaggerated the real state of affairs. Nevertheless, it was true—the final solution, so dear to the Nazi hearts, was not proceeding according to plan. "In a general way," says a police report of November, 1943, "the situation on the religious front remains unchanged . . . The clergy continues, as in the past, to disapprove of the anti-Jewish laws, under the pretense of Christianity."

*   *   *   *   *

The Church did not content itself with exhortations to the faithful; it solemnly urged them to act. Archbishop Gerlier himself sponsored and supported the activities of the anti-Nazi Christian Friendship (*L'Amitié Chrétienne*) which, under the brilliant leadership of the Jesuit Father Pierre Chaillet, fought anti-Semitism and rescued many Jews.

Father Chaillet, hero of the French Resistance, was also busy publishing the Underground paper *Letters of Christian Evidence (Cahiers du Témoignage Chrétien)* with a circulation of about 50,000 copies. But he found time to haunt the street of Lyons in search of abandoned Jewish children, whom he hid. Once he discovered four children huddling in a cave, half-dead from starvation and trembling with fear. He led the children to a monastery, where they were sheltered with several hundred others. On another occasion, Father Chaillet collected and hid a dozen Jewish children whose parents had been deported. He rescued thirty Jewish children from French police stations, where they had been brought for questioning. He prepared forged documents for the waifs and dispatched young bicyclists to surrounding villages with an appeal to French peasants, who responded by sheltering the children and even "adopting" them until the end of the Occupation. Few of the Jewish "peasant" children were betrayed. In September, 1942, the Prefect of Police demanded from Father Chaillet the surrender of 120 Jewish children reported hidden by the Jesuits. Chaillet refused and was supported in this action by Cardinal Gerlier. The priest was jailed, but the children were spirited away and distributed among Christian families in the nearby villages.

Father Chaillet's place was taken by others. One of Cardinal Gerlier's co-workers, Abbé Alexander Glasberg, succeeded in rescuing 2,000 Jews from French concentration camps. In addition, Glasberg organized a home for Jewish teen-agers, concealing sixty-five of them in the mountains. Cardinal Gerlier's secretary and chief adviser on Jewish affairs, Abbé Glasberg, was a Ukrainian Jew, born in 1902. He left Russia during the Russian Revolution and came to Paris. Embracing Catholicism, he entered a theological seminary and was ordained. During World War II this fearless and energetic man put aside all his work and devoted himself to rescue activities. Even after the Liberation his work on behalf of the Jews did not cease; he aided Jewish survivors and assisted illegal emigrants to Palestine.

In an interview held after the war with a correspondent of the Jewish-American newspaper *Forward*, Glasberg, who speaks Yiddish fluently, said: "I am not a hero ... I accomplished no heroic deeds ... The two thousand Jews I helped rescue ... this was a drop in the ocean. Six million Jews were killed ..." And he added wistfully: "We could have rescued many more if we'd had more money."

Important rescue work was carried on by a Catholic missionary organization, the Fathers of Our Lady of Zion *(Pères de Notre Dame de Sion.)* At the head of this group was the Reverend Father Superior Charles Devaux, who is credited with saving 443 Jewish children and 500 adults. At the end of 1942, Father Devaux organized a temporary shelter for his wards on Rue Notre Dame de Champs. From there he sent the children to many parts of the country, where they found temporary homes with workmen's families, among peasants, in convents and monasteries. The expenses were provided for by the group. When the relief work grew beyond their modest means, they solicited and received money from individuals, Jews and non-Jews alike, and from various organizations. The Gestapo were irked by the clergyman's ceaseless activities on behalf of the Jews. They summoned Father Devaux and cited a long list of his offenses. Theodor Dannecker, SS officer noted as a hangman of French Jews, personally dealt with Devaux. He slapped the priest's face as an initial warning, and cautioned him to cease helping Jews or accept the consequences. Father Devaux returned to his rescue work. In 1945, the brave priest was interviewed by a Jewish journalist who asked him whether he had not been aware of the great danger involved in his rescue activities. Father Devaux's answer was simple: "Of course I knew it, but this knowledge could not stop me from doing what I considered to be my duty as a Christian and a human being."

*   *   *   *   *

Pastor Vergara was a Protestant clergyman. During the massive raid staged by the Germans on July 16, 1942, when they seized 11,000 Jews, Vergara, assisted by his wife and several devoted followers, appeared at a concentration camp and boldly demanded to see the officer in charge. When the German officer came to the gate, he found himself staring down at a small man with ruffled gray hair and protruding cheekbones, accompanied by several women. Vergara reached into his pocket and pulled out an "order" for the release of Jewish children held at the camp. The order, bearing an official Gestapo mark, was a forgery, the pastor's handiwork. The officer in charge hesitated, but finally complied. Seventy Jewish children were placed at Vergara's disposal. With the aid of Father Chaillet and Devaux, Vergara distributed the children among Gentile families. The Gestapo, learning of the deception, raided Vergara's house but did not find him. Frustrated, the Germans seized the pastor's son-in-law and killed him. Mme. Vergara was tortured and their son deported. But Pastor Vergara, as soon as he came out of hiding, resumed his rescue work.

*   *   *   *   *

The legendary Father Marie-Benoit, or Padre Benedetti, as he was briefly known, was born in the French village of Bourg d'Iré, Maine-et-Loire. He entered the Capuchin Order, served five years in World War I, and was wounded at Verdun. After the war he continued his studies at the Capuchin College in Rome, received a doctorate in theology, and while still a young man, won recognition as a scholar of Hebrew and Judaism. His theoretical interest in Jewish affairs changed abruptly to the practical when Hitler invaded France.

Gifted with exceptional ability as an organizer and almost inexhaustible energy, the black-bearded, brown-robed Capuchin priest transformed the monastery at 51, Rue Croix-de-Regnier, Marseilles, into a rescue agency. A busy passport mill, located in the cellar of the monastery, fabricated and distributed hundreds of identification cards, certificates of baptism, employers' recommendations, and other documents. Procedures were set up for smuggling Jews and anti-Nazi refugees into Spain and Switzerland. The smugglers on both sides of the well-guarded frontiers demanded and received exorbitant prices. Various Jewish organizations and the French Resistance were solicited for funds.

Father Marie-Benoit's burgeoning enterprise could not long remain a secret from the Gestapo, but the suspicions of the Germans only complicated his work; they did not halt it. The first serious blow occurred with the German occupation of the Free Zone, which included the city of Marseilles, where most of Benoit's rescue centers were operating. Further smuggling forays into Spain and Switzerland were now out of the question. There was only one avenue of escape still open, the Riviera and Haute-Savoie, occupied by Germany's vacillating ally, Italy. Father Benoit, aware of the little time that stood between the Jews and annihilation, went to Nice in a desperate search for allies. He met with representatives of the Union of French Jews (*Union Génerale des Israelites de France*, UGIF) and several important Italian officials, and laid before them his bold rescue plan. Almost immediately the complicated transfer from Marseilles to the Italian Zone was arranged. Thousands of Jews began to cross the demarcation line.

The Germans, alarmed at the loss of prospective candidates for their gas chambers, protested the illegal traffic streaming across the line. No less a personage than Foreign Minister Joachim von Ribbentrop saw fit to complain about this matter to Mussolini. The Italian dictator agreed to give the problem his immediate attention, and appointed a Commissioner for Jewish Affairs, Guido Lospinoso, with the rank of general and with headquarters in Nice.

Father Benoit's enterprise appeared doomed, but he was the last one in the organization to show any concern. He decided to counter Ribbentrop's move with one of his own. Through the intercession of the aged Jesuit, Father Bremont of Nice, he met a person of influence, the Jewish-Italian financier, Angelo Donati. After a long conversation which both men found fruitful, they decided to call on General Lospinoso. There is no record of their conversation, and we do not know how Mussolini's Commissioner for Jewish Affairs was won over to the side of the man who was supposed to be his implacable foe. It is entirely possible that Lospinoso agreed to co-operate out of his own deep sympathy for the persecuted Jews. But there is also no doubt that he was captivated by Benoit's eloquence, broad humanity, and dedication. He promised to do everything he could to alleviate the plight of the Jews.

With Donati and Lospinoso co-operating, the smuggling of Jews was resumed on a formidable scale. The Gestapo and their French collaborators pounced on the fleeing Jews, but they could hardly stem the massive exodus. A new protest against the priest was lodged in Rome. Several days later, Father Marie-Benoit was summoned to appear in the Italian capital.

The fate of 50,000 Jews who subsisted in the South of France, constantly threatened with deportation, hung in the balance. While the Jews were understandably apprehensive, Father Benoit hardly had time to worry over being summoned to Rome to be censured. A new plan of action was maturing in his brain, and this prompted him to seek an audience with the Pope soon after arriving in Rome. His request granted, Benoit appeared before the Holy See to plead his new rescue scheme. His plan embodied the following: 1. gathering information concerning the whereabouts of Jews deported from France to the East, particularly to Upper Silesia whence the most dreadful news had begun to arrive about a camp named Auschwitz; 2. obtaining more humane treatment of Jews in French concentration camps; 3. facilitating repatriation of Spanish Jews who were residing in France; 4. transferring 50,000 French Jews to Morocco, Algiers, and Tunisia where, in view of Allied military successes, they would be safe, instead of bringing them to Italy.

Although the Vatican was favorably impressed with Father Benoit and his bold scheme, the plan was not worth much unless some of the belligerents, namely the Italian government on the one side and the British and American on the other, agreed to co-operate. Realizing this, Father Benoit began the delicate negotiations without delay. He had little difficulty in reaching the British Ambassador and the United States representative at the Vatican. Both diplomats listened to his rescue scheme and promised to interest their governments. Delay was feared when Mussolini was deposed on July 26, 1943, but Badoglio's government, which replaced the Duce, readily agreed to Benoit's plan, promising to supply four ships for the transport of the Jews. Israel Yefroykin, representative of the American Joint Distribution Committee, pledged to finance the project. Word was received from the British government that it was favorably disposed toward this operation and would place no obstacles in its path.

By September, 1943, all arrangements had been completed.

Approximately 30,000 French Jews in the Italian Zone were poised for flight. But the grandiose project was not destined to succeed. With the surrender of the Badoglio government to the Allies, German troops swept into the Italian Zone and the thousands of Jews fled in panic across the Alps to Italy and Switzerland.

Undaunted by the collapse of his grand scheme, Father Benoit, aided by the Vatican, prevailed upon the Spanish government to authorize its consuls in France to issue entry permits to all Jews who could prove Spanish nationality. Operating procedure was established, and in case of doubt about an applicant's nationality, final decision was to be in the hands of an impartial arbiter. In view of the fact that Father Marie-Benoit was named impartial arbiter, many Jews were rescued by the Spanish entry permits. But Benoit's days in the South of France were numbered. The Gestapo laid out its nets carefully, determined to capture him. Although Benoit eluded the Germans, he was finally prevailed upon by his colleagues to leave France. He transferred his activities to Italy, where he gained fame as Padre Benedetti.

North Italy was in the Gestapo's grip when Benoit went there. He had to move gingerly to avoid arrest. But he plunged into rescue work immediately, accepting the leadership of the Committee to Assist Jewish Emigrants (*Delegazione Assistanza Emigrati Ebrei*, DELASEM), whose director had been arrested by the Germans. The Committee had gone underground some time before, and the International College of Capuchins at 159 Via Siciliano now became their headquarters. A mill was set up for the manufacture of false documents. Contact was established with friendly Italian, Swiss, Hungarian, French, and Romanian officials. Soon hundreds of Jews who had been living in terror were provided by Padre Benedetti with new documents that established them as Aryan Romanians, Hungarians, or Swiss. Since approximately 3,000 Jews with forged documents had to be provided with food-ration cards, Padre Benedetti's mill was kept working day and night. And he worked day and night too, scorning dangers of which others constantly warned him. Alcide de Gasperi, the late Prime Minister of Italy, at that time an official in the Vatican library, was one of many who cautioned Benoit to be more careful. Even the arrest and torture of his close co-worker, Brigadier de Marco of the Italian police, failed to divert the priest from his work. Subsequent Gestapo raids deprived him of his three Jewish colleagues: Steven Schwamm, Aaron Kascherstein, and Aba Formanski. Several more arrests decimated the leadership of the group, and Benoit-Benedetti reluctantly went into hiding. The time was early 1945; the war was almost over. His work was nearly done.

Father Benoit was one of a score of giants who strode across the slaughterhouse that was Occupied Europe, aiding those whom the rest of the world cynically abandoned to the Nazi guillotine. France has bestowed numerous honors upon him, as have many of those he helped rescue. An honor he claims to cherish most is the nickname: "Father of the Jews."

CHAPTER FOUR

THE LOW COUNTRIES

The Nazi decrees against the Jews aroused deep resentment among the Dutch. The so-called "laws" aimed at the Jewish minority were considered by many as the prelude to a lawlessness that would eventually jeopardize the rights and freedoms of every Netherlander. Thus, rejection of the anti-Semitic legislation foisted on them by the occupying power was an important aspect of non-co-operation among all strata of the population. Opposition to anti-Jewish measures became one of the criteria for patriotism.

An early test of strength between the Dutch and their tormentors occurred late in 1940 when the Nazis prohibited the appointment or promotion of Jewish officials, ordered the dismissal of Jewish teachers, and introduced special benches for Jewish students. The Protestant churches reacted vigorously by lodging a protest with the German *Reichskomissar*. A distinguished educator, Professor R. P. Cleevringa, Dean of the University of Leyden, protested against the dismissal of his Jewish colleague, the prominent lawyer Professor E. M. Meijers. The dean was banished to a concentration camp as an object lesson to the rebellious Netherlanders. Far from being intimidated, the students of Leyden University, joined by others from colleges throughout the country, went on strike. The Amsterdam *Studenten Corps* voted dissolution rather than ban its Jewish members. The Christian Students' Association also dissolved as an expression of protest.

On February 9, 1941, the Nazis provoked the first of the anti-Jewish riots in the city of Amsterdam, where 70,000 of their intended victims lived. The Nazis counted on the usual stage-managed pogrom carried out by local goons, directed by a few SS men. They did not expect the Jews to strike back. They did not expect aroused Dutch workmen in Amsterdam and other cities to put down their tools, thus paralyzing the nation. The romp that turned into a savage battle and ended in a humiliating defeat for the attackers started early in the morning on February 9. A mob of collaborationist members of the Dutch National Socialist party, accompanied by German soldiers, marched noisily through the streets of Amsterdam towards the Jewish neighborhood. Roaring insults at all those they suspected of being Jewish, they held their wrath until arrival at their destination. There they smashed windows in cafés, and homes, attacked Jewish passers-by, dragged their victims from moving trolleys. It required some hours for the victims to get over the shock. Then, slowly, the Jews of Amsterdam, aided by Christians, stormed back at the invading hoodlums. A savage battle raged throughout the Jewish quarter until the invaders were forced to give ground and retreat. But they returned in the evening, their depleted ranks filled by reinforcements from the city's underworld. Now the Jews of Amsterdam were prepared. Every scrap of iron had been commandeered to create a meager arsenal. Knuckle-dusters and other "weapons" were collected and distributed among the fighters, many of whom were factory workers and longshoremen. Patrols consisting of both Jewish and non-Jewish workers stood ready to defend Jewish shops. Christian physicians pledged their aid. The hoodlums struck, were repulsed, and returned two days later for another assault. The defenders retaliated. Of the attackers, approximately 50 per cent were wounded. There were dead on both sides.

Discarding their false role as interested observers and amused outsiders, the Germans confronted the weary and outnumbered Jewish defenders with three battalions of police. (The Dutch police were not involved in this action.) The police battalions, armed with automatic weapons and tanks, were met by the Jewish *knokploegen* (fighting units) whose weapons consisted of little more than iron pipes and curses. The Germans inflicted heavy casualties on the Jews, sealed off the Jewish quarter in the old city with barbed wire, and posted guards around it. They raised the two drawbridges connecting that quarter with other sectors of the city. On the same day, several prominent Jews were summoned to appear before the German commander of Amsterdam, and instructed to form a *Jooden-Raad* (Jewish Council) on the familiar pattern established by the Nazis in all the ghettos in Poland and elsewhere. The Council's initial task was to order the surrender of all weapons without delay. The *Jooden-Raad* complied, but the Jews of Amsterdam refused to give up their arms.

A new outbreak of violence on February 19 gave the Germans the opportunity for which they had been waiting. They surrounded the isolated Jewish quarter and seized 425 young Jews in the streets and deported them to the Mauthausen concentration camp in Austria.

Dutch public opinion was outraged. In Amsterdam 2,200 workmen went out on strike. Before long, the strike movement spread to other plants in the city and elsewhere. The unprecedented mass action, while a direct result of the deportation of Jews, was also Dutch labor's warning that it was determined to fight conscription of man power to be sent to Germany.

The strike paralyzed railway yards, street railways, shipbuilding and other basic industries. Its effectiveness surprised the most optimistic among the labor leaders. It also surprised and astonished the Germans, who reacted with characteristic ferocity, arresting workers indiscriminately, deporting them to concentration camps.

The ineffectual and powerless *Jooden-Raad* was again summoned to appear before the German commander. The Nazis, having tried other measures to cope with the unprecedented action of the Dutch, now tried blackmail. They warned members of the *Jooden-Raad* that 300 Jewish hostages would be taken unless the general strike were halted without delay. The Jewish "leaders" acquiesced, but they were hardly in a position to influence the course of a strike that affected all of Holland.

Eventually the naked brutality of the Nazis prevailed. Although the strikers did not achieve their goal—the release of 425 Jews who had been seized—they put the Germans on notice that Holland would not supinely bend its knee before a tyrant. The Nazis, for their part, loosed a reign of terror throughout the land and seized an additional 390 Jewish hostages. Of the total of more than 800 Jewish youths, only one survived to relate the terrible story of Mauthausen.

* * * * *

In the fall of 1942, mass deportations of Jews began on a large scale. There were no neutral countries nearby where Jews might seek shelter, and Holland has no mountains or forests. The land is flat, like an open palm. The final solution for the Dutch Jews appeared close at hand.

In one of the most unprecedented mass acts of the war, the Dutch people came forward to offer the Jews the only shelter available—their homes. Thousands of Dutch families risked everything, including their lives, by hiding the Jews in their attics, hanging ceilings, walls, and cellars. Of the 40,000 Jews thus concealed, 15,000 survived; the rest were discovered and murdered by the Nazis, often along with those who had given them shelter. About 110,000, approximately 75 per cent of the Jewish population, were deported.

In her diary that has now become celebrated throughout the world, the gifted young Anne Frank relates, among other things, the ingenious methods used in hiding Jews. As in the tragic Frank case, accidents were often responsible for the discovery of hiding places. The two families of noble and self-sacrificing Netherlanders who helped the Franks were sent to concentration camps. But not all the endings were tragic, as was testified by the experience of the Dutch grocer Leendert Hordijk, who sheltered five Jews in his home from 1942 to 1945. He contrived to hide his Jewish friends between the ceiling and the roof of his small house in Monnikendam, a community of 3,000. For three years, in addition to risking his life and the lives of the others in his large family, Hordijk shared with his guests the food from his meager rations. Like thousands of other Dutchmen, Hordijk was motivated by principle and a deep and abiding belief that, the Nazis to the contrary, man was created in the image of God. Like the thousands whose names we will never know, Leendert Hordijk, the grocer, did not dream of reward. (In 1951, an American-Jewish industrialist, Allen B. Rabin, invited the Hordijk family to come and live in America. The Dutch grocer accepted and came to the United States, accompanied by his wife and five children. They settled on a farm in California, bought for them by the grateful American Jew who had read of their deeds during the war.)

The deportations continued; long trains dragged their human cargo eastward to the extermination ovens that belched smoke day and night. The Dutch Resistance cried to every Hollander: "Fellow countrymen: The deportation of all Jewish citizens... is the final link in the long chain of inhuman measures... It means the complete annihilation of the Jews... The Netherlands has been deeply humiliated... We must prove our honor is not lost and our conscience not silenced... We ask our fellow Netherlanders to sabotage all preparations and executions of mass deportations. Remember the February strikes when an aroused people proved what it could do! We call upon burgomasters and high officials to risk their positions, if necessary, by refusing to co-operate with the Germans. We expect everyone in the position to do so to sabotage..."

The acts of sabotage demanded by the Underground were carried on by a courageous few and on a small scale. The German military machine was still at the peak of its power, and retaliation was swift. But rescue work continued, by individuals and groups. Clandestine organizations flourished throughout the country: The National Organization To Help Those In Hiding

(*Landelijke Organisatsie for Hulp aan Onderduikers*); The Committee (*Het Comite*), founded in 1942 by a group of Utrecht students who specialized in hiding Jewish children; Center for Identity Documents (*Persoons Bewijs Centrale*) who supplied many Jews with Aryan documents. One group assigned itself the odd task of helping the Jews of Rotterdam to establish a clandestine synagogue.

* * * * *

After the Nazi invasion of Holland, the *hakhsharah* farm in Lundsrecht, which trained Jewish youths in agriculture prior to sending them to Palestine, formed a youth Underground of its own. At the head of this small Resistance group were one of the young teachers of the school, Joachim "Shushu" Simon, and his wife, Adina. With the aid of a number of friends, the Simons succeeded in establishing an underground railway to smuggle Jewish children to Switzerland. They were aided in this enterprise by the Jewish Rescue Office in Geneva. Impatient with the snail's pace of his own work while the Nazis were kidnaping and deporting the flower of Jewish youth, Shushu evolved a daring new plan. He decided to strike out across the Pyrenees to Spain, from which Palestine is easier to reach than from Switzerland. He ventured forth several times, leading groups of children across the heavily guarded borders of Holland and Belgium, through France, and across the rugged mountain ranges. The youthful Jewish teacher of agriculture became an ally of the night and was as swift and elusive as the wind. But he needed help—he could take the children only in small groups—and he appealed to the Dutch Socialist Underground. Among those who offered their assistance was a man named Joop Westerville, a principal in a Lundsrecht high school. Son of a pastor, Westerville was a noted educator and had spent six years as a teacher in the Dutch East Indies (Indonesia), where he had urged the native population to rebel against their colonial masters. Back in Holland, he established the school of which he was in full charge when Shushu Simon and Menahem Pinkhoff met with him in August, 1942. The meeting was brief, and when it was over Joop Westerville was a member of the Underground. Though Joop was long past the first flush of youth—the father of three children, a fourth on the way—he was eager for his first journey across the many borders bristling with Nazi bayonets.

Early in 1943, Shushu was captured by the Gestapo as he crossed the border from Belgium to the Netherlands. The Nazis demanded the names of his accomplices. He was subjected to the Gestapo treatment usually accorded those who chose to remain silent. His spirit as well as his body broken by the torture, Shushu slashed his veins. He died, having told nothing.

Joop Westerville was thrust into the position of leadership. It was now his job to lead the Jewish children across the Low Countries and mountainous peaks of France and Spain. This became part of his everyday existence, and he dedicated himself to it fully. At the foot of the Pyrenees where he usually took leave of the young *halutzim* (Zionist pioneers), Westerville enjoined them not to forget their non-Jewish comrades, and reminded them that they were bound to all humanity. After four days and nights of travel, sometimes by train and horse cart, but mostly on foot, he would see his beloved Holland again and find another small group of Jewish youths waiting to make the hazardous journey.

He was captured in the summer of 1944 when the Nazis, though still powerful, were beginning to reel from the blows of an aroused world. Westerville was flogged and sent to the Vught concentration camp. The Underground, which had come to rely on his brilliant leadership, felt his loss keenly. After many futile attempts, they established contact with the prisoner and evolved a plan for his rescue. Meanwhile, torture was part of Westerville's everyday diet in the camp, the Gestapo displaying particular ferocity toward this Aryan who helped save Jews. One of the notes smuggled out to the Underground by a camp physician reveals Westerville's ordeal. "I was forced to remain on my feet from Thursday noon until Saturday noon without a break, my hands fettered and bound behind my back. I am in a tiny cell in a dark cellar . . . My daily food ration is four slices of bread and a bottle of tea." This note, and others now in the archives of the Historical Institute at the *kibbutz* of the Ghetto Fighters in Galilee, Israel, goes on to say: "They interrogate me, bind and beat me . . . Each question is accompanied by blows and kicks. This morning I was advised that I would be court-martialed. They asked me if I cared to write a letter to my wife. I started eagerly to write but they stopped me and resumed the questioning . . . I have a moment of respite. But on Monday it will start all over again . . . I will not reveal any names to them. I am certain of this. I still feel strong. At night when there is a respite from the torture, my wounds have a chance to heal. Mornings, when questioning resumes, I am rested and alert. I will remain silent. I am confident of this."

The plans to rescue Westerville, so painstakingly prepared, were never carried out. The doctor who acted as liaison between the Dutch Underground and the prisoner was caught with the plan and executed. Joop Westerville was shot to death by the Germans in the woods near Vught.

Two weeks after her country had been liberated from the Nazi plague, Westerville's widow wrote to friends in Palestine: "We were freed [from Ravensbrueck concentration camp] by the Red Cross and are now in Sweden. In September I shall go back to Holland. But what is my house to me? I have heard nothing of my children since August, 1944. Write me about life in Palestine; I am interested."

The Dutch *hehalutz* survivors in Palestine remembered Joop Westerville. A forest of young trees was raised in his memory. And on the tenth anniversary of his death, a monument to him was erected in the state of Israel that his young friends had helped to establish. His widow came from Holland to attend the unveiling.

*   *   *   *   *

Of the approximately 45,000 Jews who in 1940 lived in Belgium, 25,000 were deported. The rest were snatched from Nazi deportation lists and death wagons, and hidden. Belgians from all walks of life joined in the great crusade, among them Dowager Queen Elizabeth, who rescued several hundred Jews. The Belgian police (Sûreté Publique) developed a unique skill in non-co-operation, losing and misplacing files on Jews, forging and manufacturing documents for the victims. Two department chiefs of the Ministry of Justice, Cornil and Platteau, saved many Jews from deportation by intervening directly. The Ministry of Justice made substantial sums of money available for the Jewish Defense Committee (Comité Juif de Défense). Major E. Calberg, a high official in another government department (Food and Supply), persuaded the Red Cross to surrender to him 1,000 food parcels, which he distributed to Jews in hiding.

Jean Herinckx, formerly Governor of Brabant and, during the Occupation, Burgomaster of Uccle, defied the Nazis openly by intervening several times on behalf of Jews, particularly Jewish children facing deportation. His vigorous denunciation of the badge decreed by the Nazis as part of Jewish dress encouraged a conference of Belgian mayors meeting in Brussels to condemn it. In the capital, the departments of Public Service and Social Welfare refused to make any distinction between Jews and non-Jews applying for aid. The Department of Registry helped Jews to evade deportation by facilitating mixed marriages. Officials of municipalities freely issued spurious documents of identity.

*   *   *   *   *

Jeanne Damman was an attractive young Catholic girl who made her home in Brussels. Before the German invasion she taught in a large school located in a Jewish neighborhood of the capital. In 1942, Nazi legislation excluded Jewish children from Belgian schools. A courageous Jewish couple, Professor Perlmann and his wife, established an underground school. They offered Jeanne Damman the position of principal and apprised her of the risks involved. Mlle. Damman accepted readily, but the school operated only briefly. It closed when the streets became unsafe for Jewish children. Deprived of her position, Mlle. Damman joined the Jewish Defense Committee, specializing in children's rescue, but at the same time continuing her work as an intelligence agent. After Liberation she devoted her time to rehabilitating concentration-camp returnees in a special school at Linkebeek, near Brussels.

*   *   *   *   *

Jeanne de Mulienaere, a Flemish-Catholic newspaperwoman, was active in the Belgian Underground and was introduced to the pressing problems of the Jews by her colleague, Vera Shapiro. The two women joined a Resistance ring which saved 3,000 Jewish children, dispatching them to monasteries and convents and hiding them in private dwellings. Their Underground ring manufactured false documents for Jews and advised them about escape routes.   *   *   *   *   *

The Jewish Defense Committee saved more than 2,000 young people from deportation and supplied 30,000 Jews with false documents. It financed several escape expeditions and supported Jews in hiding. A special branch of the Committee, which daily employed 300 persons, Jews and non-Jews, assisted Belgian post-office officials by intercepting denunciations of Jews mailed to the German authorities. The Jews threatened by the prospective informers were immediately warned; sometimes the incriminating information was destroyed.

One of the largest organizations in the country, ONE (*Oeuvre National de l'Enfance*), co-operated with the Jewish Defense Committee. Its director-general, Mlle. Yvonne Nevejean, served as liaison between Jewish organizations in the country and the Belgian government-in-exile, and was able to save hundreds of Jewish children by personal intervention.

Jewish partisan units (Maquis) constituted part of the Belgian Underground, which spared no efforts in order to arouse the populace against Nazi atrocities. On April 19, 1943, the Jewish Underground, aided by Christian railroad-men, intercepted and derailed a train full of Jewish deportees bound from detention at Malines to an extermination camp in the East. Several hundred Jews—more than a thousand, by some estimates—scattered in the countryside and found shelter.

* * * * *

Belgian clergymen were among the most active in aiding and rescuing Jews. A Catholic group, Our Lady of Zion *(Notre Damę de Sion)*, deprived the German deportation trains of 200 Jewish children, who were skillfully hidden in several convents in Belgium. Abbé Joseph André, vicar of the St. Jean Baptiste Church in Namur, where he presided over a house filled with Jewish children, worked closely with the Jewish Defense Committee. He was vigorously supported in his shelter and rescue operations by the Bishop of Namur, Monsignor Charue, and by the Jesuits and the Sisters of Charity, as well as other religious groups. The municipal administration supplied him with forged documents, identification cards, and food for his wards. One of the houses where Father André hid the children was less than a grenade's throw from Gestapo headquarters. Jacques Weinberg, a former guest in one of Father André's shelters, describes a typical scene: "He [Father André] used to sit up all night, napping in his chair. He would not think of undressing and going to bed. There was the constant fear of a raid. If someone knocked on the door, Father André was on his feet. In a minute he had the children fleeing through a camouflaged exit to the neighboring house, where a doctor lived. All the neighbors co-operated. Without their help Father André could not have accomplished so much. The butchers of Namur as well as the grocers and other merchants provided him with food and necessities for the children."

Father André took unprecedented action; he gave his foster children a sound Jewish education. Under no circumstances would he preach Christianity to his children; he tried, instead, to teach them the ways of their parents. He took the trouble and no small risk, during Passover, to celebrate a *seder*. In May of 1944, Father André was warned of imminent arrest. He disappeared from Namur but continued his work from hiding.

Abbé Louis Celis practically reared four Jewish children whose parents had been deported. The two boys and two girls spent three years in the priest's dwelling. The priest insisted they attend church, for security reasons, but at home he taught them the Torah and listened to their Hebrew prayers. In due time he arranged a *bar-mitzvah* for one of the boys. After the Liberation, he helped the children emigrate to Palestine. In 1950 the priest attended the wedding of one of his boys in Israel.

Father Edouard Froidure rescued 300 Jewish children without any aid from others. A Hungarian Jew who was in Belgium relates the following: "Father Edouard ran a camp of several hundred children, among them many Jews. When I brought my son to him, Father Edouard immediately gave him a false name and birth certificate. I offered to pay but he refused to accept the money." Eventually the Germans seized Father Edouard and dragged him through five prisons and three concentration camps. He was liberated from Dachau by Allied troops.

During the Occupation, the Archbishop of Malines and Primate of Belgium, Cardinal Joseph-Ernest van Roey, addressed a meeting of Catholic Action *(Action Catholique)* in Brussels: "It is forbidden to Catholics to collaborate in the formation of an oppressive government. It is obligatory for all Catholics to work against such a regime."

Catholic and Protestant church leaders in Belgium and Holland echoed Cardinal van Roey's words. The people of both these countries turned their backs on the invaders with a silent curse. But a small, valiant minority, cast in the Maccabean mold of a Joop Westerville, rose up in defiance to assert that just as there was no depth to the baseness of Nazi mentality, so there was no height to which the dignity of man could not aspire.

CHAPTER FIVE

ITALY: THE RELUCTANT ALLY

In few European countries were the Jews so much a part of the life of the country as in Italy. The 57,000 Jews (census of 1938) were represented in the economic, cultural, and political life of the land. They contributed a Prime Minister, Luigi Luzzatti; a Minister of War, Giuseppe Ottolenghi; and a Mayor of Rome, Ernesto Nathan. There were Jews among Italy's outstanding writers, scholars, industrialists, artists, and soldiers. Mussolini's leisurely march on Rome wrought no change in Italy's policy toward its Jews. During the early days of the Black Shirts only a small group in the Fascist party (Giovanni Preziosi, Telesio Interlandi, Baron di Salvotti, and a few others) displayed anti-Semitic tendencies. The Duce himself frowned on racialism, calling it un-Italian. "Anti-Semitism," Mussolini declared in 1924, "is an alien weed that cannot strike roots in Italy where Jews are citizens with full equality." In another statement to foreign correspondents in 1927, he said: "Fascism means unity, anti-Semitism division. To us in Italy German anti-Semitism appears ludicrous ... We protest with all our energy against fascism being compromised in this manner. Anti-Semitism is barbarism." After the Nazis seized power in Germany and the anti-Jewish persecutions began, Mussolini—then still at odds with the upstart, Hitler—declared in 1934: "Thirty centuries enable us [in Italy] to face with sovereign pity some of the theories now popular beyond the Alps and supported by men whose ancestors ignored the art of writing, which would have enabled them to learn something about themselves at the time when Caesar, Augustus, and Vergil lived in Rome."

With the signing of the Italian-German alliance, the Axis,

72

the opportunistic Mussolini did not scruple to eat his own words and launch, through subordinates Roberto Farrinacci, Interlandi, and others, a virulent campaign directed at the Jews.

The first anti-Jewish laws were hatched in 1938. The humiliation of Italy's Jewry was tragically dramatized by the distinguished Jewish-Italian author and publisher, Angelo Fortunato Formiggini, who flung himself to death from the tower of Modena. In view of the fact that baptized Jews were exempted from the Nazi-like decrees, 4,500 Jews embraced Christianity. The rest were forced to turn to their Christian neighbors for aid.

Like the civilized Italian soldier who refused to die for the sawdust Caesar, the populace frowned on the anti-Jewish decrees, treating them with contempt. Thus the Jewish badge did not make its appearance in Italy. Nor did the Italians build ghettos or deport Jews to death camps.

A sudden change for the worse came about after Mussolini's downfall and the Badoglio government's conclusion of an armistice with the Allies. German troops poured across the Alps and unleashed a reign of terror. In September, 1943, the Germans installed a new fascist puppet regime. Anti-Jewish pogroms were soon in full swing.

The Italians were shocked and horrified. They opened their doors to Jewish friends and total strangers. Help came from high administration and police officials—men like Mario di Marco, who worked with the legendary Father Benedetti; Mario di Nardis, Police Chief of Aquila, who risked his life to protect the Jews of his town; Giovanni Palatucci, Police Chief of Fiume, who perished in Dachau for aiding Jews; priests like Padre Mario and Francesco Repetto, secretary to the Archbishop of Genoa; Carlo Salvi; Monsignor Vincenzo Barale; Giuseppe Sala, who as the president of the St. Vincent de Paul Society of Milan built a large aid organization before his arrest; Edoardo Focherini of the Bologna Catholic daily *Avvenire d'Italia*, whose seven children died in a concentration camp because of their father's efforts on behalf of Jews.

As in other Western countries under the Nazi heel, church dignitaries limited their interventions to protests and ideological declarations, while the rescue work was being carried on by the lower clergy. Jews were hidden in monasteries, convents, and ecclesiastical buildings such as the Don Orlone Homes. Many Catholic priests were arrested and some lost their lives. Among the saviors were a few who admitted that missionary zeal was an incentive in their work. But most of them were truly doing God's work, holding out a hand to those who were threatened with annihilation. To the humble Italian—priest, monk, farmer, or laborer in the city—belongs the glory that came with saving the lives of innocents. They rescued 40,000 Jews from Hitler's death wagons; 15,000 they were unable to save.

While in Italy proper the population defied its government by helping Jews, a somewhat different situation prevailed in countries occupied by the Italian military. The Italian zone of occupation in France was a hotbed of rescue activities; Italian army and administration officials aided French Jews as well as those of Axis-controlled Yugoslavia and Greece. When the "independent State of Croatia," which the Axis powers detached from Yugoslavia and divided into two zones, published its anti-Jewish decrees, plundering and murdering of Jews and Serbs began in the German sector. The Italians in the southern zone, where 5,000 Jews lived, discouraged the fascistic Ustashis and their cohorts from committing any excesses. One Italian armored unit was credited with saving a number of Jews by a ruse. The tank unit, according to information received by the Croatian authorities, was to go into action against a group of Serb partisans. Instead, the troops rescued a group of Jews from the grasp of the Ustashi by hiding them inside their tanks. A complaint was subsequently lodged by the Croatian Nazis. The Italian soldiers who had taken part in the rescue operation were given a token punishment: several days' restriction in barracks.

Harried Jews from all parts of Yugoslavia sought refuge in the Italian Zone. Two thousand Jews, a fourth of Sarajevo's ancient Sephardic community, eluded both the Ustashi and the Germans to find safety in the Italian sector. Jews came from Cattaro (Montenegro) and Albania. Thousands found their way to such Italian-occupied towns as Ljubljana, Susak, Spalato, Ragusa, and Mostar. The Germans, whose appetite for Jewish lives was insatiable, demanded through their Ambassador to Croatia, Siegfried Kasche, that all Jews in both zones be surrendered to them. But General Robotti, Commander of the Second Italian Army, joined by Pirzio Birolli, Governor of Montenegro, refused to comply with the request. General Giuseppe Pieche in Abbazia rejected a German demand that he deliver 3,000 Jews under his protection. General Roatta, commanding Zone Two, declared he would not dishonor the Italian colors by trafficking in the lives of innocent Jews.

"We must keep the Italian Army from dirtying its hands with this business," wrote a member of the high command in Croatia. "If the Croats desire to hand over the Jews [for deportation], let them deliver them to the Germans without our playing the part of middlemen. It is painful enough for an army of a great country to permit crimes of this sort to take place, to say nothing of participating in them." Army officers who expressed such sentiments found support among certain officials in the Italian Foreign Office and with its unpredictable chief, Count Galeazzo Ciano, who was later shot by order of his father-in-law, Mussolini. Ribbentrop himself found it necessary to intervene in Rome; his plea for more Jews to stoke the death-camp ovens was echoed by the German Ambassador to Italy, Georg von Mackensen, and his aide, Prince Otto von Bismarck. Mussolini's attitude toward Ribbentrop's intervention is not a matter of reliable record. If one is to believe a report drawn by Colonel Vincenzo Carlo, General Robotti, together with the Governor of Montenegro, discussed the matter with the Duce in 1943. Mussolini, according to this report, informed them of Ribbentrop's visit and his demands, and then he said, after a mild curse directed at the German Foreign Minister, "I was forced to agree

because our treaty [with Germany] has my consent to the extra-
dition [of Jews]. But you can look around for excuses..."
However, other sources unquestionably more reliable state cate-
gorically that Mussolini readily consented to deliver the Jews.
It is further stated that he promised to punish his generals for
disobeying him.

The Italian Army respectfully listened to the Duce's orders,
then proceeded to ignore them. A number of Jews arrested by
the Croatians for deportation to Auschwitz were carried off by
Italian soldiers to the Dalmatian island of Lopud, near Ragusa.
A group comprised of 1,161 grateful Jews was interned by the
Second Army at Porto Re in Istria. Two thousand Jews were
brought to the island of Arbe in the Gulf of Quarnero from the
continental area of the Italian Zone, where frequent changes
of the demarcation line might jeopardize their lives. The fall of
Mussolini, the Italian debacle, and the armistice signed by
Badoglio created on the island of Arbe a situation similar to
that in Nice on the French Riviera. And, as in Nice, many Jews
managed to disappear before the Germans arrived; many of them
reached the areas controlled by Tito's partisans.

In another zone of Italian occupation, Greece, the presence of
the Italian army and administration was a source of comfort and
support for the persecuted Jews. The 15,000 Jews under Italian
control were not subject to any anti-Semitic decrees; they were
left alone and suffered no greater hardships than their Christian
neighbors. German pressure for anti-Jewish legislation, such as
the introduction of the badge, was ignored by General Carlo
Geloso, Commander of the Eleventh Army. A German demand
for deportation of Jews was also rejected by the Italians.

Jews from regions occupied by the Germans fled to the Italian
Zone. In many instances, Italian authorities obliged refugees by
issuing temporary certificates or passports, thus saving many
Jews from death.

In Salonika, which was not in their zone of occupation, the
Italian vice-consul, aided by several officials of his staff, organized

a smuggling ring that rescued scores of Jews. The consular officials were also aided by army officers, who saved scores of Jewish girls by claiming them as "wives." The Germans attempted to retrieve some Jews snatched from them by the Italians by sending specially trained SS units to Athens. But General Geloso turned them back.

With the end of the Italian occupation of Greece, the Germans took over. The Jews went into hiding.

In Tunisia, under joint German-Italian occupation, the presence of the Italians saved the Jews from German atrocities. Italian military and diplomatic agencies intervened on behalf of several thousand Jewish-Italian residents of Tunisia.

Heinz Roethke, head of the French branch of the Gestapo Department for Jewish Affairs, referring to the South of France where the Italians held sway and where the Jewish population almost trebled from its prewar size of 15,000, told his superiors: "The attitude of the Italians is incomprehensible. The Italian military authorities and police protect Jews ... The Italian zone of influence, particularly Côte d'Azur, has become the Promised Land for the Jews in France. In the last few months there has been a mass exodus of Jews from our occupation zone into the Italian Zone. The escape of Jews is facilitated by the existence of flight routes, the assistance given them by the French population and the sympathy of the authorities, [and] false identity cards ... The Italians have transferred 1,000 poor Jews from Côte d'Azur to the spas. The Jews are living well," Roethke ends on a petulant note. "They have been placed in the best hotels."

As we have seen, the Jews in the Italian Zone of France were not molested until Badoglio's signing of the armistice and the removal of Italian troops. Then the Heinz Roethkes took over in one of the cruelest man-hunts loosed by the Nazis.

CHAPTER SIX

HUNGARY: THE UNWILLING SATELLITE

In most of the countries occupied by Hitler, the annihilation of the Jews required several years at the least, the time depending on the size of the Jewish population, the attitude of the Christians, and a number of other factors. The Jews of Hungary lived under the stress of many restrictions, but they were without the threat of immediate extermination until 1944, when the last vestiges of Jewish life had been uprooted in most Nazi-occupied and satellite areas.

Until 1918 Hungary was less infected with anti-Semitism than most Eastern and Central European countries. Manifestations of open anti-Semitism were rare there before World War I. Of course some individuals spouted anti-Jewish harangues in Parliament, and a few small newspapers with very few readers attempted to arouse hatred against Jews. But it was the dismemberment of the country after World War I, the loss of territories, the shock resulting from the bloody terror of the short-lived communist regime of Bela Kun in 1919, that enabled Hungarian anti-Semites to peddle their gospel of hatred. The first two years of Admiral Horthy's regime were marked by pogroms and terror directed at the Jews. In 1920 attempts were made to introduce anti-Jewish restrictions, among them *numerus clausus* in the universities. But even such an openly anti-Semitic and race-minded Prime Minister as Gyula Gömbös (1933–35) did not espouse the cause of anti-Jewish legislation, despite the rising hate propaganda in the press and from speakers' rostrums.

After the *Anschluss* (the incorporation of Austria into the Hitler Reich) in 1938, Hungary found itself a neighbor of Nazi Germany. With the outbreak of World War II, the pressure applied by the Nazis became overwhelming. The Horthy government retreated under the onslaught and appeased Hitler by calling for a more virulent anti-Jewish policy. Although it avoided joining the Nazi scheme of the final solution, the Hungarian government nonetheless contributed its share by a rash of anti-Jewish decrees (in 1938, 1941, and 1942). When, because of Hitler's "magnanimity," Hungary was permitted to incorporate some Yugoslav and Romanian provinces (Bachka and Transylvania), the occupying Hungarian troops in several places committed acts of aggression against the Jewish population. Of these, the most shocking was the bloody massacre at Ujvidek (Novy Sad), where 3,300 civilians, among them about 700 Jews, were massacred in January, 1942. In spite of this, thousands of Jews from Nazi-occupied Poland, Czechoslovakia, and other areas crossed into Hungary in search of shelter. From Slovakia came 24,000; among the 200,000 crossing the border from Poland, many were Jews. It appeared to those who came from other lands and to the native Jews that they might escape the tragic fate of their brothers in Nazi-occupied areas; Hungary, though an ally of Germany, was "independent," with legal opposition parties. Moreover, an Allied victory seemed near.

But the sword fell upon them. The Jews of Hungary and those who came to Hungary to seek shelter were struck down with unprecedented savagery and cruelty.

According to the census taken in 1941, there were 725,000 Jews in Hungary and approximately 100,000 Christians of Jewish origin. With their characteristic single-mindedness matched only by their capacity for murder, the Nazis pressed for their usual "solution of the Jewish problem." Prime Minister Nicholas Kallay appeared willing to surrender Hungary's Jewry, providing that the Germans guaranteed the lives of those deported would not be placed in jeopardy. Regent Nicholas Horthy, however, balked at the notion of turning over the Jews because he knew they inevitably would be slaughtered by the Nazis. On April 17, 1943, Hitler summoned Horthy to Germany and verbally lashed the Kallay government for its lack of interest in what his pathological mind hoped would be the final solution. "In Poland," Hitler told his visitor, "we settled the problem by very simple means. We shot those Jews not willing to work. Those unable to work we exterminated." Horthy begged his wrathful host to keep in mind that Hungary was bound by a constitution, and that any action he undertook required the consent of Parliament. In retort, Hitler made disparaging remarks about the parliamentary system and declared that Hungary's troubles stemmed from the fact that it was not yet a totalitarian state.

In March, 1944, German troops occupied Hungary. Admiral Horthy, who had just returned from another visit to Hitler (the "invitation" was carefully synchronized with the German blitz action), summoned the Crown Council to an extraordinary meeting. He declared that one of the chief reasons for the German move was Hungary's hesitation in introducing "the steps necessary to settle the Jewish question. We are accused of the crime," Horthy added, "of not having carried out Hitler's wishes, and I am charged with not having permitted the Jews to be massacred."

The Kallay government resigned, and a new quisling cabinet headed by Doeme Sztoyay was appointed. A harsh policy aimed at the Jews was one of the main objectives of the new puppet regime. German SS and Gestapo headquarters were put in charge of such practiced assassins as Adolf Eichmann and Dieter Visliczeny. In 1944, sweeping anti-Jewish decrees were proclaimed. Ghettos were set up and deportations arranged. From all parts of the land the death trains filled with Jews streamed toward Auschwitz. Only the capital was spared. In a brief period, as though aware that their own days were numbered, the Germans kidnaped 435,000 Hungarian Jews and sent them to their doom.

The beleaguered Jews of Budapest frantically appealed to Horthy to intervene. The Jewish Council, representing Hungary's decimated Jewry, published a desperate appeal aimed at their millions of Christian fellow countrymen. They also sought intervention from another quarter—the legations of neutral powers like Sweden, Switzerland, Portugal, and several Central American countries. Nor did they neglect to seek aid from the Papal Nuncio, as well as from representatives of the International Red Cross.

As the appalling news of the mass deportations and atrocities spread beyond Hungary's frontiers, King Gustav V of Sweden communicated personally with Horthy, who promised to do "everything in [his] power, under existing conditions," to safeguard "the principles of humanity and justice." A similar exchange of letters between Pope Pius XII and Horthy took place on June 25 and July 1. In Budapest, the Papal Nuncio, Monsignore Angelo Rotta, and the Swiss, Swedish, Portuguese, and Spanish representatives accredited to Hungary intervened with the Foreign Office. On June 26, President Roosevelt, in a sharp note forwarded through the Swiss legation (the United States and Hungary were at war), called upon the government to cease deportations of Jews without delay, threatening reprisals if the plea were ignored. Regent Horthy, impressed by the voices of outraged humanity, summoned the Crown Council to a meeting on June 26 and called for a stop to deportations.

The Nazis, loath to abandon the large prize within their grasp —Budapest's Jewry—accused Horthy of being a "Jew-friend" whose family was "infested by Jewish intermarriage." All of Hungary was informed by the Germans and their native followers that Horthy's son was tainted, having married a Jewess. "Young Horthy is a personal friend of the Jews," Joseph Goebbels, one of the architects of the Thousand-Year Reich, noted in his diary. Not averse to a little blackmail, the Nazis circulated rumors that the Regent himself was not free of the taint: he too was married to a Jewess.

While on the one hand the Nazis and their native collaborators reviled Horthy, they made slight concessions in order to still the indignant outcries and protests from many parts of the world. They granted Horthy the power to exempt from deportation

Jews who submitted to him a personal application endorsed by the professional group to which they belonged. By mid-September of 1944, no less than 30,000 petitions for exemption were received by the Regent. But only 616 were granted.

Meanwhile, the Germans, vexed by Horthy's dilatoriness, decided on a *coup d'état* to force him out of office. Their plan, which had the support of the pro-Nazi Arrow Cross party, *Nyilas,* failed miserably because Horthy appeared to have the army on his side. He relieved Doeme Sztoyay of his duties as Premier and invited a non-political general, Geza Lakatos, to form a new government.

By midsummer, as the Allies on all fronts were tightening their iron hold on *Festung Europa,* the deportations of Hungarian Jews were halted by order of Regent Horthy. The cessation was in the nature of a lull while the various contending parties jockeyed for positions. The Germans threatened to resume deportations by the end of August. The neutral legations in Budapest, in an attempt to frustrate the Nazi plan, protested to the Hungarian government. Simultaneously, Regent Horthy was carrying on secret conversations with the Russians, and it was finally agreed that an official announcement about an armistice would be proclaimed by the Hungarian government in mid-October. However, the Germans wrecked Horthy's plan; they seized the Regent and his son and appointed the chief of the fascist Arrow Cross party, Ferencz Szalasi, as Prime Minister.

The fate of the Jews appeared sealed. The *Nyilas* gangs were unleashed to plunder and massacre their victims at will. Deportations were resumed on a massive scale, accompanied by a brand of savagery sometimes mistakenly referred to as medieval. The neutral legations protested vigorously, but more than notes and verbal interventions appeared necessary.

Between October 15, 1944, and January, 1945, approximately 100,000 Jews perished at the hands of German and native Nazis, or were deported to Auschwitz. The Budapest orgy of blood has no equal in the black pages of Nazidom. Those few who survived the massacres and death trains owe their lives to men and women of the neutral legations and to fellow Hungarians of the Christian faith.

The neutral legations extended help by granting Jews passports, certificates of citizenship, promises of visas, certificates of baptism (issued by the Papal Nunciature), and any other protective documents that offered hope of reprieve. As the massacres raged unabated, the legations opened special buildings and invited the Jews to move in. How these sanctuaries operated will be described in another chapter, along with the story of the legendary Raoul Wallenberg who saved thousands of people. For the time being, suffice it to say that 15,600 Jews moved into the sanctuaries established by the neutral powers. The Swiss harbored almost 8,000; about 4,500 lived in the Swedish legation buildings; 698 were sheltered by the Portuguese; 100 by the Spanish; 2,500 by the Nunciature; an undisclosed number were protected by documents issued by the Republic of El Salvador. The official figures quoted here were disputed by Raoul Wallenberg, who was in a position to know. (According to Wallenberg, 33,000 Jews found shelter in the neutral legations.) In addition, thousands armed with forged documents fled to the International Ghetto.

Many Jews, particularly Christians of Jewish origin, found shelter in various ecclesiastical institutions. Professing Jews were rescued by friends, colleagues, business associates, and sometimes by strangers whose hearts had not turned to stone. But the Jews of Budapest were also saved by time. The Russians were storming the approaches to the city. Had it not been for the collapse of the German front in Hungary, it is doubtful that many Jews would have been saved.

Both the Christian scholar, Istvan Bibo, and the Jewish-Hungarian writer, Robert Major, agree that the attitude of the Christian populace at large toward the ordeal of the Jews was one of complete indifference. Among officialdom and the officer corps, there were many who participated in the anti-Jewish excesses. However, the crude savagery displayed by the Arrow Cross horrified and alienated many of those who, up until then, had passively condoned the harsh anti-Semitic decrees. A few bold voices were raised in protest.

In Hungary there were no feats of matchless courage such as those performed by the Danes, or valorous deeds like those of Joop Westerville. There were men and women who came forward to help those who appeared beyond help. But there were few of them. When the terror was at its worst, a number of army officers and policemen demonstrated their sympathy for the Jews and aided them in various ways. According to rumors, General Igmandy-Hegyessi stated in the upper house of Parliament that he would refuse to wear the uniform of the Hungarian Army unless the *gendarmerie* ceased its role in the deportation of Jews. It is a matter of record that on several occasions the army foiled and delayed deportations by drafting Jews into labor battalions, a practice it followed during the early months of the war. Jews were employed in the building of fortifications and trenches. According to Laszlo Endre, Under Secretary of the Interior and a prime Jew-hater, 80,000 were saved from deportation by the army draft. There are recorded instances of officers and soldiers hiding Jews, helping them across the Romanian frontier, rescuing them from deportation.

Colonel Laszlo Ferenczy, in charge of concentration camps and deportation, compiled for his superiors a list of those discovered helping Jews. In May, 1944, according to Ferenczy, Hungarian soldiers helped smuggle forty Jews to Romania; in Maros-Vasarhely, conscripts assigned to round up Jews accepted messages from the captives to deliver to friends and relatives; Dr. Janos Schilling, Under Sheriff of Szolnok-Doboka, feigned illness in order to avoid taking part in the roundup of Jews; in Naszod, Colonel Vazul Nemes, Commander of the Twenty-second Frontier Battalion, warned Jews of raids; police officers in several small towns concealed the property of Jews in their homes with the intention of returning it to their rightful owners;

in Maros-Vasarhely and Szaszregen, heads of the local military and public administration "arbitrarily took over the management of rounding up Jews and adopted such measures as greatly hindered its execution."

To this incomplete list of the hard-working colonel should be added the name of Police Officer Alfred Miller, now a resident of Israel. An enemy of the Nazis, Miller joined the Hungarian police force with the avowed purpose of aiding Jewish victims of German terror. According to his story, corroborated by the Rescue Department of the Jewish Agency, Miller assembled food from rich peasants and stored it in a vacant house in Budapest, distributing it to the Jewish Underground. His aid saved 240 Jewish orphans from death by starvation. He is credited with saving twelve Jews from deportation by providing them with forged documents.

* * * * *

The role of the churches in Hungary, during the time of the Jewish catastrophe, followed a two-track policy: first, the aiding of Christians of Jewish (non-Aryan) origin; second, the aiding of professed Jews. When the Hungarian cabinet, on March 31, 1944, issued a decree ordering all Jews to wear the yellow Star, both Catholic and Protestant churches claimed exemption for the converts. Prince Primate Justin Cardinal Seredi declared: "The six-pointed Star is not the emblem of the Jewish race but of Jewish religion. Consequently, the display of it is, in the case of Christians, a contradiction, and constitutes a renunciation of faith." Similarly, Senior Bishop Laszlo Ravasz of the Reformed Church protested against the yellow Star for non-Aryan members of his church.

During the eventful days of July, 1944, a message communicated to all Protestant churches stated: "The Hungarian Calvinist and Lutheran churches intervened repeatedly with the authorities in connection with the Jewish question, especially where baptized Jews are concerned. They will continue their efforts in the future." On another occasion, Prince Primate

Seredi wrote to Prime Minister Sztoyay: "The fact that the government's so-called 'Jewish decrees' . . . have been augmented by new ones and will apparently be implemented fills me with deep sorrow and great anguish. . . . I have in mind those decrees which without the legal basis cause injury to Hungarian citizens, my Catholic brethren . . . I herewith insistently request the Royal Government . . . to consider the baptized Christians and distinguish them from the Jews."

Yielding to pressure by the churches, the government issued an order on July 12, 1944, allowing converts to found their own organization: Union of Baptized Jews. More than 70,000 persons received membership certificates in the Union during the initial week of its founding and thus were saved from deportation, at least temporarily. New converts streamed into its ranks by the thousands. However, the Union of Baptized Jews was a fragile body; it was smashed by the Arrow Cross in the middle of October when the *Nyilas* became the power in the land. Subsequently, the extermination of *all* Jews, including those who no longer considered themselves as such, became the order of the day. Confronted by the naked savagery loosed on a helpless minority, church dignitaries, led by Angelo Rotta, Papal Nuncio, spoke out in protest.

The Nuncio did not content himself with personal interventions. On June 27, he informed Prince Primate Cardinal Seredi of the Pope's wishes to call the Consistory of Hungarian Bishops to take action in defense of Christian principles and to aid baptized Jews.

Simultaneously, the Protestant churches, through Bishop Laszlo Ravasz, protested to Prime Minister Sztoyay against anti-Jewish atrocities. Moreover, Bishop Ravasz wrote to Cardinal Seredi suggesting that both churches co-ordinate their protest action. On June 23, a joint memorandum of the two Protestant churches, Lutheran and Calvinist, was submitted to the Prime Minister. It called for a halt to the deportations. These actions were concerned with both baptized and non-baptized Jews.

Protests were also voiced on a local level. The Catholic Bishop, Vilmos Apor, intervened against the evacuation of the ghetto of Györ, in his diocese. He requested an audience with Sztoyay but was refused. Archbishop Gyula Czapik of Eger voiced his indignation several times, but without results. The bishops of Kolozsvar, Pecs, Kassa, and other cities denounced the atrocities, but they were small voices in a wilderness.

Realizing that little or nothing was being achieved by protest notes and verbal interventions, the churches turned to direct action. Judging by the cries of indignation from some government officials, the relief work done by the churches must have been effective. "We must state openly," declared the Under Secretary of the Interior, Laszlo Endre, "that as far as aid to the Jews is concerned, priests and clergymen . . . unfortunately are in the first rank. Protection and intervention has never been on such a large scale as today."

The chief means of rescue was concealment. The Jews were sheltered by humble clerics; by monks, nuns; in Jesuit colleges; in foreign missions. Outstanding in the field of rescue was the work of the Nuncio; he was aided by a group of courageous young priests and nuns who distributed safe-conducts and other certificates issued by the Nunciature and helped victims in other ways. During the death march of the Jews to Hegyeshalom in November, 1944, when trains were not available and the Nazis forced their victims to walk the full distance, Sandor Ujvary, a voluntary worker of the International Red Cross, was permitted by the Nuncio to distribute hundreds of blank safe-conducts. Ujvary, who had told the Nuncio he worked with forged documents, received from the cleric the following benediction: "My son, you need have no qualms of conscience about what you are doing, for the rescue of innocent people is an honorable and virtuous deed that God Himself will approve. Continue your work for the glory of God!"

The Bishop of Györ, Vilmos Apor, organized collections of food, money, and clothing, and he instructed the clergy in his diocese to assist, in every way possible, the deportees passing through. Similarly, help was extended by Endre Hamvas, Bishop of Csanad; Archbishop Czapik; Bishop Virag; Chief Abbot of the Benedictines Krizosztom Kelemen; the prelates Meszlenyi, Mihalovics, Drahos, Grosz, Beresztoczy, Shvoy, Mikes, Kovacs, Zichy, and others.

In Budapest the Church sent priests to houses marked as "ghettos," for the purpose of feeding and consoling those inside or bringing them letters of safe-conduct.

Twenty-five refugees hid in the home of the Social (Charitable) Sisters. They were denounced by an employee, a *Nyilas* sympathizer. One of the Sisters, Sarah Salkhaz, was taken away with a group of refugees and murdered. The Charitable Sisters continued their work of mercy, under the fearless guidance of Margit Slachta, and hid scores of refugees.

The Lazarist Fathers sheltered thirty Jewish males, all of whom were saved. Father Koehler rose in the town hall of Hegyeshalom to speak for the deportees who were being led to their doom. He was attacked by *Nyilas* hooligans on more than one occasion for helping Jews. "Shoot if you dare!" the Lazarist priest told them with scorn. "I am not afraid of you!"

Jews were hidden by the Sisters of Mercy, in the Sophianium, by the Oblatas, in the Zion Convent, by Franciscan Missionary Sisters, by the nuns of St. Elizabeth, in the convent of *Sacré Coeur*, by the Society of the Girls of *Sacré Coeur*, in the Regnum Marianum.

Jews were hidden in the Collegium Theresianum, in the College of St. Anne, by the Carmelite Sisters, in the Champagnat Institute, by the Order of Mary. The clerics and nuns who were denounced to the Gestapo suffered torture at the hands of the Nazis and their Hungarian henchmen. But the work went on. The Sisters of the Divine Savior gave shelter to 150 Jewish children whom the *Nyilas* finally exposed. Both children and adults were sheltered by the Order of Divine Love. The Ranolder Institute established a spurious "war plant" for the purpose of giving employment to 100 Jewish girls and saving them from deportation.

One hundred and fifty Jews were hidden in the Jesuit College. They were in charge of the Prior, Father Jacob Raile, who became a legendary figure in Budapest during the days of the carnage. Either he was on the move wheedling, begging, and procuring false certificates of baptism for his "guests," or matching wits with the murderous *Nyilas* gangs that were constantly stalking him or the Jesuit home. One day Father Raile converted his monastery into a "police station" by outfitting 100 men in police uniforms. The *Nyilas*, wildcats when it came to unarmed and outnumbered Jews, ceased molesting the home for fear of reprisals.

The Good Shepherd, run by the Calvinist and Lutheran churches of Hungary and aided by the Red Cross, hid 1,500 Jews. The Convent of the Good Shepherd saved 112 Jewish girls. The English Sisters sheltered 100 children and 40 adults, all of whom were saved.

Heroic work was performed by the Scottish Mission in Budapest. The Mission's building was for a time headquarters of the Union of Baptized Jews, and contained a workshop for the manufacture of false documents; seventy Jewish children were sheltered there, including forty adults. On April 25, 1944, the Gestapo raided the premises and seized the two women whom many harried Jews of Budapest had come to love and revere— a Miss Hanning and a Miss Lee; the latter survived the Nazis, but Miss Hanning was murdered in Auschwitz.

"It is not too much to say," stated an article appearing after the war in the semi-official Catholic publication, *Church and Society*, "that Budapest Jewry in no small degree owed their lives to the churches." The author of the article, William Juhasz, concludes with satisfaction that those who helped the Jews "facilitated conversion in every way possible."

Even as late as the summer of 1944, Hungary was a center of Jewish Underground liaisons and rescue activities for Jews in adjacent countries. Rescue agencies (the Jewish Agency, the United States War Refugee Board) operated a lifeline that stretched from Istanbul through Sofia and Bucharest to the capital of Hungary, where contacts were maintained with Slovakia, Austria, and Poland. Money, letters, people, particularly members of youth and *halutz* organizations, were smuggled into Hungary from the northern border countries and dispatched by an underground railway to Palestine and other places. During the days of the *Nyilas* terror, Underground groups attempted the rescue of Jews by bribery, ruse, and on occasion by force. There are several recorded instances of Jewish Underground units being aided by members of the Christian Resistance movement. Two leaders of the Smallholders party, Laszlo Jekely and Paul Fabry, organized a mixed Christian-Jewish fighting unit whose purpose it was to guard Jewish "protected houses" from the marauding *Nyilas* gangs.

In the autumn of 1944, when the situation of Budapest's Jewry was desperate, a plan was drawn up for co-operation between Jewish and non-Jewish Resistance groups. The leaders of the Jewish community appealed to the Hungarian National Independent Front for immediate admission. A contribution of 100,000 pengös was made to the fighting fund by the Jews, whose representatives, Gergely and Beer, met with Lt. Gen. Charles Lazar, Commander of the Regent's Guard and the person in charge of organizing the Resistance; negotiations were also carried on by Dr. Bela Fabian of the Committee of Jewish War Veterans with Generals William Nagy and William Schroeder. An agreement was reached that, in the event it proved necessary and feasible, the 25,000 members of labor companies garrisoned in Budapest, all of them Jews, would be armed by the military to strike back at the Nazis and the *Nyilas*. The uprising did not take place. The Nazis sent additional troops across the borders to reinforce the *Nyilas* regime on October 15. Deportations and massacres were resumed on a large scale and raged unabated for three months.

The Jews of Budapest were liberated on January 16 and 17, 1945, when the Russian armies that had been storming at the gates of the city for several days broke through and captured the Central and International ghettos. But before the Germans were routed and their Arrow Cross accomplices dispersed, a half million Hungarians of Jewish origin were dead.

CHAPTER SEVEN

"WE LET GOD WAIT TEN YEARS"

"I pray for the defeat of my country. Only in defeat can we atone for the terrible crimes we have committed . . ." These searing words were uttered by a Protestant pastor, Dietrich Bonhoeffer, at Geneva in 1941, where he had journeyed in the interests of the German Underground. Bonhoeffer, who was subsequently murdered by the Nazis, along with his family, was an exception among the clergy in Nazi Germany. During the years of Nazi rule, most of the clergymen who dared raise their voices did so on behalf of baptized Jews and partners of mixed marriages. Few dared protest the crimes being committed against a small minority, the Jews who were marked for extermination. This chapter will deal with those few courageous clerics who defied the truncheon and the death camp to assert their rights as men.

After Hitler consolidated his power, in the middle thirties he imposed upon all churches the so-called "Aryan paragraph," ordering the elimination from ecclesiastical offices of all "racial Jews" and "Aryans" married to Jews. The number of Jewish converts had reached 50,000, and there were, according to statisticians of the Thousand-Year Reich, 300,000 half-Jews and quarter-Jews living in Germany in 1933. After the incorporation of Austria in 1938, these same statisticians were confronted with an additional 100,000 baptized half- and quarter-Jews. Alarmed by the Nazi plans, Catholic and Protestant churches were moved to form organizations for the protection of their non-Aryan members. They were supported in these endeavors by a large number of Germans who displayed strong partisanship in favor of the *Mischlinge* and members of mixed marriages. To cite only one instance: When, on February 27, 1943, the 10,000 Jews remaining in Berlin were being deported, the Christian wives of those arrested, supported by German public opinion, were able to wring concessions from the Nazis, who released the men. The Nazis further yielded to the clamor of the populace, excepting Jewish *Mischlinge* and members of mixed marriages from the anti-Jewish laws.

On occasion a courageous voice was heard on behalf of those condemned to die—the Jews. Sometimes the references were oblique, as in the case of Michael Cardinal Faulhaber of Munich, who in his sermons delivered before Christmas, 1933, stressed the high "religious, social and moral values of the Old Testament," and firmly defended Judaism against Nazi slanders. The Cardinal limited his discourse to biblical Jewry, claiming that his competence as a scholar did not transcend the ancient epoch. However, as Nazi persecution of Jews gained in virulence, Cardinal Faulhaber put aside his previous reservations and spoke out vigorously on this matter. "History teaches us," he stated, "that God always punished tormentors of . . . the Jews. No Roman Catholic approves of the persecutions of Jews in Germany. . . . Racial hatred is a poisonous weed in our life." In addition to denouncing Nazi anti-Semitism, the Cardinal helped converts and Jews in individual cases. In October, 1938, when the rising tide of anti-Jewish violence convinced the chief rabbi of Munich that his synagogue was in danger of being put to the torch, Cardinal Faulhaber came to the rescue by providing a truck for the removal of Torah scrolls and other devotional objects, to be stored in his palace. Nazi mobs, infuriated by the Cardinal's defiance of Hitler, demonstrated before his dwelling and shouted: "Away with Faulhaber, the Jew-friend!" But the man who was later named "Lion of Munich" continued his activities on behalf of non-Aryan Christians as well as Jews, particularly during the deportations to the East.

* * * * *

In the Western German provinces the Bishop of Muenster (later Cardinal) Clemens August Count von Galen, delivered vigorous sermons against the anti-religious character of the regime and its racial policies. His was a lone strong voice in a land where silent obedience had become the accepted way of life. On occasion others were heard. Conrad Cardinal Count von Preysing of Berlin denounced in a pastoral letter the Nazi persecutions in the following words: "Every human has rights that cannot be taken from him by an earthly power. . . . These rights cannot be denied him simply because he is not of our blood. . . . We must realize that depriving him of those rights is a grave injustive, not only toward the stranger, but toward our own people." These words, so vague in meaning, so mild in their rebuke, were considered treason in Germany in the year 1942.

The Catholic church as a body protested against racial persecution in 1943, when the German bishops were called upon to declare: "The extermination of human beings *per se* is to be deplored even if it is allegedly in the interest of the commonwealth; it is particularly evil when directed against the innocent and defenseless, the mental cases, the sick, hostages, POW's, people of alien races or alien descent."

*   *   *   *   *

Bernard Lichtenberg was priest at the St. Hedwig Cathedral Church in Berlin. In August, 1941, he declared in a sermon that he would include Jews in his daily prayers because "synagogues have been set afire and Jewish businesses have been destroyed."

"I came to St. Hedwig's Cathedral one evening," an American described his visit in 1940. "No service was scheduled, but people were walking up the steps. I entered the church. . . . It was dark inside. Worshipers were kneeling in the pews. The only spot of light was the tiny flicker of the sanctuary cup. Only one voice could be heard . . . of a priest imploring his God. . . . On occasion he would pause and the people would cry, 'Lord, have mercy! Christ, hear us!' Then he would be heard again. . . .

There was no allusion to politics, the affairs of the world, and yet every sentence had a meaning reflecting the troublous times. It was like a protest of the crucified church against oppression, like the community of all the faithful crying out to God, in deepest distress."

One evening Monsignor Lichtenberg did not appear at his church. A brief announcement in the newspapers informed his followers that he had been arrested for "subversive activities." He was sent to prison and, after serving his term, sent to a concentration camp for "re-education." A poor student, so far as the Nazis were concerned, the ailing old priest asked to be deported to the Jewish ghetto of Lodz. His plea was ignored. He died November 3, 1943, on the way to Dachau.

* * * * *

Considerable aid was given Jews during deportation by the Caritas Catholica, an organization which was founded primarily to help non-Aryan Christians; as time went on, it also extended help to professed Jews, particularly to children. (The Caritas organization had a similar record of helpful assistance in other countries, such as Poland, Hungary, and Czechoslovakia.)

In the spring of 1943, the Gestapo, aware of the Caritas activities, arrested its leaders, among them Dr. Gertrude Luckner and Grete Wuensch. Frau Luckner was flung into Ravensbrueck concentration camp, where she was found by the Allies two years later. (In 1950, five years after the Hitler nightmare had ended, Dr. Luckner visited England on the invitation of Rabbi Dr. Leo Baeck, and in 1951 she went to Israel as a guest of that government. In both countries she was enthusiastically welcomed by German Jews who owed a great debt to her. In 1955, the Israeli government invited her to christen a ship delivered by Germany under the reparations agreement.)

* * * * *

The Protestant church, although in the majority among the 70,000,000 Germans, and unhampered by such an agreement as the Concordat (the agreement signed in July, 1933, between the Vatican and Hitler about the organization and the rights of the Catholic Church in Germany; incidentally, an agreement which Hitler never kept), was hardly more effective in aiding Jews. The voice of the Protestant church was blunted by the fact that it was split into twenty-nine independent regional organizations and into several denominational congregations, as, for example, the Lutheran and the Reformed churches. Under Nazi pressure the Protestant churches were united into one national German Evangelical Church, presided over by a Reichsbishop. However, the highly esteemed and popular Bishop-elect, Pastor Dr. Friedrich von Bodelschwingh, was before long forced by the pro-Nazi wing of the Church to resign, and a Nazi stooge, Dr. Ludwig Mueller, took his place. Under the new Bishop's leadership the synods of the Church resolved to introduce the "Aryan paragraph" into all Protestant congregations. This decision resulted in a schism. Two thousand pastors, led by several courageous members, left to found the Pastors' Emergency League and later the Confessional Church. Despite harassment by the regime, the Confessional Church grew steadily, claiming 9,000 pastors in 1936. In an estimate made two years after the schism, 40 per cent of the German Protestants were said to belong to the new church, 10 per cent remaining with the old Evangelical group, while 50 per cent remained neutral in this struggle for supremacy.

One of the outstanding leaders of the Confessional church was Dr. Martin Niemoeller. A gifted orator, organizer, and politician, he began by sympathizing with the program of nationalist regeneration, until he discovered that this was not what the Nazis had in mind. The introduction of the humiliating "Aryan paragraph" and the regime's slanderous campaign against the Bible decided for Niemoeller where he stood. He became a severe critic of the Nazis, but confined his opposition to the regime to the defense of biblical Judaism and the Old Testament, ignoring the ordeal suffered by his Jewish neighbors. However, his attitude underwent a metamorphosis as the Nazis became more blunt in their methods of savagery. On May 27, 1936, the leadership of the Confessional Church submitted a memorandum to Hitler: "When blood, race, nationality, and honor are regarded as eternal values, the First Commandment obliges the Christian to reject this evaluation. . . . Anti-Semitism of the Nazi *Weltanschauung* forces one to hate the Jews, while Christianity directs one to love one's neighbor."

The leaders of the Confessional Church were arrested, among them Pastor Niemoeller. After he had served his term in prison, Nazi physicians recommended for him a period of "convalescence" in a concentration camp. He was sent for his cure to Sachsenhausen, and later to Dachau.

After Niemoeller's arrest, his congregation in Berlin-Dahlem was in charge of the courageous Pastor Dehnstedt. A German painter, a Protestant of Jewish descent, Valerie Wolffenstein, visited the congregation at the beginning of 1943 and made notes of her observations. In view of the fact that by Nazi laws she was a Jewess and therefore was forced to lead a stealthy, undercover kind of life, Fraülein Wolffenstein visited the church after dark. "The first time I entered it," the visitor related, "the whole congregation was reciting the 126th Psalm: 'When Jehovah brought back those that returned to Zion, we were like unto them that dream.' January 30 was the tenth anniversary of Hitler's coming into power. At the end of the service, where a prayer for the Fuehrer was prescribed, Pastor Dehnstedt intoned: 'Lord, do what seems impossible, perform a miracle, turn the obdurate heart of our Fuehrer.'" After the November, 1938, pogroms against Jews, "atonement services" were held in the packed main church at Dahlem.

A month later, the Synod of the Confessional Church, taking exception to anti-Jewish riots sponsored openly by the regime, cautioned its followers: "We remind our congregations and

members to take note of the physical and spiritual hardships of
our Christian brethren of Jewish descent and to pray for them."

*   *   *   *   *

Pastor von Jan in Oberleuningen was moved after the November riots to address his congregation in the following words:
"Much evil has been done, openly and covertly. . . . Parents are
held in contempt, as are teachers. Wedlock has been broken,
property taken, honor of neighbors sullied, lives taken. Lord
God, we confess before Thee these our sins and those of our
nation."

Soon after he delivered his sermon, Pastor von Jan's residence
was surrounded by Nazi hooligans shouting: "Jew-lackey." His
vicarage smashed, the pastor was brutally beaten and flung into
jail. To make his stay in prison official, the authorities issued a
warrant for the pastor's arrest.

The shouts of "Jew-lackey" greeted others who summoned
the courage to assert that man's dignity had not been completely
uprooted by the Storm Troops. In Wuerttemberg, Landbischof
Theophil Wurm was arrested as early as 1933 for his protests
against the Nazi efforts to create a "Nordic hybrid religion."
The Bavarian Bishop, Hans Meiser of Munich, shared a similar
fate for his public anti-Nazi manifesto. Both churchmen were
eventually released because of public clamor. After the riots in
November, 1938, Bishop Wurm addressed an urgent plea to the
Reichsminister of Justice "to do everything in order that authority, law, and justice be restored." In the spring of 1943, the
Bishop sent the following memorandum to the authorities:
"There must be an end to putting to death members of other
nations and races who are not even accorded trial by either civil
or military courts. What is happening weighs heavily on the
conscience of all Christians. . . . A day will come when we will
pay for this." Bishop Wurm was firmly convinced that the day
of reckoning for the sins committed by the German nation was
not too far distant. He saw as "just retribution" the screaming

Allied bombs that gutted houses and churches, smashed walls, and put to flight thousands of Germans. "All of this," the Bishop cried, "is a reminder to the Germans of the suffering the Jews recently endured" at their hands.

Encouraged by Bishop Wurm's bold stand, the Confessional Synod of the Old-Prussian Union went on record condemning Nazi atrocities: "The right to exterminate human beings because they belong to . . . another race, nation, or religion was not given by God to the government. The life of all men belongs to God and is sacred to Him." In the practical sphere, the Confessional Church operated several rescue organizations, helping converts as well as professing Jews. Non-Aryan Protestants were also aided by a group named *Paulsbund*, and non-Aryan Catholics by the *Rafaelsverein*.

One of the most successful aid organizations was *Buero Grueber*, established in 1936 by Pastor Heinrich Grueber of Berlin-Kaulsdorf. While primarily concerned with aiding Protestants of Jewish descent, the group helped a number of Jews to emigrate between the years 1936-40. The activities of Pastor Grueber were tolerated by the Gestapo, for it was the policy of the regime to get rid, by emigration and by other means, of as many Jews as possible. However, a sharp change in the government's emigration policy occurred in 1940; Jewish emigration from Germany and other Nazi-controlled areas was forbidden. The *Buero* was closed and Grueber was flung into a concentration camp. But Protestant rescue action was carried on by others, among them Pastor Werner Sylten, who was eventually arrested and deported to a camp where he perished. The work was entrusted to Pastor Martin Albertz and his three non-Aryan secretaries. Eventually this group was discovered, and twenty-six of its members were tried and sentenced. The Berlin office smashed, the work was carried on in some of the provincial branches. One of those surviving was the Heidelberg office. It was in charge of Dr. Hermann Maas, a Christian Zionist since 1903 and an enthusiastic admirer of Jewish colonization in Palestine, where he had visited in 1938. Maas, whose daughter Brigitte helped found a vocational school for weavers in Jerusalem, began his rescue activities soon after Hitler came to power. As an initial warning, the Nazis deprived Maas of his office as pastor of the largest church in Heidelberg, the Church of the Holy Spirit. His obduracy resulted in a death sentence, which was commuted, and he was sent to a concentration camp. (After Liberation, Maas wrote numerous articles stressing German guilt toward the Jews. He was the first German to be invited by the Israeli government to visit Israel. Upon his return from Israel, which he visited twice, in 1950 and again in 1953, Maas wrote enthusiastically of his journeys and addressed members of the German Parliamentary Society at Bonn, touching as he previously had on "our guilt toward the Jews.")

Hermann Maas was not alone in his profession of guilt. Others spoke in the same vein, indicting not only the hangmen but also the millions who acquiesced.

"Nobody wants to take the responsibility for the guilt," Pastor Martin Niemoeller stated in one of his first postwar sermons. "Nobody admits to guilt but instead points to his neighbor. Yet the guilt exists, there is no doubt about it. Even if there were no other guilt than that of six million clay urns, the ashes of burnt Jews from all over Europe. And this guilt weighs heavily on the German people and on the German name and on all of Christendom. These things happened in our world and in our name. . . . I regard myself as guilty as any SS man." And yet very little had been done to help rescue the Jews during the years of Hitler's terror. Said Niemoeller: "We let God wait ten years."

CHAPTER EIGHT

THE UNVANQUISHED

Czechoslovakia

It is odd that Czechoslovakia, with virtually no anti-Semitism to soil its long proud record, had a lower percentage of Jewish survivors than any other Nazi-occupied country. The Czechs were always friendly toward their Jewish countrymen, and this attitude did not change, even after 1938-39, when the country suffered the consequences of Munich and was finally dismembered.

From the start, the Nazis plotted the involvement of the native populace in their anti-Jewish depredations. *Volksdeutsche* groups sprouted throughout the truncated country, but they failed to win adherents among the Czechs. Leaders of political parties issued statements condemning anti-Semitism. The Czech war veterans appealed to their countrymen: "Let us not lose our heads. Anti-Semitism is not in the interest of the Czech nation."

Characteristically, the Nazis passed from incitement to acts. Imbued with the missionary zeal which the Fuehrer instilled in them, they proceeded to burn down synagogues, rob, loot, and steal. No object was too small to engage their attention. In Moravska Ostrava they set fire to a Jewish almshouse. A crowd of irate Czechs intervened in an attempt to put out the fire. German police were summoned to disperse the angry knots of people. On the following day, the almshouse was still intact, guarded by a crowd of Czechs. Thwarted, the representatives of the Thousand-Year Reich set fire to a house of worship. A Czech fire engine was summoned, but this time the German police made certain that the Fuehrer's will was done. The pitiful little house was reduced to ashes. Of such triumphs was the glory of Nazi Germany compounded.

As in other countries they occupied, the Nazi decreed that all Jewish shops be designated by the Star of David. But instead of shunning the Star-marked establishments, the Czech public favored them, thereby displaying both moral and material support for the persecuted.

Early in 1939 there were, in the "Protectorate of Bohemia and Moravia," approximately 120,000 "racial" Jews, including 15,000 non-professing Jews. Of these, only a pitiful 13,000 survived—3,000 in Czechoslovakia, of whom 500 were hidden by Christians; 7,000 were freed from the Terezin camp and later returned from temporary refuge in Switzerland; approximately 3,000 returned from camps in the East. The rest were murdered.

Why did so many perish? Why were so few helped? The most plausible explanation, in view of the Czech friendliness toward their Jewish fellow countrymen, was the Nazi terror. After the assassination of Reinhard Heydrich in June, 1942, this terror was intensified. In a small nation so thoroughly intimidated, the possibilities of rescue action apparently were reduced to the vanishing point. Another reason might be the fact that most of the Jews in the Protectorate were isolated from the rest of the population by confinement in camps, among them the huge ghetto camp, Terezin. Contact between Czechs and their Jewish countrymen was maintained largely through the *gendarmerie* recruited from pro-Nazi elements. But even among the *gendarmerie* there were those who displayed a spark of humanity and on occasion offered help, as was witnessed by the case of the fourteen Czech *gendarmes* executed by the Nazis for aiding Jews.

In those few instances when contact was established even briefly between Jewish and Aryan Czechs, harmony and good will prevailed. A survivor of a Nazi camp near Pilsen tells the following story: On a certain day, the Nazis brought a group of camp inmates for a short stay in town. The Czech population greeted them warmly. The mayor, priest, doctor, and other citizens of note arranged a reception for the Jews. Instead of putting the prisoners in a barn or stable, as they were advised to do, the people prepared temporary billets in the local motion picture theater, brought linen and clothing, and supplied them with food and medicine. A few of the prisoners succeeded in escaping; they found refuge in nearby towns among the Christian populace.

A friendly regard for the Jews on the part of the Czech government-in-exile is a matter of record. On more than one occasion were their words of courage directed at their Jewish countrymen. But words, even so noble as theirs, were not often enough translated into deeds by those among the Christians who heard them. As a consequence, those marked for annihilation by the enemy died.

*　*　*　*　*

Rudolf Masaryk was a relative of the great Czech patriot and founder of the Czechoslovak republic, Thomas Masaryk. An officer in the Czech Army, Rudolf was married to a Jewish girl who came from a distinguished Prague family. He was twenty-eight years old. In 1942, the Nazis decreed that Rudolf's Jewish wife (who was pregnant) be deported to Poland. Rudolf decided to accompany her. Their destination, according to the Germans, was a "health resort somewhere in Poland." Actually, the place was Treblinka.

At the death camp, Madame Masaryk met the fate of all the other non-Aryans. Rudolf was spared. He attempted suicide twice, but failed. When a group of Jewish inmates of the camp began plotting an armed uprising, Rudolf joined them. Plans were made to gain entry to the camp's arsenal, to seize the guards, to destroy the camp's gas chambers and crematoria as well as the instruments of torture, to blow up Treblinka itself, this product of a monster-mind, and to liberate those of its inmates who could still walk or crawl. A small group of bold, desperate men took over the leadership of the planned revolt. Masaryk became part of that group. On Monday, August 2, 1943, the skeletal fighters struck. They fought with their bare hands and a curse; they had nothing to lose. They took the Nazi guards by surprise and seized weapons. Masaryk grabbed a machine gun, turned it on a knot of bewildered SS guards, and opened fire. Above the chatter of the bullets and the screams of the dying men, his own shouts could be heard. "This is for my wife!" Rudolf Masaryk bellowed. "This is for my unborn child!"

Of the 200 bold and desperate men, no more than a score broke through the German fire, the barbed wire enclosure, the mine fields, and only a few of those made their way back to safety to relate the monstrous story of Treblinka. But Masaryk the Czech was not among them. He died.

Yugoslavia

The recital of the fate of the Yugoslav Jews is brief. The Germans murdered thousands of them in co-operation with the puppet government of "independent" Croatia. The Jews who had fled to the Italian zone of occupation were rescued. A small number saved their lives by escaping to the partisans; but not many reached the guerrilla units because they operated in remote mountain areas and were continually on the move. A small number of Palestinian-Jewish parachutists were dropped into areas controlled by Tito's guerrillas to organize the rescue of Yugoslav and Hungarian Jewry.

In 1941, partisans attacked a concentration camp near Nish, in Serbia, and liberated the imprisoned Jews. The Germans counterattacked, and the retreating guerrillas called upon the younger men among the camp inmates to join their ranks. But only a small number availed themselves of the opportunity. The others remained to lend aid and comfort to the old and the sick in their families. They all perished.

Bulgaria

Although in the German camp, Bulgaria had a record second to none in its successful rescue activities on behalf of the Jews. The courageous stand of the Bulgarians in opposing the introduction of the Jewish badge has been described in another chapter.

While the government partially acquiesced in the anti-Jewish policies of the Nazis, the Bulgarian people, representatives in Parliament, municipal councils, leaders of unions and the Church, manifested their resentment of Nazi racism in many ways. Between 13,000 and 15,000 Jews in Yugoslav and Greek territories occupied by the Bulgars were deported to German extermination camps. However, the Jews of Bulgaria were spared. The first abortive attempt to deport Bulgarian Jews aroused a storm of protest. Constant German pressure on King Boris to make Bulgaria *judenrein* proved of no avail. The Germans were able to wheedle from the Bulgarian authorities a promise to put the Jews in labor camps. The fulfillment of this promise, however, proved difficult, for Bulgarians crowded the railroad stations and interfered with the deportations. As a result, no more than 10 per cent of Bulgaria's 50,000 Jews reached German concentration camps.

Rescue operations in Bulgaria were comprised of many facets. One tactic that proved successful was the veritable epidemic of "mercy baptisms" during the German occupation. Another was mixed marriages; in the years 1938–41, approximately 10,000 mixed marriages were concluded between Christian Bulgarians and Jews trying to evade Nazis racist decrees. After 1941, conversions were administered on a mass scale with both parties tacitly agreeing that the convert could renounce his vow after the war. Several priests were censured and removed by the government for being too generous with their dispensations. A government order placed a deadline on conversions, ruling that only Jews who had been baptized prior to the publication of the racist laws were exempt. However, in many instances priests readily stated that a Jewish applicant for formal baptism had in fact been converted to Christianity some time earlier. The Bulgarian public wholeheartedly supported the clergy in this and other lifesaving deceits.

Greece

The pattern of repression, persecution, and deportation of Jews was the same in Greece as in other countries occupied by the Germans. Here, too, almost from the beginning, a small, gallant minority of Christians risked death to help their fellow countrymen. The great bulk of the population, while not indifferent, played the role of an interested if shocked spectator. However, this situation began to change after Archbishop Theophilos Damaskinos, who later became a regent, intervened forcefully on behalf of the Jews threatened with deportation. The Archbishop's vigorous protest about the action contemplated against the small Jewish population of Greece created a stir throughout the country. Damaskinos' intervention was enthusiastically supported by the president of the Greek Academy; the rectors of the University and the Polytechnic Institute; the chairmen of the Association of Physicians; the Union of Newspapermen; the Association of Writers, Painters and Artists; by lawyers, surgeons, dentists, industrialists, and chambers of commerce. Joined in a group, these distinguished Greeks petitioned the Germans to stay the deportation of Jews and permit them to remain in the country under Greek police supervision, or on some island, if so desired by the occupying power. The Germans rejected this plan and proceeded with their own.

The Gestapo struck before rescue work could be organized by the indignant Greeks. Salonika, where the largest number of Jews dwelt, was chosen as the first target. Only a few Jews succeeded in eluding the Nazi net. The Italian army and civilian administration saved a number of victims. But despite this, and the intervention of the collaborationist Prime Minister, Logothetopoulos, virtually all of Salonika's Jews were either slaughtered or deported. According to Rabbi Michael Molho, religious leader and historian of martyred Salonika Jewry, only 615 survived and most of those were partners of mixed marriages. Ten Jewish families were saved by Christian friends. Of the 45,000 Salonika Jews this pitiful few remained.

In Athens, where the Italians held sway, the Jews were still free to go about their business. But in the autumn of 1943, after the Badoglio armistice, the Italians moved out of Athens and the hobnailed boots of the Germans were heard in all the city streets. Acting swiftly, as though fearing the loss of his prospective victims, Dieter Visliczeny, Gestapo deportation expert, summoned Athens' Chief Rabbi, Elie Barzilai, and ordered him to submit a list containing the names and addresses of all Jews living in the city. Given twenty-four hours in which to complete his task, Rabbi Barzilai called an emergency meeting of Jewish community leaders and informed them of the Nazi order. After the meeting, he set fire to all the files and archives containing any information about Athens Jews. Two days later, he appeared before Visliczeny and pleaded inability to comply with the order, the community archives having been destroyed during military operations some months before. The SS officer ordered Rabbi Barzilai to provide the list from memory, if necessary, and gave him forty-eight hours in which to do it. Word about the German ultimatum reached the Jews of Athens, who were urged to take advantage of the few precious hours of grace and seek shelter with Gentile friends. Leaders of the Jewish community insisted that Rabbi Barzilai take refuge, a notion he rejected until Archbishop Damaskinos prevailed upon him to change his mind. A Greek lawyer, aided by the Underground, transferred the rabbi and his family to a small village in Rumelia. Simultaneously, almost all Athenian Jews and an undisclosed number of refugees from Salonika and other places vanished from the city overnight.

The effective rescue operation of the Athenian Jews could not have been carried out without the active co-operation of a large number of Greeks who risked their lives and the lives of their families. For one thing, the Jews required new identity papers and family names. With this in mind, the Greek Chief of Police, Ebert, issued secret orders to his subordinates empowering them to grant identity papers to all who applied for them. During a brief period, 6,000 Jews were equipped with false papers. There was hardly a Jew in all of the province of Attica who did not have a *taflotita*, a forged document issued by a competent police official.

The second and equally important phase of the rescue operation was the finding of living quarters for the new Aryans. According to the chroniclers of Greek Jewry, Rabbi M. Molho and Joseph Nehama, such aid was granted "unconditionally, cordially ... They [the Jews] were billeted, fed, protected" by people who asked nothing in return. (A small number of Athenian Jews did not go into hiding. There were, among the several hundred who registered with the Germans, sick, disabled, or old people, and—strangely enough—a few stubborn souls who believed the Nazis would not harm them. All of these people, in addition to 500 caught in their hiding places, were deported.)

To provide funds for those in hiding, various committees and assistance groups were formed throughout Greece. Some of the wealthier Jews, assisted by the Greek Resistance, crossed the Aegean Sea and landed at such places in Turkey as Izmir (Smyrna) or Yeni Tchecme (Nea-Vrissi), where small reception committees met them and found shelter for them, arranging for their passage to Syria, Egypt, and Palestine. Approximately 1,500 Athenian Jews escaped along this route. Many youths among the escapees enrolled in the Allied armed forces (Palestine Brigade, Free Hellenic Forces) after their arrival in Egypt and Palestine.

The Jews of Chalkis, capital of Euboea Island, emulated their brothers in Athens and vanished one day after they had been ordered to register by SS General Juergen Stroop, exterminator of the Warsaw Jews. They disappeared in the rugged mountain country of Euboea, where Greek peasants and herdsmen gave them shelter. Some of them crossed the Aegean Sea to Turkey; the rest returned to their homes after the war.

While persecutions were raging all over Greece, the 275 Jews on the island of Zante (Zakynthos) in the Ionian Archipelago were enjoying a brief immunity. Their commander, an Austrian, delayed the introduction of anti-Jewish legislation. When, eventually, he was compelled to fall into line with his colleagues and issue the anti-Jewish decrees (particularly those concerning forced labor and registration), the whole Jewish community vanished. Many found refuge in the mountains; others joined Greek Resistance groups.

Greek partisans facilitated the escape of Jews by providing safe-conduct passes or escorting them to remote places and supplying them with provisions. In isolated mountain hamlets and on small islands, the illiterate among the local population eagerly took advantage of those among the Jews who could acquaint them with the magic of the printed word. Jews were hidden whenever rumors spread of probable German raids. Once a German patrol was ambushed on Olympus while twenty Jewish families escaped from nearby Larisa. Greek partisans helped hundreds of Jews to reach the Aegean Sea, where a shuttle service was operating to the Turkish mainland. Trucks driven by partisans hauled passengers to designated spots on the rugged Greek coast where fast motorboats waited. A Greek Jew connected with *Ellas*, the Left-Wing Underground organization, arranged the sailings. A Greek boat making the dash across the treacherous Aegean usually carried between eight and ten refugees. The route became so widely traveled that both Allied and Axis espionage agents were said to make use of it, for reasons of their own.

The Greek Orthodox church, always a power in the political life of the country, used its considerable influence to oppose anti-Jewish laws and, later, to help rescue the victims. The humblest *papas* of remote villages as well as the highest dignitaries of the Church enlisted in the crusade to help Jews. Itzhak Kabeli, a Greek-Jewish writer, relates an incident to illustrate the attitude of the clergy: A number of Jewish refugees came from Athens to a small village whose inhabitants had never seen a Jew. The local population displayed signs of hostility, and their priest upbraided them. "Do you know that Jesus was a Jew?" the clergyman asked the assembled villagers. "He lived and died a Jew. Therefore, I beg you in His name to save His brethren."

Virtually the entire Jewish population of the town of Volo was saved by the intervention of the local Metropolitan, Joachim. One day the rabbi of Volo received a secret report from the mayor that the Germans planned to seize all the Jews on Rosh Hashanah (Jewish New Year). The rabbi immediately ran to Metropolitan Joachim to plead for aid. The Metropolitan invited the Greek prefect to come to his house without delay, and held a conference with him on ways and means of saving the Jews of Volo. It was decided to evacuate them all. The Metropolitan gave Rabbi Moshe Pessah a letter of recommendation to a partisan group operating in the neighborhood of the town. Soon after the meeting, the Jews of Volo were alerted and quietly spirited out of town. Of the 822 Jews living in Volo, all but 130 were rescued.

CHAPTER NINE

"FOR YOUR FREEDOM AS WELL AS OURS!"

The largest Slavic country conquered by the Nazis in the early phases of the war was Poland. As a matter of fact, Poland was the first target of German aggression and the first to be occupied. And yet, despite the fact that Poland suffered Nazi terror longer than any other country, the national spirit of its freedom-loving citizenry was not crushed. The Germans tried desperately, but never succeeded in creating a quisling regime as in Norway, France, and other lands. The Poles early formed guerrilla units and many paid with their lives.

Since the attitude of the Poles toward the invader was hostile and uncompromising, one would assume this anti-German feeling would bear a relationship to the persecution of the Jews who were the first victims. We have seen in Western countries how opposition to Nazi anti-Semitism became an important criterion for patriotism. However, things were entirely different in Poland.

Emanuel Ringelblum, who was in Warsaw during the German Occupation, made the following entry in his world-famed diary: "The opinion is prevalent that anti-Semitism has increased during the war and that the majority of Poles are pleased with the calamity which struck the Jews . . . However, the attentive reader of our material [material collected by the clandestine Jewish Archives in the Warsaw ghetto] will find hundreds of documents proving the contrary. In the reports from many a town he will read how friendly the Polish population has been towards the Jewish refugees. He will learn of hundreds of instances where, for many months, a Polish peasant has given shelter and food to Jewish refugees from neighboring towns . . ."

The same author noted in his entry of February 21, 1940, a considerable improvement in the relations between the Polish intelligentsia and the Jews, citing the fact that on the first day after the closing of the ghetto, confining the Jews behind the nine-foot wall, many Christians came to offer bread to their imprisoned acquaintances and friends. He described the friendly attitude toward Jews on the part of officials in municipal councils and even at police headquarters during the early part of the Occupation. He recorded instances of Poles taxing themselves in order to help Jews, of Polish hostility toward hooligans attacking Jews. Ringelblum also took note of the metamorphosis that took place in Cracow, where all Polish parties, including the PPS (Polish Socialist Party) on the left and the ONR (Camp of the National Radicals) on the right, instituted a tax to help refugees of Jewish origin. Polish customers sent parcels to their Jewish merchants in payment of debts. On the other hand, Ringelblum did not fail to record unfriendly acts and instances of hostility. He was not unaware that the anti-Semitic sentiments of the Polish population provided a fertile soil for Nazi agitation. Even some of the underground publications of the Camp of National Unity praised Hitler's policy toward the Jews, although condemning the methods employed. Ringelblum devoted a great deal of space to the phenomenon of virulent anti-Semitism, the pogrom psychology and pogroms, and took the trouble to record instances when Poles had failed to return Jewish possessions. However, Ringelblum's conclusion concerning the future of the Jews in Poland was optimistic. Describing the anti-Jewish riot in Warsaw (October, 1939), he made the following comment: "Today I witnessed schoolboys from the Konarski High School beating up Jews in the streets. Several Gentiles intervened. A crowd gathered to watch. Such things happen frequently of late: Poles protesting against assaults by Gentiles, a thing unheard of in prewar Poland."

The well-known Polish actor Alexander Zelwerowicz, who, with his daughter Lena, performed courageous rescue and relief work on behalf of Jews, expressed a somewhat different view: "Polish society during the Occupation, regarding its attitude toward the Jewish tragedy, can be divided into three groups. The first group consisted of a great many individuals and organizations that heroically and spontaneously offered aid, realizing the peril involved ... The second group, most likely the largest one, consisted of those who restricted themselves to mere expressions of sympathy, more or less sincere, and to ... condolences. And lastly, I believe only a small minority acquiesced in the final solution as proposed by the Germans ... These people followed the German deeds with alacrity and pleasure and became *de facto* accomplices of Nazism."

*   *   *   *   *

In the latter half of 1942, when Nazi persecution reached its apex in Poland, organizations as well as individuals came forward with offers of help. "Jews were taken into theological seminaries disguised as clerics," according to Maria Czapska, social worker and writer. They were placed in "sanatoria as patients, hidden on landed estates, in parsonages disguised as house servants ... Special hiding places were built for them with double walls and underground bunkers. They were armed with forged birth certificates and German identification cards *(Kennkarten)*."

Among the archives of the *Judenrat* in Lodz, most of whose Jews perished, there are records of instances where Poles displayed open sympathy and offered aid. A Christian bakery-owner in Brzeziny, near Lodz, produced bread beyond his allotted quota, and sent this rare, priceless commodity to the starving ghetto. Both the baking of nonquota bread and smuggling of food to the ghetto were considered crimes. The baker enlisted the co-operation of children, who carried the bread to specially designated spots near the reservation wall, where they were met by messengers who took the precious cargo inside for distribution. Generous Christians on the outside provided the ghetto, in the same manner, with quantities of fat and meat.

A striking example of an awakened conscience in regard to Jews is found in the case of the lawyer and politician, Jan Mosdorf. A leader, before the war, of the rabid anti-Jewish Camp of Radical Nationalists noted for staging anti-Jewish riots, Mosdorf was arrested for Underground activities and deported to Auschwitz. At the camp, Mosdorf altered his views in regard to Jews. Some of the food parcels he received from friends (Christian inmates were allowed such privileges) Mosdorf distributed among Jewish prisoners. As an employee in the camp office, he sometimes warned Jews of imminent selections for the gas chambers.

The Jewish writer Wolf Glicksman, an alumnus of Auschwitz, mentioned incidents of Christian aid to Jews: "When I arrived at Auschwitz I happened to meet Josef Cyrankiewicz (he later became Prime Minister of Poland) on the very first day. His initial act was to give me a sizable slice of bread. This was the highest expression of human charity at the camp. Another person of note, the prewar leader of the anti-Semitic youth movement in Poland, Jan Mosdorf, frequently risked his life to carry letters from me to a relative in the women's camp at Birkenau. Mosdorf worked at Birkenau and often brought me vegetables . . . and sometimes a slice of bread or articles of clothing." Eventually the Germans shot Mosdorf.

Stanislaw Piasecki, editor of the prewar anti-Semitic journal *Prosto z Mostu* (Straight from the Shoulder) and an admirer of Hitler, had a change of heart in the early months of the Occupation. Similarly, Adolf Nowaczynski, a well-known journalist, underwent a metamorphosis. Several lawyers who had in the past professed anti-Semitism balked at co-operating with the Nazis and were punished. "Nowodworski and other anti-Semitic lawyers," Ringelblum noted in a May, 1940, entry in his diary, "have now been arrested . . . They were invited [by the Nazi authorities] to make statements of their attitude toward the Jews. They refused. They said this was not the propitious time to raise the Jewish question." Ringelblum cited two additional "conversions" of a similar nature. "The former leader of the ONR in the Warsaw city council, Koziolkiewicz, speaks now about Jews in an entirely different manner from that before the war, simply unrecognizable." In another entry of the same period, the eminent historian noted: "An attorney who formerly voted for the 'Aryan paragraph' now carries with pride his notice of removal from the list for having a Jewish assistant."

Witold Rudnicki, a member of the anti-Semitic National-Democratic party, repudiated his past and aided a Jewish girl, an Underground courier, to get in touch with representatives of the Polish Home Army (*Armia Krajowa*, A.K.). As commander of an Underground unit, Rudnicki, who was sixty years old, ordered the execution of four blackmailers who threatened to inform the Germans of Jews hidden in the village of Pustelnik, near Warsaw. His apartment in Warsaw eventually became a shelter for Jews who escaped from the ghetto. He was killed during the revolt in Warsaw in the autumn of 1944.

Aleksander Witaszewicz, landowner and member of the above-mentioned anti-Jewish National-Democratic party, sheltered and fed on his estate near Siedlce, nine Jews for a period of two years. In 1942, Witaszewicz was compelled to send five of his "guests" to Warsaw, where they were hidden in the apartment of his former farmhand. Witaszewicz often came to Warsaw for the purpose of bringing food to the hidden Jews. An attack on his manor in 1943 resulted in his death. The assassination was interpreted by neighbors as an act of political vengeance by an anti-Semitic guerrilla unit.

Dr. Franciszek Kowalski, a lawyer from Zakopane, declared: "I was an anti-Semite before the war. Hitler's bestiality toward the Jews changed me. I had not imagined that human debasement as displayed by the Germans could sink to such depths." Kowalski concealed a twelve-year-old Jewish girl in his home.

There were those among the anti-Semites who helped Jews, and others who co-operated with the Germans in their persecution. There were both anti-Semites and philo-Semites among clergy, professional people, workers, and peasants.

Rachel Auerbach, a Jewish writer and survivor of the Warsaw ghetto, writes of those who helped Jews: "They were university professors, railroad workers, bus drivers, priests, wives of high officers of the army, peddlers, merchants, peasants, particularly peasants who, for a single act of charity, giving of a loaf of bread to a Jew, a pint of milk or a night's accommodation in the barn, were cruelly punished, often killed, and their homes set on fire by the Germans."

Ringelblum noted the following: "I heard from Jews of Glowno how peasants helped them during the whole of the winter. A Jew who went out to a village in search of food usually returned with a bag of potatoes ... In many villages, the peasants showed open sympathy for the Jews. They threw bread and other food [through the barbed-wire fence] into the camps ... located in their neighborhood."

Eve Horn-Rosenthal tells in her memoirs of an old acquaintance who agreed to shelter her and her husband in his attic for the price of fifty dollars per month. The police found out that Jews were being hidden in the village and made several searches. They did not find the Rosenthals. "But the villager was frightened and anxious to get rid of us. However, he appeared unable to bring himself to ask us to leave. He knew we had no place to go." Eventually, anxious for the safety and peace of mind of their benefactor, the Rosenthals left to search for another shelter. After a number of miraculous escapes, they returned to the village, exhausted and without any means. "When the peasant saw us," Mrs. Rosenthal related, "he hugged and kissed us. He had been certain that we were no longer alive." During their second stay, Mrs. Rosenthal bore a child with the aid of a peasant woman who cut the umbilical cord with a pair of rusty scissors. Mrs. Rosenthal became very ill and was nursed by their host. The newborn child appeared healthy, but its lusty screams frightened the landlord as they aroused suspicion among villagers. Eventually the child was placed with a wealthy peasant who believed the infant to be a foundling.

Although there was not in Poland among professionals and intellectuals the open indignation against Nazi savagery that existed in France or the Low Countries, where Dutch physicians refused in a body to co-operate in the sterilization of Jews, and professors and students struck and demonstrated their hatred of the foe, nevertheless scores of Polish intellectuals concealed Jewish colleagues and aided in other ways. Thus, Wladyslaw Szpilman, a well-known pianist, was saved from the Warsaw ghetto by Polish friends who took care of him in the Aryan part of the city. The world-renowned bacteriologist, Professor Ludwik Hirszfeld, a baptized Jew, found refuge in homes of Polish landowners. The prominent scholar and historian of Polish literature, Professor Julius Kleiner, of Jewish origin, was rescued in a similar fashion. The actor and stage manager, Jonas Turkow, author of a touching and often brilliant book about the Jewish ordeal *(The Way It Was)*, cites other instances of Christian colleagues who offered help. Dr. Jan Wladyslaw Grabski, son-in-law of the former President of Poland, Wojciechowski, offered refuge on his estate to the well-known writer of Jewish descent, Dr. Emil Breiter, his wife, a Jewish attorney, Dr. Stanislaw Tylbor, a Jewish girl from Drohobycz, and a family who had lived in the neighborhood.

In Poland, the big landowners and members of the nobility formed an important part of the intelligentsia. In spite of the fact that this group was, in the main, conservative and Catholic, their attitude toward Jews was in many instances helpful. Sometimes landowners requested Jewish man power from the Germans and thus saved many from deportation. The wealthy nobleman, Count Stefan Humnicki, saved fifty Jews from deportation by employing them on his estate. After a Nazi order forced the withdrawal of Jews from private agricultural enterprises, Count Humnicki hid several of the laborers.

O. W. Maslak, a noted painter and librarian in Lwow, gave

shelter to 100 Jews during one period when the Nazis embarked on a murder spree. Several of those hidden by Maslak escaped from Poland, but others joined his group. Maslak sheltered, fed, and looked after his "guests" until the Liberation. Professor Tadeusz Zaderecki, the renowned orientalist of Lwow, gave shelter to several Jews in his tiny one-room flat, sharing with them the crumbs to which he was entitled on his ration card. The writer of this book hid twice in Zaderecki's apartment for periods of several weeks.

Many Polish writers, both Gentile and Jewish, created works dealing with the impact of Nazism on their land. A mere listing of books, poems, stories, and essays written during the war and afterwards would run into the hundreds. Most of the works expressed sympathy for the Jews who bore the main brunt; some revealed a deep sense of guilt.

"For every Christian the slaughter in the ghetto was a bitter experience," Jerzy Zawiejski wrote. "The more so, because we realized that we had condoned these crimes for a long time. We did not rise against this evil when it was in the process of being hatched." Another writer, Jerzy Andrzejewski, noted on the third anniversary of the Warsaw ghetto uprising: "When they were fighting in the ghetto, where was our conscience? ... The anniversary of the Jewish heroism is still a bleeding wound ...Repentance is not enough. What we Poles ought to do is actively fight anti-Semitism among ourselves."

Stefan Otwinowski declared: "I don't wonder that words of bitter reproach are heard from my Jewish comrades again and again. We would like to disregard these words but cannot... The terrible truth is that part of the Polish nation behaved toward the Jews in a cruel fashion."

* · * * * *

Although the Polish Underground was organized in an early period of the war, its concern with the anti-Jewish atrocities perpetrated by the Nazis was a later development. In his recently published memoirs, Stefan Korbonski, head of the Committee for Civil War in the *Delegatura* (governing body of Underground groups), declares that organized protest action against the Nazi slaughter did not begin until July, 1942. The frantic coded messages sent by Jewish Underground organizations through the *Delegatura* to the government-in-exile in London elicited no response from that body to the Underground's warnings of disaster. A month passed before the British Broadcasting Company informed the world that 350,000 Jews in Warsaw and thousands in other cities and towns throughout Poland were facing annihilation. Several additional months passed before the *Delegatura* received a reply from London. The authorities in exile, according to their reply, doubted that such crimes as described by the Jews had been committed by the Germans or were contemplated by them. Altogether, they considered the news from Poland as exaggerated anti-Nazi propaganda. In September, the Committee for Civil War issued a declaration: "In addition to killing Poles, the enemy has been carrying on ... planned slaughter of the Jews. The scale on which this mass murder is carried on has no parallel in history ... Jews are undergoing a hell of agony and degradation; they are thrown out of buildings, murdered, gassed, buried alive. The atrocities to which they are subjected dwarf everything in history ... The number murdered exceeds one million and grows each day."

The Committee further stated: "While we [Committee for Civil War] cannot rise to oppose this, we protest in the name of the Polish people. All Polish social and political organizations join in this protest. The responsibility for these crimes belongs to the Germans and their collaborators."

Two months elapsed, added to the precious time previously lost, before the first steps were taken to give tangible help to the Jews. The noted Polish writer Sophia Kossak-Szczucka, known in the Catholic Underground as "Veronica," joined Wanda Filipowicz (wife of a former Polish Ambassador to the United States), known to the Underground as "Alina,"

Czeslawa Wojenska, and others to form in October, 1942, the Temporary Committee to Help Jews. A proposal to establish an all-national Council for Aid to Jews was submitted to the *Delegatura* and received approval. The first clandestine national convention took place in Nazi-infested Warsaw in December, 1942. All political parties in the *Delegatura* were on hand. Julian Grobelny, a Socialist whose undercover name was "Trojan," was selected as chairman of the new organization. Grobelny, often invalided by tuberculosis, was an indefatigable ally of the Jewish Fighters' Organization (ZOB), aiding them in the purchase of arms. Neither his illness nor the Gestapo diverted this gallant man from his course. He witnessed the liberation of his country, then was struck down by his malady. Standing beside the courageous Grobelny were Tadeusz Rek of the Peasant party, Marek Arczynski of the Polish Democratic party, Wiktor Bienkowski and Wladyslaw Bartoszewski of the Catholic Front of Polish Renascence. In July, 1943, the Catholic Front withdrew from the organization, but the Left Wing of the Polish Socialist party joined. The Jewish Underground was represented by Dr. Leon Feiner of the Socialist Bund and Dr. Adolf Berman of the Jewish National Committee.

The Committee's aim was to give financial aid to Jews hiding on the Aryan side, providing these Jews with spurious documents, finding shelter for them in Christian homes, establishing contact with forced-labor camps and lending assistance to their inmates, establishing and maintaining contact abroad with Underground organizations and partisan units. Abandoned and orphaned children were on the list of those to be helped. By the end of 1943, some 600 Jewish children were placed in various municipal, ecclesiastical, and social institutions in Warsaw. The successful results achieved in the children's department could not have been possible without the inspired leadership of Irena Sandlerowna, a social worker whose undercover name was "Jolanta." Furthermore the Warsaw headquarters of the Committee found shelter for 4,000 Jews and obtained Aryan documents for them; the Jewish National Committee aided approximately 6,000 people, and the Bund 2,000.

It is estimated that 20,000 Jews were hidden in Warsaw and its environs alone during the crucial years 1943–44. Branches of the Committee, known as the RPZ, functioned in Cracow and Lwow. A special department for field operations, headed by Stefan Sendlak, sent its emissaries to various towns—Radom, Kielce, Piotrkow, and others—to establish channels of communication with Jews in nearby labor camps. Attempts were also made to aid the thousands of Jews roving the countryside, hiding in gullies, in caves, and trenches, or lying somewhere by the wayside, exhausted from starvation, awaiting death.

The RPZ had to contend with the Nazis, the local anti-Semites, and with hundreds of extortionists who plagued Jews clinging to the Aryan sectors of Polish cities. These extortionists, recruited from the dregs of society, frequently operated as well-organized gangs and made a lucrative livelihood from mulcting Jews they threatened to expose. And emulating these hundreds of professional and amateur extortionists were the street urchins who ran after strollers and passers-by, threatening to expose them as Jews unless they parted with their dwindling supply of zlotys.

By March, 1943, the RPZ urged the *Delegatura* to take strong measures against blackmailers, recommending the death penalty. The *Delegatura* promptly responded and published in its bulletin a statement which ended with the ringing words: ". . . The KWC warns that the blackmail incidents are recorded. The culprits will be punished by all the vigor of the law, if possible at the present time; certainly in the future."

The warning, however, proved no deterrent at all.

In 1942, having reached the limit of its endurance, the Jewish Underground began preparations for a final clash with the Nazis, the outcome of which was a foregone conclusion. The skeletal remnants of Jewry in the ghettos of Warsaw, Bialystok, Vilna, Cracow, and other towns were determined to force the Germans to pay dearly for achieving their avowed goal of making Poland *judenrein*. The handful of Jews knew beyond any doubt that they were doomed to die, and they were resolved to die fighting. But in order to fight, arms were essential. Their own niggardly stores were woefully inadequate, and they sent out an urgent appeal to like-minded Christians. The leadership of the Polish Underground, however, was opposed to a large-scale uprising in 1943. They were concerned lest such a Jewish uprising involve the Polish Underground in a premature clash with the enemy. As a result, the desperate efforts to obtain arms and munitions through the *Delegatura* brought only trifling results. At the end of December, 1942, during a period when the Nazi extermination squads seized Jews by the thousands and turned the ghettos of Poland into blazing infernos, the Jewish Fighters' Organization of Warsaw received from the Home Army a gift of ten pistols and ammunition. Fifty grenades and revolvers were delivered in February. The Jews, faced by a terrifying array of steel, sent out frantic appeals for more arms, but the Home Army and its chiefs proved adamant on that score, refusing to send anything further. The Jewish Fighters' Organization of Bialystok failed to receive even the small number of guns promised it. In Vilna, the request of the ghetto fighters was turned down altogether.

The Jews rose, nevertheless, fighting the iron-clad foe almost with bare fists. The German incendiary bombs set the ghettos on fire, but the fighters burrowed underground. On the fifth day of the Warsaw uprising, the Jewish Fighters' Organization appealed to the Christians outside the wall: "This is a fight for your freedom as well as ours. Poles, citizens, soldiers of freedom! Above the din of German cannon . . . machine guns . . . through the smoke of the burning ghetto . . . we, the slaves of the ghetto, convey heartfelt greetings to you. We are aware that you have been witnessing our ordeal with horror and compassion . . . Every doorstep in the ghetto . . . shall remain a fortress until the end. All of us will perish in the fight, but we will never surrender . . . This is a fight for your freedom as well as ours, for your dignity and honor, as well as ours. We shall avenge Oswiecim, Treblinka, Belzec, and Majdanek!

"Long live freedom!

"Death to the hangmen and murderers!

"Our struggle against the enemy must go on until the end!"

The impact of the manifesto on Polish readers was not so impressive as its authors expected it to be. And yet it cannot be said that on the Aryan side people did not shake their fists at the unparalleled barbarism of the Germans. There *were* verbal protests, but not enough help came from any source. The commander of the armed Underground forces in Warsaw promised on several occasions to relieve the ghetto fighters by additional arms shipments and diversionary acts, but these promises materialized on only a small scale. Aid of a nonmilitary nature was given when the Polish Underground provided the JFO with several men who worked in the Warsaw sewer system. A number of routes were mapped which enabled the besieged ghetto fighters to reach sewer exits located in the Aryan part of the city. Thus, ways for smuggling limited quantities of food and weapons to the ghetto were secured. After the Nazis had converted the ghetto into burning heaps of rubble, these routes served as avenues of escape for a few Jews, among them several small units of ghetto fighters. Seventy Jewish fighters who escaped through the sewers were transferred by the Polish Underground to the woods neighboring Warsaw, where they formed several small partisan units. However, constant German raids, the difficulties in obtaining food, the lack of arms, and their inexperience in guerrilla warfare decimated these groups. Some of the fighters disappeared under mysterious circumstances, and it is assumed that they were murdered by a Polish anti-Semitic group.

During the final agonizing days of the ghetto uprising, General Stefan Rowecki ("Grot"), commander of the Polish armed forces, issued instructions to "incorporate the fighters leaving the ghetto with their arms" into units of the Home Army. But only on very rare occasions were the Jews received into the ranks of the A.K. For one thing, the rank and file of the Home Army units were often hostile to the Jews. Some partisan groups were virulently anti-Semitic. There were instances when Home Army groups attacked and murdered Jewish refugees hiding in the woods, even Jewish partisan units. During the Warsaw revolt in 1944, several Jews were killed in the streets. Murder was committed by members of the National Armed Forces (*Narodowe Sily Zbrojne*), an independent military organization affiliated with the Home Army; another group, a part of the A.K. known as *Jedrusie*, fell upon the pitiful remnant of Polish Jewry hidden in the woods and slaughtered them indiscriminately. There is no record that these assassins were punished or even censured by the chiefs of the Home Army or the *Delegatura*. Of course there were some in the ranks of the A.K. who reached out to help the Jews, but they were the exception, not the rule.

A few men of the cloth came forward to perform what was in their opinion Christ's true work. Monasteries and convents opened their doors to Jews. In Otwock, Pludy, and certain other places, the convents of the Sisters of Maria's Family were outstanding in their rescue activities. No less effective was the work performed by the Ursuline Sisters (in Warsaw-Powisle and the provincial convents); the Franciscan Sisters in Laski; the Sisters of the Order of the Lady Immaculate (*Niepokalanki*) in Warsaw, Szymanow, and Niepokalanow; the Sisters Szarytki of the municipal hospitals in Warsaw; and in Otwock, by the Catholic personnel of the orphanages and hostels of the RGO (Polish Relief Council). Although a strong missionary zeal influenced their work, the aid these groups extended saved countless Jewish lives. In Lwow, after the Nazis occupied the city, according to the collaborationist *Gazeta Lwowska*, no less than 4,000 Jews attempted to evade the German net by baptism (Lwow had a Jewish population of 170,000). *Gazeta Lwowska* violently castigated the Catholic Church for accepting the applications. A particularly vicious attack was directed at one of the priests of the Church of St. Vincent a Paolo who had approved of the conversions and defended the baptized Jews in his church sermons.

In Warsaw, more than 6,000 baptized Jews were ordered by the Nazis to move into the ghetto, where they established their own churches. Food parcels were sent them by the Caritas Catholica, and several priests moved in among them to minister to their spiritual needs.

Emanuel Ringelblum notes in an entry in his diaries dated December 31, 1940, that priests in all of Warsaw's churches exhorted their parishioners to bury their prejudice against Jews and beware of the poison of Jew-hatred preached by the common enemy, the Germans. In an entry of June, 1941, Ringelblum tells of a priest in Kampinos who called on his flock to aid Jewish inmates of the forced-labor camps in the vicinity. A priest in Grajewo similarly enjoined his parishioners to help Jews.

During the early days of the German occupation, in October, 1939, eleven Jews were seized in Szczebrzeszyn. Aid was sought from the local priest, Cieslicki. He promptly formed a committee of Christians to plead with the German authorities. In Pruzany, Catholic nuns rescued scores of Jewish women by disguising them in the clothes characteristic of their Order.

Several Jews of Siedlce survived in a bunker in the woods near Miedzyrzec, thanks to a monk who, having discovered their hiding place by accident, brought them food every day.

In July, 1941, the Germans imposed a staggering fine on the Jews of Zolkiew; a Roman Catholic priest contributed a large sum of money to help the Jews.

Andreas Gdowski, priest of the famous Ostra Brama Church in Vilna, saved the lives of several Jews by concealing them in the house of worship. According to Hermann Adler, a Jewish poet who survived the Vilna ghetto, Father Gdowski, in addition to saving the lives of Jews, also took care of their spiritual needs by setting aside a well-camouflaged room in his church to be used by his "guests" as a synagogue.

In Szczucin, on the Day of Atonement, 1939, the Germans staged a raid on all the synagogues. They harassed and beat the worshipers, ridiculed and spat upon them; they tore the garments off young Jewish females and drove them naked through the market place. At noon, the vicar of the local Catholic church appeared in the market place in his sacerdotal vestments and implored the Germans to cease torturing the Jews and permit them to return to their prayers. The SS men, however, were not to be denied their afternoon of fun and frolic; they burned down the synagogues.

A number of priests in the neighborhood of the death camp at Treblinka gave food and shelter to Jews escaping from transports on the way to the camp.

Father Urbanowicz of Brzesc-on-Bug was shot by the Germans in June, 1943, for aiding Jews. For the same crime Canon Roman Archutowski, Rector of the Clerical Academy in Warsaw, was sent to the Majdanek concentration camp, where he died of torture in October, 1943. Similarly, the Deacon of Grodno parish and the Prior of the Franciscan Order were sent to Lomza in the autumn of 1943, and were shot.

In 1942, during the massive German raids on the Jews in the Warsaw ghetto, the three remaining rabbis received an offer of asylum from members of the Catholic clergy. The rabbis graciously declined the proffered chance of escape and perished with their congregations.

When, in 1940, the Nazis drove the millions of Polish Jews into the ghettos as a prelude to extermination, the major groups in the Polish labor movement issued a joint declaration: "There are no degrees in slavery and there are no better or worse categories of slaves. The Polish people understand this and reject with contempt the Hitlerian notion that they become a superior type of slave due to the fact that they are not enclosed in a ghetto. In the face of the savagery unleashed by the invaders, the Polish people recognize only two categories: those who submit and compromise with the oppressors, and those who oppose them." Much precious time elapsed and millions of lives were lost before these declarations were fashioned into deeds. At a conference of the Polish Socialist party held in Cracow in 1941, the majority rejected active opposition to Nazi depredations against the Jews. As a result, representatives of the two Jewish Socialist parties, the Bund and Poale Zion Right, left the conference in protest. However, local socialist organizations, trade unions, and individual Socialists established contact with Jewish groups in the ghettos. Antoni Zdanowski, Secretary General of the Polish Trade Union Federation, came forward to offer help; Runge, leader of the transport workers, was another.

A Polish Socialist, Pluskowski, was a clerk in the Warsaw city administration assigned by his superiors to work in the ghetto. He found the Jewish Underground, provided forged documents for many of their members, served as a liaison between the ghetto and the outside, was a source of valuable information, and supplied the fighters with ammunition. His wife, not to be outdone, on one occasion supplied the ghetto with ninety-seven grenades. Pluskowski, who lived on the Aryan side, concealed eight Jewish families in his apartment. He continued giving aid even after the uprising had been crushed. The Germans eventually caught up with Pluskowski and flung him into a camp. He was freed by the American Army in 1945, and was sent on to Paris through the efforts of the Jewish Underground group *Brihah*. After his untimely death, Pluskowski's family was aided by the Jewish Labor Committee of New York.

Relief activities on behalf of Jews were initiated in Cracow by the Secretary General of the Socialist party, Joseph Cyrankiewicz, later Prime Minister of Poland. During his confinement at Auschwitz, Cyrankiewicz and another Socialist leader, Stanislaw Dubois, aided Jewish inmates. The Socialist combat units were in constant touch with Jewish Socialists in the Warsaw ghetto, organized the escape of many from the ghetto, provided hiding places and protection. Outstanding in this phase of operations were Dr. Wlodzimierz Kaczmanowski, Dr. Maciej Weber, and Rytel Jan Szeliga. However, the aid provided was unfortunately far from adequate, especially during the period when the remnant of Warsaw's once-proud Jewry rose to make its last stand.

The Communists, who after the outbreak of the Soviet-German war increased their Underground activities, sought to attract new adherents by indulging in spectacular actions. The Communist PPR (Polish Workers Party) sent a number of pistols to the ghetto fighters and engaged in several diversionary military actions on the outskirts of the ghetto during the uprising. However, these actions were carried out on a small scale and had no bearing on the ghetto battle.

Toward the end of 1939, a Resistance group containing Jews and Christians was organized by a Polish youth of Jewish descent, Kazimierz Andrzej Kot. It attracted to its ranks physicians, lawyers, technicians, teachers, and musicians. The Gestapo smashed the group early in 1940, seizing 250 of its fighters. In and around Warsaw, Jewish fighters were active in Resistance groups, often in positions of leadership. In the Lublin district, close co-operation prevailed between Christian and Jewish armed groups. A Jewish youth named Szymek organized the peasants of Polichno into a partisan band. After he was killed in battle, the peasants, who had idolized him, buried Szymek in the Catholic cemetery. Even while the war against the invader was still raging, and afterward too, peasants brought flowers to his grave; songs were written about him; he became a local legend. Yet few were cognizant of the fact that their gallant Szymek was a Jew.

"Grab" Widerkowski, a former officer in the Polish Army, was in charge of a partisan group in the Lublin area. The group numbered 1,000 men and contained two Jewish units, one of them led by Hil Grynszpan, the other by Mietek Gruber. One daring action devised by the Grynszpan unit was an attempt to liberate 770 Jewish prisoners from the labor camp in Krasnik.

Liaison was established with the Jews inside the camp, who were supplied with thirty revolvers and a number of hand grenades. A plan for concerted action was carefully elaborated; the revolt inside the camp was to flare up simultaneously with the partisan attack from the outside. Unfortunately an informer revealed the plans to the Nazis. Several days before the scheduled revolt was to take place, the Nazis seized the armed rebels inside the camp, killed the bulk of them, and transferred others to the camp at Budzyn. During the transfer, several scores of prisoners escaped and joined Hil Grynszpan's unit.

A Jewish veterinarian, Dr. Mieczyslaw Skotnicki, was the commander of the mixed partisan unit operating in the woods of Parczew. Skotnicki's group fought many successful battles. He was killed in one of the skirmishes.

In Poland, as in so many of the other lands where Hitler ruled briefly by fire, there were many unnamed heroes who helped during the days of the Jewish catastrophe.

CHAPTER TEN

EASTERN EUROPE

The Ukrainians

Several months prior to their invasion of the Soviet Union, the Nazis set up a plan for the total extermination of Jews in "Communist-infested areas," and for this task they prepared specially trained assassins, the *Einsatzgruppen*. These murder gangs, dignified by the name "commandos," followed the advancing German armies and methodically destroyed the remnants of the Jewish population (many Jews escaped to Central Russia and Siberia).

The vast territory over which these assassins operated may be divided roughly into two areas. Area A was comprised of the former Polish Belorussia, Polesie, Volhynia, Eastern Galicia, and the Baltic countries. Area B consisted of Soviet Belorussia, Soviet Ukraine, parts of Western Russia, the Crimea, and parts of the Caucasus. In Area A, the *Einsatzgruppen* failed in exterminating the Jews completely, partly because of the quick advance of the German armies, whom they were bound to follow, but mainly on account of economic reasons. Thus, a part of the Jewish population, particularly skilled industrial workers and craftsmen, managed to survive until 1943–44 in several ghettos, such as Vilna, Kaunas, Bialystok, and in several smaller towns, particularly in Eastern Galicia. In Area B, the *Einsatzgruppen* arrived when the advance of the German armies had been halted and the front was stabilized for a longer period; they were able, as a result, to accomplish their murderous task in a more leisurely manner, annihilating the entire Jewish population within a period of several months.

Taking full advantage of the deep resentment of the peasant

population against Communist rule, the Germans shrewdly attempted to link the grievances of the people with anti-Semitism under the name of *Judeo-Communa*. To carry out their plan of exterminating "all Communists, professional revolutionaries, Gypsies, and Jews," though not necessarily in the order named, the Germans sought to enlist the co-operation of the populace to a much larger degree than in Poland or in the Western countries. Their formation of Latvian, Lithuanian, Belorussian, and Ukrainian auxiliary police (militia) was not only for the purposes of security in the vast area; these units were frequently used in massacres, or as concentration-camp guards. The zeal and enthusiasm the auxiliaries displayed in their work, prompted their German masters to dispatch them to other occupied areas, particularly to Poland, where they helped in the murder of hundreds of thousands of Jews. The Nazis also succeeded in inciting many peasants and city-dwellers to commit excesses against the Jewish minority. The enlightened segment of the populace, among them the intelligentsia and the clergy, were outraged at the orgy of blood. With the exception of the radical chauvinistic groups collaborating fully with the Germans, virtually all social, political, and ecclesiastical groups remained aloof or made efforts to counteract the Nazi gospel of death and destruction. But these groups were weak, small, without any co-ordinating superstructure, and their hold on the people was insignificant. They were weakened by years of oppression and the loss of leaders who had either been forced to flee by the Stalin terror or had been jailed. Their protests were quickly silenced by German truncheons.

According to statistical estimates of 1939, approximately 1,500,000 Jews lived in the Soviet Ukraine and 600,000 in the former Polish sector (Volhynia and Eastern Galicia). Probably 400,000 were evacuated eastward in 1941 before the arrival of the German armies. But this was partly offset by a forced migration of Jews from the West, several hundred thousand Jewish refugees from Nazi-occupied Poland, and also Jews from

Hungary and Romania, deported to the area as forced laborers. These were all threatened with annihilation.

Even before the outbreak of the Russo-German war, the Nazis had made overtures to the nationalistic Ukrainian leaders. Hope was kindled among the Ukrainians when, in 1940, the Nazis supported the creation of a Central Ukrainian Committee in the city of Cracow. As the German armies swept through Galicia, many Ukrainians were led to believe that the hour of liberation had struck. On June 30, 1941, the Ukrainian National Assembly formed a government in Eastern Galicia and nominated a president and a cabinet. The Germans reacted quickly, arresting members of the government that had hardly began to function, as well as the leaders of all the factions contending for power. On August 1, 1941, Eastern Galicia was incorporated into the Gouvernment General and became an adjunct of the German Empire. Other former Polish provinces, Polesie and Volhynia, were joined with the Soviet Ukraine under the rule of the Reich Commissioner for the Ukraine, Erich Koch. Ruthless economic exploitation, mass deportations to Germany, and persecution at home all embittered the Ukrainians; illusions of German benevolence were shattered. Even the nationalist parties which had formerly relied on the Germans were driven into opposition. A Ukrainian partisan movement grew rapidly, and the Ukrainian Partisan (Insurgent) Army enlisted 200,000 fighting men. In addition, numerous bands and guerrilla units sprang up to wage war against one another, against isolated German garrisons and small military units and Communist guerrillas; they also declared war against the Poles and Jews living in the Ukraine.

Among the dregs of Ukrainian society, among Fascists, thwarted politicians, and a segment of the peasantry, there still prevailed a respect for the Nazis and a hope to share in their booty. It was from these elements that the Germans succeeded in recruiting their auxiliary police and the mobs that participated in looting and massacring of Jews. These elements also supplied the Germans with a native *Waffen SS* and units of a regular army.

Under such incredibly difficult conditions, the giving of any aid to Jews must be considered as nothing less than heroic. And yet acts of heroism did come to pass, and by a miracle of self-sacrifice or compassion a peasant, a merchant, or a member of the clergy or intelligentsia might rise to that summit which is reserved for saints.

*   *   *   *   *

Metropolitan Andreas Szeptycki, Archbishop of Lwow, was the titular head of the Ukrainian Greek Catholic church in Galicia. Born in 1865 of a distinguished Polish Roman Catholic family, he was the son of Count Ivan Szeptycki, a descendant of a Ukrainian aristocratic family that had become Polonized over a long span of time. His mother was the daughter of Count Alexander Fredro, a Polish playwright and political leader. From early youth Alexander Szeptycki was attracted by Ukrainian national ideas. He left the Roman Catholic and Polish milieu of his parents at the age of twenty-three and entered a Uniate (Greek Catholic) monastery, calling himself Andreas. In 1900, he was appointed head of the Ukrainian Greek Catholic church in Galicia. A trained scholar, author, and Hebraist (he once wrote a letter in Hebrew to a group of Jews petitioning for aid), he was the founder of the Ukrainian Religious Scholarly Society and of a journal. His extensive travels on behalf of Ukrainian political and ecclesiastical groups brought him to the United States in 1921.

He was an old man in 1941 when the Germans spread like the locust over his land. But he rose up with magnificent scorn to castigate the barbarians. His own people he cautioned: "Thou shalt not kill!" When, in November, 1942, the Germans were massacring Galician Jews with the aid of many Ukrainians, Szeptycki threatened with "divine punishment" all individuals who "shed innocent blood and make of themselves outcasts of human society by disregarding the sanctity of man." He prohibited the rendering of religious services to individuals who embraced the Nazi gospel of murder. After the Rohatyn massacre in which a number of Ukrainians were involved, Szeptycki wrote an indignant letter to Heinrich Himmler protesting the employment of Ukrainian auxiliary police in such actions.

Although the Metropolitan's interventions and pastoral letters failed to dampen the zeal of Ukrainian collaborationists, they made an impact on a great many peasants and workmen as well as on the clergy and intelligentsia. His became the ringing voice of protest. But he did not content himself with words. In his Cathedral Church on the Mountain of St. George in Lwow, Szeptycki hid fifteen Jewish children and several adults, among them Rabbi Dr. David Kahane, who after Liberation was appointed Chief Rabbi of the Polish Army and is now a resident of Israel. On orders of the Metropolitan, 150 Jews, most of them children, were hidden in convents of the Order of the Studites in Eastern Galicia. Among these children was the daughter of Rabbi Kahane, the sons of the martyred Rabbi Dr. Chameides of Kattowitz, and two sons of the rabbi of the great temple on Zolkiewska Street in Lwow, Dr. Yehezkiel Lewin, who was killed by the Germans. One of the "guests," Itzhak Lewin, later wrote a book and several articles describing his experiences in the Studite monastery. Approximately 500 monks and nuns, according to Lewin, had knowledge of the Jews' presence, but there was not one instance of betrayal and none of the Jews fell into Nazi hands.

In his memoirs, Dr. David Kahane describes his first encounter with Metropolitan Szeptycki during the fateful days of August, 1942, when 55,000 Jews in Lwow were slaughtered by the Nazis: "Together with my colleague, Rabbi Dr. Chameides of Kattowitz," Kahane writes, "I decided to go to the Metropolitan and plead with him to save the several hundred Torah scrolls which were stored in the cellars of the Jewish Community building at 12 Bernstein Street. Through the good offices of a friend of mine, the priest Dr. Gabriel Kostelnik, we got an appointment and were received by the Metropolitan in his residence at the St. George's in Lwow. The Metropolitan was then an old man of seventy-seven, with a majestic white beard. He was half-paralyzed—had been for a decade—and lived in a wheel chair. He told us of his indignant letter to Himmler and the latter's rude rebuff, of his pastoral messages to the Ukrainian people warning them against committing murder ... He agreed to store the Torah scrolls and to receive in custody Jewish children, but only girls. Hiding boys, he said, was dangerous, as they were circumcised and could be easily detected. However, he did not rule out the possibility completely and promised to consult his brother, the *ihumen*, Supervisor-General Clement Szeptycki, head and archimandrite of all Ukrainian monasteries ... A half hour later we were received by the *ihumen*, who was only a few years younger than his brother ... The *ihumen* gave us a letter to *ihumine* Josephine, Mother Superior of all nuneries. This was on Friday, August 14, 1942. Sunday morning I went to the convent in Lyczkow at 4 Ubocz Street. Sister Josephine received me warmly and told me of her deep compassion for the suffering of the Jews."

Eventually Dr. Kahane found shelter in the Metropolitan's palace, where he spent almost three years working in the library and giving Hebrew lessons to monks.

Itzhak Lewin tells the following story: "My father was a friend of the Metropolitan. In 1942, when I found that the situation was hopeless, I visited Metropolitan Szeptycki and asked him for help ... Almost immediately he began a planned campaign to save lives. I spent two years in the monasteries of the Fathers Studites in Lwow, Luzki, and Uniw, in the beginning as a lay worker and, during the final and most dangerous phase of the war, disguised as a monk. Had I been discovered by the Germans, not only I, but all the monks and priests would have been killed ... During one of his visits, the Metropolitan said to me: 'I want you to be a good Jew, and I am not saving you for your own sake. I am saving you for your people. I do not expect any reward, nor do I expect you to accept my faith.' "

Not all of his subordinates who hid Jews followed the Metro-politan's course. Either for reasons of safety or out of a strong missionary zeal, all the hidden children were by the end of 1942 converted to the Greek Catholic faith. After the war only a small number of the children, and only those whose parents or relatives survived, returned to the Jewish fold.

Szeptycki lived to see the Nazis crushed and driven out of his country. He died soon after the Liberation. A petition submitted by Archbishop Ivan Buchko for the beatification of the noble priest has been approved by the Vatican.

The Lithuanians

SS Brigadefuehrer Franz Stahlecker, Commander of *Einsatz-gruppe A*, operating in the Baltic countries, wrote to Heinrich Himmler on October 15, 1941: "On the basis of our instructions, the Security Police has initiated the solution of the Jewish ques-tion with all possible dispatch. However, we deemed it advisable that the Security Police should not put in an immediate appear-ance, as the extraordinarily harsh measures pursued might have a negative reaction, even in German circles. It is our purpose to show the world that the native population itself undertook to suppress the Jews."

However, Stahlecker, who proceeded to recruit his mercen-aries from fascist partisan units, jobless police, and the under-world, discovered to his surprise and chagrin that Lithuanians, as a rule, shied away from the opportunity offered them by the Thousand-Year Reich. "It was not a simple matter," Stahlecker complained, "to organize an effective action against the Jews." But the Nazis did not give up. Their perseverance was crowned with success when an obscure journalist, Klimatis, organized a small band of cutthroats who volunteered to kill Jews. He staged a pogrom in Kaunas on instructions and advice from a small detachment of an *Einsatzgruppe*. The Germans remained aloof from the action advertised as spontaneous in nature and purely native in character. Subsequently, on June 25 and 26, Lithuanian bands massacred 1,500 Jews, destroyed several synagogues, and burned down a Jewish district of sixty houses. In succeeding days, 2,000 Jews were killed.

The Klimatis unit, consisting of 300 men, was soon enlarged with the aid of the grateful Germans, who were quick to recognize its leader's talents. The enlarged group was sent on similar missions to other places. "This unit," Stahlecker reported enthusiastically, "was assigned for pacification work not only in Kaunas, but in numerous other places in Lithuania. It did particularly well in extermination actions," the commander concluded rhapsodically. Similar units of voluntary Lithuanian police were formed in Vilna and Shavli for the purpose of aiding the Nazis in "eliminating useless and undesirable people." In a period of less than three months, almost 150,000 Jews were massacred in the Baltic countries of Lithuania, Latvia, and Estonia. Having satisfactorily completed their task in these areas, Stahlecker and his superiors assigned a number of units to other areas, particularly to the Gouvernment General and Belorussia, where they further distinguished themselves as among the most outstanding of Himmler's pupils. Two battalions of Lithuanian snipers of about 500 men, trained in mass murder, were dispatched to Lublin, Minsk, Lida, Slonim, and other places. Nor should their contribution to the German cause in the Warsaw ghetto be forgotten.

Among enlightened Lithuanians there were expressions of horror and indignation. Several church leaders protested, urging their countrymen to abstain from the orgies of blood. "Are we to be Europe's hangmen?" one group demanded in a leaflet seized by the Germans.

The Fatherland Front, an Underground newspaper, on June 1, 1943, appealed to Lithuanian policemen: "It should be clear to all that the German aim is to destroy the Lithuanian people. First they attempt to destroy us morally, taking pains to turn all Lithuanians into executioners. Later the Germans will shoot us as they do the Jews, and will justify their acts to the world by saying that Lithuanians are depraved hangmen and sadists."

The Nazi terror was denounced in other Underground publications, but these were isolated voices; generally the dilemma of the Jews was not mentioned at all—almost as though it did not exist.

Among the Lithuanian people there were murderers like Klimatis and there were the reverse—those made in the image of God, like Anna Simaite. There were assassins, collaborationists, and informers; there were others who risked their lives to help the Jews. There were valorous men like Joseph Stokauskas of Vilna, who gave refuge in his office to several Jews escaped from the ghetto. He hid twelve Jews in a well-concealed section of the archives department of which he was the director. He informed two other officials of the archives department of his secret: the nun, Maria Mikulska, and a former mathematics instructor, Zhemaitis.

Dr. Marc Dworzecki, chronicler of the Vilna ghetto, cites seventeen Lithuanian scholars and university professors who helped Jews in various ways.

A group of Lithuanians, among them former Minister of Agriculture Audenas, a professor of gynecology, a former editor of *Lietuvas Zinos*, and two teachers, became adept at hiding Jews, particularly Jewish children.

Often the combined efforts of several families were required to save one Jew or a Jewish family. Professor Movshowitch, a well-known botanist in Vilna, found shelter in the home of a carpenter; was transferred to the residence of Professor Bielukas, a geographer, where he spent several weeks; was forced to flee to the home of Anna Nekrashovna, an assistant professor at the University; escaped by jumping out the window during a raid, and spent the remaining months before the Liberation in a fourth hiding place.

The scholar and student of Jewish mystics, Julian Jankauskas, who was friendly with several Jewish writers, supplied his pen-colleagues who had joined the JFO with twenty guns and one machine gun.

A minor clerk in the Labor Office in Vilna, Rutkauskas, drafted and sent 150 Jews to work in Germany on the basis of faked Aryan documents. Moreover, he hid a Jewish girl in his home, and gave another Jewish girl the documents left behind by his daughter, who had been deported to forced labor in Germany.

"To be sure, Gentiles helped us," Zelig Kalmanovitch, the famed Jewish philologist of Vilna, observed. "They purchased food for us and sold it to us in secret [the Germans imposed the death penalty for such crimes]. Our gratitude to them! The sympathetic attitude of many people was a great solace to us. We should be very grateful for these sentiments."

Some Christians went further, according to Kalmanovitch. "Saw a letter of a girl who is hiding with a Lithuanian peasant . . . Hundreds have saved themselves in this manner. Clergymen and peasants are concealing people."

Before his death in a camp, Kalmanovitch observed: "Man is still better than is generally assumed. The Gentile woman in the market place who sells her goods cheaper to the Jewish woman buying from her clandestinely is good. Or the woman who meets Jews in the street and exhorts them not to lose faith . . ."

Thaddaeus, a poor Lithuanian peasant, was an old man whose cottage in the forest was filled with Jewish "guests." He and his wife Barbara spent many hours foraging for food to maintain those whom they sheltered. They accepted no money and sought no glory for their deeds. "I am not sheltering you for the money," Thaddaeus explained. ". . . I only want to prove that not all Lithuanians are like Klimatis."

*   *   *   *   *

The attitude of the Catholic hierarchy in Lithuania toward the ordeal of the Jews differed according to locality. In Vilna, in the early days of the invasion, the Nazis pressed the higher clergy to issue a pastoral letter condemning Bolsheviks and Jews. The clergy complied, with a message containing a vigorous condemnation of communism, but failing to mention the Jews. This omission, according to Anna Simaite, was in itself an act of great courage. The Bishop of Vilna, Rainis, went a step further, boldly enjoining his parishioners to help the Jews in every way possible. He refused to give ecclesiastical blessings to a Lithuanian regiment joining the Nazi cause, since it took part in an anti-Jewish pogrom.

Father Krupovitchius, leader of the Christian Democratic party and former Minister of Agriculture in independent Lithuania, lodged a vigorous protest with the German authorities for the murder of Jews. He was deported and sent to a forced-labor camp.

Several priests in Vilna delivered sermons admonishing their parishioners to refrain from taking Jewish property or shedding blood; eventually these clerics disappeared.

A priest who baptized a seventeen-year-old Jewish girl and aided her in other ways was tried in public, flogged by the Gestapo, and sentenced to forced labor for life.

Father Lipnianus castigated publicly those who took part in anti-Jewish riots. He was seized by the Gestapo and carried off.

The 200 Jews of Vidukle were driven to the local synagogue to be murdered. The local priest, Jonas, succeeded in smuggling thirty children out of the condemned building. He hid the children in his church. An informer brought this fact to the attention of the Germans, who ran to the church to retrieve their loss. The priest blocked their path, shouting: "If you kill the children, you'll have to kill me first!" The Germans did just that, and afterward massacred the children.

Father Vaitchkus, a poet, friend of the Jewish librarian and writer, Balosher of Kaunas, baptized several Jewish girls in the hope of saving their lives.

Father Dambrauskas, of Alsedzhiai (Olshad), concealed Jewish Torah scrolls until Liberation. From his pulpit he hurled thunderbolts at those who plundered and killed Jews, denying such killers the confessional. He sent large quantities of food to Jews hidden in the countryside by peasants. He was denounced and banished to a monastery in Calvaria.

Latvia and Estonia

In a report to his superiors, Stahlecker wrote: "It proved much more difficult to set in motion . . . cleansing actions in Latvia. . . . It was possible, however, through the exploitation of certain channels to set in motion a pogrom against the Jews in the capital city, Riga. During this action, carried on by the Latvian Auxiliary, 400 Jews were killed and all synagogues destroyed."

In Riga, the Germans were able to secure films and photographs proving beyond any doubt that the "spontaneous executions of Jews and Communists [had been] carried out by the Latvians themselves."

Of the third Baltic country, Estonia, Stahlecker reported: "By reason of the relatively small number of Jews, no opportunity presented itself to instigate riots." Half of Estonia's 4,500 Jews had fled before the German invasion. All Jewish males over sixteen years of age were executed by Estonian Auxiliaries under the supervision of the Nazis; Jewish girls and women from sixteen to sixty were sent to forced-labor and concentration camps. The rest were executed.

Belorussia

Evidently Stahlecker's jurisdiction did not include Belorussia; if it had, he would have been called upon to write a most unsatisfactory report to Himmler. The population of Belorussia showed no eagerness to co-operate with the Germans. Belorussia became, from the start, the classic field of guerrilla warfare against the invaders. Its numerous forests and swamps offered excellent protection for the fighting units. A considerable number of Jews escaped to the woods and, as time went on, formed Jewish partisan groups.

"Now as ever it is to be noted," an *Einsatzgruppen* report of October 7, 1941, declared, "the population . . . refrains from any action against Jews. . . . They are not prepared to take part in any riots, in spite of our painstaking endeavors." In a later report, the attitude of the Belorussians was more extensively analyzed: "No Jewish problem exists for the White Ruthenians," the writer declares, either deliberately or mistakenly referring to the Belorussians as Ruthenians. "Jews are the objects of pity and compassion. The Germans are regarded as barbarians and hangmen."

According to a German observer, the massacres of Jews and particularly the carnage in Borysow in October, 1941, revolted the native population. "The eyes of the latter (non-Jews) expressed horror at the ghastly scenes."

Jewish survivors have reported aid given them by Belorussian Christians. In Minsk, seventy Jewish children were hidden by Gentiles. Dr. Vladimir Lukashenia, a physician, aided his Jewish colleagues in Baranowicze. The people of Byelovyezh helped Jews in various ways. Machol, SS and police officer tried as a war criminal by a postwar tribunal in Poland, admitted in his deposition that the relation between the Jews and Belorussians was friendly in the district of Bialystok.

CHAPTER ELEVEN

"WE WILL NOT SURRENDER THE JEWS!"

Finland was one of the few countries in Europe where anti-Semitism was practically nonexistent. The 2,000 Jews of the small republic were completely integrated in the economic and cultural life of the country. After the Nazis took power in Germany, the Finns looked askance at the sweeping anti-Jewish decrees in the Reich. They were aroused to a fever pitch of indignation and disgust in the late thirties when the Hitlerites turned to looting and jailing German Jews.

Wipert von Bluecher, German Ambassador to Finland in the years 1935–44, wrote in his memoirs: "A wave of compassion for the German Jews was evident throughout the country. . . . The situation became even more aggravated when the first Jewish refugees from Germany arrived in Finland. . . . An appeal published in all newspapers was signed by distinguished men in Finnish cultural life. . . . Money was collected for the refugees." Although the Finnish government took no official steps, the Ambassador observed ruefully that "members of the cabinet unanimously disapproved of the German action against the Jews. . . . One of the most distinguished Finnish diplomats [Hjalmar] Procope [Finnish Ambassador to the United States], revealed to me his sympathy for the Jewish people. According to him, Finnish culture derives not only from Greek, Roman, and German, but owes a great deal to Jewish influence, first of all the Bible, but also to Spinoza and Lord Beaconsfield . . ." The Ambassador was cautioned by a wealthy Finnish businessman that Germany's treatment of her Jews was losing for her all her Finnish friends.

The loss of German respect and influence in Finland did not prevent these two countries from becoming allies in the war

against Russia. The small republic, fiercely proud of its independence, was soon forced to rely on its powerful partner
for food as well as arms. The north of Finland was occupied by
German troops, and Nazi ideological pressure made itself felt in
the political life of the country.

The first move to introduce anti-Jewish legislation was made
in April, 1942, by three pro-Nazi members of the City Council
in Helsinki. While this action was being indignantly overruled
by a large majority, eight local Hitlerites in the Finnish Parliament offered their own brand of anti-Jewish legislation. A wave
of indignation swept through the country. The powerful Social
Democratic party held an impressive mass demonstration, condemning the native Nazis and urging Parliament to reject the
anti-Jewish measure.

Although frustrated by a vigilant people, the Nazis were in a
position to increase pressure because the Finns were now almost
wholly dependent on them. After long and seemingly fruitless
attempts, the Gestapo had gained a foothold among the pro-Nazi
elements in the Finnish police. Bluntly they demanded the surrender of 300 Jewish refugees from Germany and Austria who
were held in a labor camp at Suchsari Island. The Jewish community of Helsinki intervened with the Finnish government, and
the 300 refugees were hastily packed off to neutral Sweden.

In July, 1942, the Germans began to press for a final solution
of the Jewish problem in Finland. To impress the Finns with the
importance of this matter, the Nazis sent Heinrich Himmler to
negotiate many matters, including the "problem." Among
Himmler's entourage on the journey to Finland was his personal
physician, Dr. Felix Kersten, and by this circumstance hangs
a tale.

Born in 1898 at Dorpat, Estonia, Felix Kersten was graduated
from high school in Riga, and during the civil war in Russia he
enrolled as a volunteer in the Finnish Independence Army under
General Mannerheim. After the war he became a Finnish citizen
and went to Germany to study chiropractic. Settling in Holland,

he gained a measure of recognition in his field. In 1939, Dr. Kersten received an urgent invitation to come to Germany to treat Heinrich Himmler for a neurogastric condition. Kersten accepted the invitation and impressed Hitler's chief henchman with his method of treatment. After the Netherlands was occupied by the Germans in 1940, Himmler found Dr. Kersten and offered him the opportunity to serve as his personal physician. The doctor sought the advice of his friend, T. M. Kivimaeki, Finnish Ambassador to Berlin in 1940–44, and a professor at the University of Helsinki. Kivimaeki urged Kersten to accept the offer—in the interests of Finland.

As personal physician, Kersten spent most of his time with the hypochondriacal Himmler and accompanied him to Finland, where Kersten was to play an important role in the negotiations that were to seal the fate of Finland's 2,000 Jews. Kersten was not ignorant of Himmler's intentions in regard to Finnish Jews. He knew that Himmler intended to press for an immediate solution; Himmler was prepared to demand of Finland's President Ryti and Minister of Foreign Affairs Witting the following: 1. the surrender of Jewish refugees from Germany and Austria; 2. the deportation of all Finnish citizens of Jewish descent whose names Himmler had brought with him from Germany. Aware of the facts, Kersten got in touch with Minister Witting soon after arriving in Helsinki. Witting listened intently to Dr. Kersten's report, and then explained his own position and that of the Finnish people in regard to this delicate matter of the Jews. The Finns, Witting declared, would not countenance Himmler's demands despite the country's precarious military and economic position; an obdurate position on Himmler's part would succeed only in further exacerbating the differences between the Finns and the Germans; an official note spelling out such outrageous demands might have disastrous consequences, since Finland could not be expected to yield.

On the following day, Himmler informed Kersten that he intended to press the Finnish government for a quick solution.

The physician made a cautious overture, offering his services in any and all phases of this matter in which his employer saw fit to make use of him. He volunteered to conduct preliminary talks with Finnish leaders, who were extremely sensitive about the Jewish question; in his opinion nothing would be lost if he, Kersten, were empowered to sound out Prime Minister Rangell; the German note, he reasoned, might be presented later, if necessary. Although this was a roundabout way of dealing with a vexing problem, Himmler gave his reluctant consent. The Finns annoyed him, but his hands were full elsewhere.

Understandably, the small Jewish community of Finland was alarmed at the visit of the Chief of the German Security Police. They viewed Himmler's mission with the gravest concern, and petitioned their government to remain steadfast. Only a miracle, it appeared, could save them.

While negotiations were in progress between Himmler's emissary and Prime Minister Rangell, Finnish Intelligence agents penetrated Himmler's apartment in Helsinki and photographed the contents of his portfolio, which contained detailed plans for the "final solution" after the Finnish Jews had been relinquished to the efficient Nazis. The Finnish cabinet, briefed by its own Intelligence about their extraordinary discovery, met in emergency session to chart a course. The meeting was extremely brief and dramatic. It was decided, with surprising unanimity, to reject Himmler's demands, to refuse the surrender of a single Jew, refugee or native. However, in order not to offend a powerful ally, a course of dilatory action was chosen.

"I had lunch with Foreign Minister Witting for two hours," Dr. Kersten noted in his diary. "He told me in regard to Himmler's demands, 'Finland is a decent nation. We would rather perish together with the Jews. . . . We will not surrender the Jews!' "

In his report to Himmler, Dr. Kersten summarized the situation: The Finnish cabinet agreed in principle with Himmler's viewpoint in regard to the Jewish problem. However, Finland,

being a republic, was bound by certain laws. In order to surrender the Jews to the Germans, authorization from Parliament
was necessary. Unfortunately Parliament was in summer recess
and would not reconvene until November, at which time ap-
propriate action could be expected. Kersten did not fail to inform his employer, also, of the Finns' attitude toward Jews and
the consequences flowing from too hasty a decision. Himmler
was not pleased. He reported by telephone to Hitler, who agreed
reluctantly to wait until November when the Finnish Parliament
reconvened.

In the meantime, news of the delicate negotiations leaked out
to the press and the public. The influential newspaper *Suomen
Sosialidemokraatti* published an indignant editorial in defiance of
the censor, assailing Nazi racial theories and appealing for aid
for the refugees. "The position of the fugitives," the editorial
stated, "is in no wise enviable. There is no reason for making it
worse. Let us take care . . . that with the return of peace no
shadow is cast across Finland that might dim our otherwise
bright . . . course."

The government, in an unprecedented move, placed three
vessels at the disposal of the Jewish community in Helsinki.

November passed without any untoward incidents. Himmler
held his fire until December and then demanded action from the
Finns. Dr. Kersten, who again represented Himmler, returned
to inform his powerful employer that the Finnish Parliament
had sat only briefly in November because of the deteriorating
military situation; the Finnish cabinet, Kersten further reported,
had hesitated about bringing the Jewish decree before the legis-
lators, fearing complications. Himmler flew into a rage and
threatened to solve the Jewish problem in his own way. The
Gestapo was alerted to proceed with its own proven methods.
However, in view of the non-co-operative attitude of the government agencies, action was instituted on a police level. Four
Jewish refugees were seized and charged with crimes they did
not commit. Gestapo-fashion, the innocent Jews were deported

to an extermination camp. When news of the deportation reached the Finns, a wave of indignation swept the country. Co-operation at police level ceased.

Late in October, 1943, Himmler returned to the vexing problem of Finland's 2,000 Jews. He demanded of the new Foreign Minister, Ramsay, that the Jews of the small republic be placed at his disposal. When Dr. Kersten was informed of the blunt demands made by his boss, he confidentially advised the Finnish diplomat that in view of Germany's deteriorating military position, it was possible to conclude that Himmler's bark was becoming worse than his bite.

Thus were Finland's 2,000 Jews delivered from Hitler's Chief Hangman. As for Dr. Felix Kersten, the wars he subsequently fought will be described in another chapter.

CHAPTER TWELVE

MIRACLE OF THE EXODUS

At the outbreak of World War II, the Jewish population of Denmark was estimated at between 6,000 and 7,000 people. Most of them lived in the capital city of Copenhagen. The only other Jewish community of any consequence was in Randers, East Jutland. After 1933, approximately 1,200 Jewish refugees from Germany settled in the country. In addition, 500 refugees from Czechoslovakia worked as *halutzim* on various farms while awaiting transportaton to Palestine. In view of the later developments, mention should be made of the 1,376 half-Jews and an indeterminate number of baptized Jews living in the country.

As in Finland, there was no so-called Jewish "problem" here. The Jews were completely integrated into the life of the country, having been granted full rights of citizenship in 1814. It was not until 1933 that the poisonous weed of anti-Semitism was planted on Danish soil. It took root in South Schleswig, where a small but noisy German minority of 50,000 lived. In other parts of Denmark, the political rumblings from Germany were either ignored by the populace or dismissed with lofty indifference verging on contempt.

The pogroms loosed against German Jews in the middle thirties made a deep and painful impression on the Danes. Their King, Christian X, found occasion to demonstrate his and all of Denmark's attitude on the matter when, on April 21, 1933, he joined in the celebration of the one-hundredth anniversary of the Crystal Synagogue in Copenhagen. It was rumored that the German Ambassador to Copenhagen had tried to dissuade the King from attending, citing the harm it would cause to German-Danish relations. The King disregarded the warning. He came, with the royal family and members of the government, and cheered his Jewish subjects with a brief address.

On April 9, 1940, the Nazis invaded Denmark in blitz fashion without bothering with the formalities of declaring war. After a brief and unequal struggle, the small Danish Army was crushed and the country placed under German "custody." Although a fiction of "independence" was maintained, the Germans did not delay in launching their campaign of repression. As was customary, the Jews were to be dealt with first. Nazi cells were formed, nourished, and then released to contaminate the bloodstream of one of the most democratic nations in the world. Collaborationist periodicals financed by the Germans carried on a vicious anti-Semitic campaign.

In a desperate attempt to counteract the flood of propaganda, two Copenhagen rabbis, the Orthodox Wolf Jacobson and Reformed Dr. Marcus Melchior, quickly prepared a book, in Danish, of Jewish writings, tenets and principles of Judaism, and Jewish ethics. This small voice of truth ranged itself in unequal combat against the deafening roar of the Nazis. We do not know how the two gallant rabbis hoped to distribute their book to the Danish populace. However, a copy was submitted to the King, who promptly voiced his gratitude in a widely publicized letter. In his letter, the King took occasion to touch on another matter. He expressed satisfaction that the attempt to destroy the synagogue in Copenhagen had been frustrated; Christian did not mention the perpetrators, but it was known to all they were Nazis.

Early in 1943 the Germans began to prod the Danish government for anti-Jewish legislation in spite of the warnings from their representative at Copenhagen, Dr. Werner Best, that such a move was premature. In a report to Ribbentrop on January 28, 1943, Best declared: "Any anti-Jewish legislation copied on the German pattern would encounter the strongest opposition from the entire population, Parliament, the Government and the King. Prime Minister Scavenius informed me that in the event such a move is made, he will resign, as will all members of the Cabinet."

Dr. Best's intervention was scornfully rejected by his superiors in Berlin. The obdurate Danes were bluntly ordered to proceed with anti-Jewish legislation, establish a ghetto, and enforce the wearing of the Jewish badge. King Christian balked, declaring he would be pleased to move from his palace to such a ghetto and would regard wearing the so-called "Jewish badge" as an honor. Opposition to the German plans of repression was voiced in all parts of the country. Pastoral letters were issued by the Bishop of Zeeland and others, protesting in the name of Christianity the introduction of humiliating anti-Jewish measures.

The Germans retaliated. They arrested Danish officers and soldiers. The Danes, in turn, retaliated by scuttling the Danish fleet. Martial law was declared, Parliament dismissed, and the King placed under virtual house arrest in his palace. Dr. Werner Best was summoned to Berlin and accused of timidity in handling the Danes. Rising in his own defense, the representative to Denmark from the Thousand-Year Reich promised to take any and all measures necessary to expedite the "Jewish problem," including the Fuehrer's favorite, deportation to death camps. His plan was approved by Hitler. A group of SS deportation experts in charge of the infamous Rolf Guenther arrived in Copenhagen to make arrangements.

The Jewish New Year in 1943 fell on October 1. This was the day chosen by the Germans for the start of their mass arrests and deportations. They prepared their snares with characteristic German thoroughness and in complete secrecy. It is difficult to predict what might have happened had not Count Helmuth von Moltke, who later was executed as a member of the German anti-Nazi opposition, received intelligence of this plan and passed it on to friends in Denmark. The shocking news also reached the Danes from another unlikely source. Captain Georg Ferdinand von Duckwitz, German shipping expert in Denmark, was in possession of a strictly confidential letter from his superiors ordering him to prepare four cargo ships. The four ships, in the estimation of Berlin, would be adequate to transport all Danish Jews in one mass deportation. Disregarding the personal danger involved, Duckwitz sought out Hans Hedtoft and H. C. Hansen (both of whom served as Prime Minister after the Liberation), and the Swedish Ambassador to Denmark. Duckwitz informed the three men of the danger facing the Jews.

C. B. Henriques, president of the Jewish community in Copenhagen, heard the fateful news from Hedtoft and Hansen. At first he refused to lend any credence to their report. "I don't understand how this can possibly be true," he repeated over and over again.

Only a small number of Jews attended the synagogue on the morning of September 29, and thus only a very few were apprised of the German plan. Those warned of the coming disaster ran from the synagogue to sound the alarm among their relatives, friends, neighbors, and all Jewish acquaintances they chanced to meet in the streets. Members of the Danish Underground mobilized swiftly for the purpose of alerting the Jews of Copenhagen and other communities. Throughout Denmark, people were stopped in the streets and asked whether they were Jews or had Jewish friends or acquaintances. Danish families offered their Jewish countrymen temporary shelter while rescue action was being organized.

The Swedish government, having learned of the German plan, instructed its Ambassador in Berlin to inform the Nazis that his government would undertake to transfer all Danish Jews to Sweden. The Germans ignored the offer. The 6,500 Danish Jews were within their grasp. There was only one avenue of escape for the Jews, and that was by sea, to Sweden. And German gunboats were stationed along the water route to make certain not a single Jew tried to escape.

And yet that is how the Jews escaped—by sea.

The story of the survival of Danish Jewry is the story of Denmark's Christian freemen, who defied all the might of Germany to carry out one of the most miraculous sea rescues in history.

Prior to 1943, the smuggling of people to Sweden had taken place on only a small scale. Occasionally a leader of the Underground was ferried across, or a former Danish officer who had earned the enmity of the invader, or a Jew with a premonition of things to come. Only small fishing craft had been employed in these operations. But the imminent Nazi roundup of all Danish Jewry presented the rescue workers with a gigantic task. The Jews had to be evacuated without delay. Even under the most favorable of circumstances this would have been a formidable task. The difficulties appeared insurmountable. In addition to warships blocking the sea, the Gestapo and German soldiers were thick as fleas at all ports of embarkation.

How, then, were the Jews saved? As soon as the sobering news of the impending action against the Jews got around, a secret meeting of the Protestant higher clergy was convened in the home of the Bishop of Copenhagen, Fogelsang-Dagmar. With swift unanimity the clergymen present resolved to form an organization whose avowed purpose it was (1.) to rescue Jews and (2.) to rescue Jewish devotional objects such as Torah (Holy Writ) scrolls and other synagogue treasures. A group of young men belonging to the Danish Underground was empowered to break into the Great Synagogue of Copenhagen, whence they removed 100 scrolls and other precious objects, including prayer books. This sacred treasure was stored in the cellars of Protestant churches in Copenhagen. Soon after the raid, a pastoral letter issued by the Protestant Synod urged all clergymen to become active in the rescue of Jews.

A Pastor Gildeby who lived in Erslew, Jutland, where a Jew had never been seen, wrote an urgent letter to the Copenhagen rabbi, Dr. Marcus Melchior, inviting him and his family to take shelter with them. The rabbi, moved by the offer, cited the risks involved for the pastor and his family in inviting Jews to his home. Pastor Gildeby persisted, and Dr. Melchior came with his family to take shelter in the Jutland home. A special guard was organized to patrol the grounds outside the pastor's house. The townspeople, their curiosity checked by security regulations imposed by themselves, sent gifts and food parcels to Gildeby's house. The pastor's immediate superior, Bishop Flums, was given all the details of Gildeby's visitors. Incidentally, the Bishop had a secret of his own; his palace was the headquarters of a rescue organization that ferried Jews to Sweden.

All over Denmark rescue groups, varying in size and effectiveness, sprang into action. Jews were escorted out of towns and taken to small villages near the sea, points of embarkation where they were hidden while they waited to be smuggled across to Sweden. The rescuers came from all walks of life; they were bishops, like Flums, farmers, businessmen, fishermen.

Dr. Aage Bertelsen, for instance, was a pedagogue. Principal of Aarhus Cathedral College and an outstanding biblical scholar, he had shunned politics before the outbreak of the war. With his wife Gerda and several friends, Bertelsen formed a rescue organization that eventually numbered sixty people. Known as the Lyngby Group, after the town in which it operated, these modern vikings who struck only at night smuggled 1,200 Jews past a flotilla of German warships, depositing them safely on Swedish shores. Eventually the Germans learned of Bertelsen's operations and surrounded his home. But Bertelsen successfully eluded the Gestapo noose, slipped out of town, and continued to direct the rescue operations from hiding places. Finally he was forced to escape to Sweden. The Germans arrested his wife Gerda, but she refused to divulge any of the group's secrets. In reply to the bludgeoning Gestapo official who pressed her to confess that she had participated in the smuggling of Jews to Sweden, the gallant woman asserted: *"All* decent people do!"

*   *   *   *   *

Berge Aaudze was a newspaperman. During the German occupation, in addition to organizing a network of Underground publications, he actively participated in the smuggling of Jews to Sweden. "Without the passive attitude of the [German] soldiers," Aaudze declared after the war, "we would not have been able to save so many Jews. . . . Some German officers, Socialists . . . cooperated with the Underground by warning us of imminent deportations." The Gestapo captured Aaudze and attempted to blackmail him by threatening to deal severely with his wife, children, and parents. Aaudze withstood the threats and the torture. One day he received a note from the Underground informing him that the British had captured the family of the Gestapo chief in Denmark. Several days later, the Gestapo official received the following impertinent note from one of his prize prisoners: "I hope my family will be treated by you exactly as you wish your family to be treated by the British. Signed: Aaudze."

*   *   *   *   *

Peter Freuchen's name is familiar to many Americans who read books about Arctic exploration. Those who frequent the United Nations in New York may more than once have seen the majestic figure of this giant with gray beard and the manner and dress of a sea captain. His wooden leg, the result of surgery performed by himself during an expedition to the frozen North in 1921, adds a touch of mystery and perhaps glamour to Freuchen's personality. Freuchen, a newspaperman, in a recently published autobiography refers to himself as a "vagrant viking." Like Bertelsen and Aaudze and countless others, he belongs to the breed of free and fearless men that only a democracy can nourish.

Freuchen crossed swords with Hitler long before the Nazis invaded his beloved Denmark. After the outbreak of World War II, Freuchen (then in his fifties) returned to Denmark and together with friends organized the Society to Help Nazi Victims. He offered his island, Enehoie, as a refuge for anti-Nazis and Jews smuggled out of Germany. He also carried on rescue work of his own—long before the Germans invaded his native land. This work, of which both his Committee and the police were ignorant, consisted of singlehandedly rescuing German political and social refugees who jumped from excursion boats. "My island was strategically located," Freuchen writes in *Vagrant Viking*, "and as the boats filled with gay holiday crowds sailed peacefully through the Baltic Sea, I ran out to meet them in my speedboat. Passengers jumped overboard and I picked them up from the ice-cold water. Some of them were shipped to Sweden in small fishing vessels; others returned to Enehoie with me."

With the Nazi invasion of Denmark, the guests at Enehoie were quickly evacuated to Sweden. But Freuchen chose to remain in Denmark, where he joined the Underground. Seized by the Germans and placed in a concentration camp, he escaped during an air raid. His renewed Underground activities resulted in a second arrest. This time the Nazis robbed him of his wooden leg—to make certain he would not attempt another escape. But with the aid of the resourceful Danish Underground Freuchen escaped a second time.

*   *   *   *   *

Money to carry on the vast rescue operations was always forthcoming, sometimes from mysterious sources. Pastor Paul Boxenius, nicknamed by the Nazis "The Shooting Priest" because his activities in the Underground included, in addition to rescuing Jews, the blowing up of German communication lines, declared after the war: "When you needed money you simply went to a bank and asked the teller for 5,000 or 10,000 kroner, stating your purpose, and the money was promptly handed to you." The recipient, according to the pastor, was not required to identify himself or present any authorization for the request. Significantly enough, there were no records of any misrepresentation. According to Bertelsen, one means of securing money to defray the rescue expenditures was the ringing of doorbells. (Even children were busy collecting funds.) The Danish writer Per Moeller believes that 1,000,000 kroner was collected in this fashion in one day. However, it becomes clear in retrospect that the most important source of money was the Danish government itself, making its contributions through secret channels to the Resistance groups. "Within a period of ten days I borrowed 148,000 kroner from a timber merchant I never met before," Aage Bertelsen states in his book *October, '43*, dealing with those fateful days. One day the head of a department in the Ministry of Commerce called on Bertelsen and left with him a brown package containing 70,000 kroner, the first installment on the money owing the timber merchant. Moreover, the Danish government informed the Swedish Ambassador in Copenhagen, Baron Dardell, that it was prepared to reimburse the Swedes for all the monies expended on Danish Jews who found refuge in Sweden.

Records were meticulously kept of all books, libraries, archives, and other assets belonging to Jewish individuals and organizations, so that they could be returned to their rightful owners after the war.

A man responsible for one of the most important aspects of the rescue work—transportation—was Viggo J. Rasmussen, who after the war became European director for the Scandinavian Airlines System. "I had two offices during the Nazi era," Mr. Rasmussen explained during an interview, "one for my formal business, the other for my work as Underground communications officer. Our Resistance movement . . . was broken down into groups." So tight was the security system of the Danish Resistance that even Rasmussen did not know the exact number of people evacuated. It is estimated that more than 6,000 Jews were rescued within three months of the day the Nazis began their roundup on October 1, 1943. Several hundred people fell into German hands during the raids, before the general alarm had been sounded.

After the war, when the Danish-Jewish refugees returned to their country, each one of them was granted 4,050 kroner. The Jewish homes that had not been burned or looted by the Nazis were returned to their rightful owners. Some repatriates even found that their lawns had been mowed. A Jewish girl who came back to Copenhagen from the Theresienstadt concentration camp was greeted by her Christian neighbors with flowers and keys to her apartment. Entering her dwelling, she found an envelope on the kitchen table with a large sum of money. "This is for your initial expense," a note read.

In his *October, '43*, the gallant Aage Bertelsen makes the following observation: "I do not know whether Jews feel more intensely than we do, but I have often been impressed how strongly and spontaneously they express their gratitude."

CHAPTER THIRTEEN

RAOUL WALLENBERG: HERO OF BUDAPEST

Raoul Wallenberg was thirty-two years old in 1944 when he was catapulted into the field of Jewish rescue activities. Scion of a distinguished Swedish family (his grandfather had been Ambassador to Japan and to Turkey, and his father a prominent banker), Raoul's only contact with Jewish affairs was a casual visit to Palestine before the outbreak of World War II. Earlier, he had studied law in France, and architecture and engineering in the United States. After his return to Sweden, Wallenberg embarked on a business career and became, at the beginning of the war, co-director of a large export and import firm in Stockholm, the Mellaneuropeiska Handels A.B. His partner was a Hungarian Jew, Koloman Lauer, whose wife and in-laws were stranded in Hungary.

After March 19, 1944, when the situation of the Jews in Hungary became extremely precarious, there were a number of people in the capital of neutral Sweden concerning themselves with devising and executing rescue activities. Norbert Masur of the World Jewish Congress, who had such plans, was diligently searching for a prominent non-Jew to go to Budapest and organize the rescue activities, with the aid of the Swedish Embassy and the financial assistance of the United States. Offers of American aid had been made through the United States Ambassador to Stockholm, Herschel Johnson, who had asked the Swedish Ministry of Foreign Affairs to designate a prominent Swede who would be prepared to carry on rescue work in Budapest. Wallenberg's selection may have come by sheer accident. His partner's offices were adjacent to those of Ivar C. Olsen, who was financial attaché at the United States Embassy in Stockholm. Lauer and

Olsen became friendly, and the former told the American about his partner Raoul Wallenberg, who was disturbed over the predicament of Hungarian Jewry and desired to be of assistance. It soon appeared to all concerned with the problem that Wallenberg was the suitable choice for the delicate and, as it eventually turned out, dangerous mission. The nominee at first demurred, but finally agreed. In order that he might have diplomatic immunity in Budapest, he was appointed an attaché of the Swedish Embassy in the Hungarian capital.

He arrived in Budapest on July 9, 1944, his only luggage a briefcase containing a list of Jews to be given rescue priority and the names of Hungarian anti-Nazis whose assistance he might seek. He set to work without delay, establishing a new department under his charge in the embassy, the so-called "Section C," whose sole function was the rescue of Jews. From the initial twenty voluntary workers, the staff of Section C burgeoned to number 660 persons, including their families. It goes without saying that all these officials and their families enjoyed a precarious immunity, being under the protection of the Swedish Embassy, and were reasonably safe from deportation or the harsh anti-Jewish decrees of the Hungarian government. The safety of his staff was not Wallenberg's sole concern; its expansion reflected the magnitude of his plan—which was the rescue of as many Hungarian Jews as possible. Through Section C, he issued several hundred Swedish passports to Hungarian Jews with relatives or business ties in Sweden. Moreover, he devised the "protective passport," a certificate emblazoned with the Swedish colors, the embassy stamp, and his signature. Within a short time, more than 1,000 people were placed under Swedish protection in this manner.

Other neutral countries followed suit; the Papal Nunciature, the Swiss, Portuguese, and Spanish embassies issued protective passports. The Budapest director of the Red Cross, Waldemar Langnet, issued several thousand "protective letters" over his signature. In a short period of time the protective documents numbered tens of thousands. This sudden increase, however, was partly caused by uncontrollable factors. Underground printing plants sprang into action, manufacturing counterfeit passports on a large scale to fill the desperate need of Budapest's 300,000 Jews threatened with deportation. They operated independently of Wallenberg, but he did not denounce them, and when such documents were presented to him, he did not invalidate them.

The Nazis and the Hungarian police accepted many of the spurious documents, often out of ignorance, occasionally on the logical deduction that the German battlefront, both East and West, was collapsing, and it was therefore advisable to establish and maintain friendly contact with representatives of neutral powers. Wallenberg, not unaware of this sentiment among the Nazis and Hungarian officials, took full advantage of it. On one occasion, learning that a group of Jews had been assembled at the railroad station of Josefvarosy for deportation, he drove there speedily, summoned the commander, and said: "I have it on good authority that among the people arrested by you for deportation are persons protected by the Kingdom of Sweden. This is an outrage. I demand that you instantly release them or I will complain to your superiors!"

While the bewildered German was gathering his wits for a retort, Wallenberg addressed the crowd of Jews: "Whoever has a Swedish protective passport, please step out." A score of persons responded. Wallenberg continued: "Whoever has any provisional protecting documents in the Hungarian language, please step out."

Now a great many Jews responded. They stepped forward eagerly, holding up mail receipts, certificates of vaccination, ration cards. Wallenberg solemnly examined the meaningless scraps of paper, nodding affirmatively in each instance, while the Nazi commander, who did not know Hungarian, watched his transport dwindle.

But Wallenberg did not rely solely on hit and run tactics. He established excellent relations with neutral legations and several high-ranking Hungarian officials and political leaders. He did not hesitate to promise certain influential government officials eventual Swedish protection and diplomatic services in the event the Axis should collapse—if they were helpful in his enterprises. Some Hungarian functionaries were won over by the prospect of cold cash. Wallenberg used the funds at his disposal freely, bribing, when necessary, in order to save lives.

Together with other neutral legations he formed Section A of the International Red Cross, headed by the chairman of the Zionist organization in Hungary, Otto Komoly. He created a number of children's centers protected by the International Red Cross. These centers sheltered 8,000 Jewish children.

On October 15, 1944, Regent Horthy announced to the nation his decision to negotiate with the Allies. A few hours later, the Germans struck, toppling the Horthy regime. The Regent was taken into custody and the government entrusted to Ferencz Szalasi, the Hungarian fuehrer of the Arrow Cross party. Losing no time, the Szalasi government, which had little or nothing to learn from the Nazis, proclaimed as one of its main tasks the "solution of the Jewish question."

The Budapest Jews, living during this period in houses marked with a yellow Star (a closed ghetto was not established until November) were ordered to remain inside their homes for ten days. Jews who dared to leave their homes were murdered; their unburied bodies littered the streets of the city. In the meantime, the Szalasi gangs went from home to home, looting, flogging, and selecting victims for deportation. As this orgy of blood raged unabated, Wallenberg organized groups of young Hungarian Jews into commando units whose function it was to bring food and medical aid to the home-blockaded Jews. Often disguised in the uniforms of the SS or the Arrow Cross, these commandos effected the release of prisoners from deportation transports, and defended Jews from looters and terrorists.

Having loosed its gangs on the hapless Jews, the Szalasi government attacked in another vital sector, declaring that only those armed with legitimate neutral passports were to be treated as privileged foreigners. Thousands of Jews who had pinned their hopes to the protective letters were threatened by this ukase. Wallenberg acted without delay. He got in touch with the wife of Baron Gabor Kemenyi, Minister of Foreign Affairs in the Szalasi cabinet, whom he knew to be of Jewish origin. He succeeded in winning over the lady, and her considerable influence with her husband resulted in the rescinding of the order. Subsequently, Kemenyi interceded on several occasions to help Jews.

--But the Szalasi government and SS Lieut.-Col. A. Eichmann were not to be diverted from their ambitious and not unattainable plan of murdering the rest of Hungary's Jews. Even the news that the railway leading to Auschwitz had been destroyed by bombing did not deter them. They issued orders that the thousands of Jews herded together at assembly points be dispatched to the death camp on foot. The victims were put in charge of young Szalasi fanatics, who drove them on forced day-and-night marches with the aid of truncheons, whips, gun butts, and bullets. The victims were compelled to march without food or drink, and those who faltered—and thousands did—were shot. Even such a practiced assassin as the German Rudolf Hoess, commander of Auschwitz, who was on an official visit to Budapest, was moved to remark on the naked brutality and savagery of the Hungarian Fascists in charge of the columns. Wallenberg followed the columns, riding in his car, comforting the victims with bandages, warm clothing, and shoes. His example was emulated by members of the Swiss Embassy and by Catholic nuns offering bread, water, and clothing to the Jews.

Back in Budapest, Wallenberg devised a new technique of saving Jews from deportation. He organized an intelligence service that provided him lists of Jews arrested for deportation. Section C in the Swedish Embassy was put to work manufacturing protective letters for some of the deportees. The documents were placed in the police files, and the Hungarian authorities were urged to remove all holders of such protective letters from the deportation transports. Usually Wallenberg had to appear in person at the assembly centers in order to prevail upon the commander in charge to release holders of letters. It has been estimated that by using this method Wallenberg saved approximately 4,000 Jews from deportation. Other estimates place the number at 10,000.

By November, 1944, only 100,000 Jews remained in the city of Budapest; the rest had been sent to their death. To speed up the extermination action, Szalasi decreed that all Jews move into a small, closed ghetto. More than 80,000 complied, moving into a cramped space, the so-called "Central Ghetto." The enclosure was not unlike the ghettos of Warsaw, Vilna, and Lodz, the only difference being that here the mercenaries were Hungarian, instead of Ukrainian, Lithuanian, or Lett. Only those Jews possessing neutral passports were exempted; they remained in residences marked with the yellow Star and signs indicating they were under the protection of a neutral power. With defeat inevitable, the Szalasi mobs ignored the neutral protective signs on the buildings to wreak their vengeance on the Jews inside. The neutral embassies protested, but to no avail. As the embassies were located in Buda, on the right bank of the Danube, while the largest number of Jews were in Pest, news of attacks by the mobs was late in reaching them. Against the advice of his friend, the Swedish Ambassador, Wallenberg transferred his offices to Pest in order to be nearer at hand. He rented thirty-two large buildings, in addition to those already in operation, put them under the protection of the Swedish Embassy, and filled them with Jews seeking shelter. The Swedish Red Cross and embassies of the other neutral countries followed Wallenberg's example, and the so-called "International Ghetto" came into existence. It sheltered about 15,000 Jews.

The Nazis, despite their assiduous courting of neutrals, decided to do away with Wallenberg, who had been a thorn to them since his arrival in Budapest. He went underground, but did not cease his operations.

By December, 1944, the Russians had laid siege to Budapest. The fascist mobs, enraged at facing defeat, went out of control. They looted and murdered, attempting to accomplish in the few days left to them what they had failed to do in all the preceding months. Hundreds of SS men, accompanied by a like number of Hungarian policemen and several detachments from the Arrow Cross, converged on the two ghettos, the Central and International. Wallenberg, apprised of their action, came out of hiding to warn General Schmidthueber, commander of the German forces in the city, that he would be held responsible if a massacre were perpetrated and that Wallenberg himself would spare no efforts to have Schmidthueber hanged for the crime. As a result of this interview, German troops were ordered into the threatened areas. In addition, several Hungarian police officials, bribed by Wallenberg's promise to protect them, helped to frustrate what was to have been the final massacre of the Jews in Hungary.

The Russians broke through to the International Ghetto on January 16 and conquered the Central Ghetto on the following night. Although street fighting flared in other parts of the city until February 13, the Jews of Budapest were safe from the Nazi scourge.

Even as the guns were still firing, the people of Budapest—the Jews in particular—sought to show their gratitude to Wallenberg, a modern Moses who had come to them out of the frozen North. At the Jewish Central Hospital they named a building in his honor; the sculptor Paul Patzay was commissioned to create a statue of him. And soon there appeared a Wallenberg Street in Budapest. Elaborate preparations were made to celebrate his valorous deeds, but Wallenberg, the bright star of the occasion, was nowhere to be found. He seemed to have vanished from Budapest.

The following facts are known: On January 10, 1945, Wallenberg met with his staff. On the same day he was seen in various parts of the city, attempting to secure food for his many "guests." Anxious to obtain Russian protection for the thousands of Jews, he moved his headquarters to the International Red Cross building, which was nearer the fighting front. On January 13, a Russian patrol entered the Red Cross building and was met by Wallenberg. He requested that protection be given his charges. The soldiers were not authorized to negotiate, and they referred the Swedish diplomat to a Soviet officer, one Major Demchenko. Wallenberg was placed under Russian guard. On January 17, he appeared briefly at his former office at 6 Rue Tatra, accompanied by three Russian soldiers. Upon leaving, he told several of his co-workers that he was on his way to meet Marshal Malinovsky, Russian commander, at his headquarters at Debrecen, adding: "Whether as a guest or a prisoner—I do not know." He was seen no more.

The fact that he was placed under the protection of the Russian military was several times confirmed by the Russians themselves: in January, 1945, by the Budapest commander, General Tchernishev, and by the Deputy Commissioner of Foreign Affairs, Dekanozov, who spoke of it to the Swedish Ambassador to Moscow, S. Soederblom; and a few weeks later, by Mme. Alexandra Kollontai, Soviet Ambassador to Stockholm, who similarly informed Wallenberg's mother. His co-workers in Budapest were interrogated by Soviet authorities, but none of them was detained. The Swedish government several times requested that Soviet authorities investigate Wallenberg's whereabouts. In his native land, a campaign for his release was launched, with more than a million Swedes signing the petition. Two biographies have been written about him, and many articles in magazines throughout the world have drawn attention to this heroic figure and his mysterious disappearance. Several former Axis officials released from Russian prisons in 1952 claimed they had seen or spoken with Wallenberg in a Moscow prison. On February 7,

1957, a news dispatch from the U.S.S.R. revealed that Wallenberg had died, allegedly from a heart attack, in the dreaded Lubyanka Prison in Moscow on July 17, 1947.

In Budapest, chiseled in bronze, the record of Raoul Wallenberg's deeds is preserved for all time.

CHAPTER FOURTEEN

FELIX KERSTEN AND FOLKE BERNADOTTE

Sweden was the only Scandinavian country that did not become embroiled in World War II. Surrounded by Nazi-occupied and Nazi-controlled areas, its main naval outlet, the Baltic Sea, completely controlled by the Germans, the Swedish government, as well as the man on the street, was constantly aware of the precarious position in which the country existed. German invasion could not be discounted. Despite the ever-present threat poised like a Damocles sword, the Swedes did not hesitate to give shelter to many thousands of refugees from German-occupied countries and to thousands of prisoners released from German concentration camps, among them approximately 12,000 Jews.

It is not necessary to record here the official deeds of the Swedish government on behalf of the Jews of Belgium, Holland, and Hungary; it is our purpose to show that the people of Sweden acted out of a deep conviction and humanitarianism. In a democratic country such as Sweden it is difficult to draw a line between popular and governmental action. King Gustav, Count Folke Bernadotte, or Raoul Wallenberg were certainly motivated, in their efforts to save Jews and other victims of Nazism, by humanitarian rather than political considerations. Their words as well as deeds in this matter represented the people of Sweden.

In the early years after Hitler's rise to power, the highly civilized Swedes refused to believe the atrocity stories frequently told by visitors to the Third Reich. Their traditional sympathies for Germany and its culture deceived even independent minds. A change in the attitude of Swedes became discernible after the November, 1938, pogroms in Germany. It is true that a small number of Jewish refugees from Germany had entered Sweden as early as 1933. There had been some misgivings at that time among certain Swedish university students about a possible "invasion" of their medical profession by "foreigners." But these mild protests disappeared with the outbreak of World War II, particularly after the German occupation of Denmark and Norway in 1940. A number of non-Jewish refugee committees energetically set to work rescuing victims of Nazism. Simultaneously, Jewish relief groups organized by the Jewish community of Stockholm, the Swedish Zionist Organization, and the Swedish section of the World Jewish Congress made efforts to secure entry permits for Jewish refugees from Denmark, Norway, the Baltic countries, Germany, Austria, and Poland.

The first significant rescue operation jointly operated by the Swedes and Norwegians was the rescue of Norway's 1,700 Jews. In Norway itself rescue work was carried on by *Nansenhjaelp*, a committee led by Odd Nansen, son of the famous explorer Fridtjof Nansen. This committee also secured asylum in Scandinavian countries for a number of Nazi victims from Austria, Czechoslovakia, and Poland, among them many Jews. (In January, 1942, Nansen was seized by the Nazis after the German occupation of Norway, and held as a hostage in the concentration camp at Grini. While other Norwegian hostages were released, Nansen failed to win his freedom because of a "stubborn unsusceptibility" to Nazi ideas, and his continued sympathy for the Norwegian Jews who passed through Grini on the way to Auschwitz. Eventually the Nazis sent him to Sachsenhausen camp, where he languished until the end of the war.)

In Norway, there were some who lived with the quixotic hope that, because of their insignificant number, the Jews would be left alone by Quisling and his Nazi lords. After the outbreak of the Russo-German war in June, 1941, the Nazis began harassing Jews. Arrests became a common practice; anti-Jewish legislation was introduced. The vigorous protests of the Norwegian Church had no effect on the invader. On the night of October

25, 1942, the Germans descended on the homes of the Jews and arrested all males sixteen years of age and older. A month later, Jewish women and children were seized in the same manner. All were driven onto the German ship, *Donau*, and deported via Stettin to Auschwitz. Of the 770 deported, twelve survived and returned to Norway after the war.

But not all Norwegian Jews were taken by the Nazi raids. Rumors of probable action had reached many Jews prior to the raid. The Norwegian police, instructed to co-operate with the Nazis, instead gave warning to the Jews. Those warned, took the only route of escape open to them—Sweden. But Sweden was not a goal easily attainable. The frontier zone was an area of thick forests, wilderness, and mountainous terrain made even more inaccessible after the first fall of snow. The fugitives were spirited away from towns in buses or trucks, and driven to Eastern Norway. There they were hidden by Norwegian families in sparsely-populated districts. Often the refugees remained in hiding for many days; sometimes months passed before they were able to make the crossing. Several Norwegian Underground organizations took part in the smuggling operations that brought into Sweden 930 Jews and 100 persons labeled by the Nazis as half- and quarter-Jews. Upon their arrival on Swedish territory, the refugees were provided with transportation and living quarters. Food was supplied by government officials and representatives of Jewish and non-Jewish committees. They remained in Sweden until the collapse of the Thousand-Year Reich.

* * * * *

Heinrich Himmler introduced Dr. Felix Kersten to Count Ciano, Mussolini's son-in-law, as "the magic Buddha who cures everything by massage." Himmler suffered from intestinal spasms, and neither narcotics nor injections gave him any relief. Kersten was the first to treat the Hangman by manual therapy, and the results (unfortunately) were astonishing. During World War II, as the physical and mental strain multiplied, particularly when the Reich appeared to be losing the war, Himmler was subject to frequent attacks and became ever more dependent on Kersten. An intimacy developed between the two men. Himmler confided in Kersten about matters pertaining to politics. According to Kersten, he became confessor and consultant to this man, one of the most powerful and evil men in the world, and attempted to use his considerable influence in aiding victims of Nazism, an ism of which his employer was the outstanding symbol. From reading his memoirs, it becomes apparent that Kersten's influence frustrated his master's plan to murder the Jews of Finland, foiled the plot to deport 3,000,000 Dutch citizens to Eastern Europe, and helped in the release of thousands of Norwegian and Danish prisoners of war.

Kersten, it appears, learned from Himmler directly of the Nazi plan to exterminate all of Europe's Jews. Himmler told him of this plan in the beginning of November, 1941. Himmler called a meeting of top representatives from various branches of the German government, police, SS, and the Nazi party, in order to discuss the implementation of what was to be the "final solution of the Jewish question." (The conference was postponed and convened on January 20, 1942, in Wannsee, a suburb of Berlin.)

According to Kersten, he discussed the monstrous Nazi plan with his employer on several occasions with a view toward changing Himmler's mind. But Himmler remained adamant; he was determined to destroy what remained of Europe's great and proud Jewry. Kersten abandoned the notion of the frontal attack and resolved on winning small concessions, wherever possible, and modifications of the total scheme. His first opportunity came when he successfully intervened on behalf of Finland's 2,000 Jews. In 1943, Kersten obtained leave from Himmler to settle his family in Sweden. This was the beginning of fruitful journeys between his villa near Berlin, and Stockholm. In the autumn of 1943, he initiated secret discussions with the Swedish Minister for Foreign Affairs, Christian Guenther, about the possibility of working for the release of Danish and Norwegian internees held in German prisons and camps; several additional months were required, Kersten stated, to win Himmler to the idea. In his talks with Himmler, Kersten expanded the categories of prisoners who might be freed. On December 8, 1944, he noted in his diary that Himmler had agreed to let him bring home the following "Christmas present": a number of imprisoned Danish and Norwegian women, students, policemen, and children; 1,000 Dutch women, 800 French, 400 Belgian, and 500 Polish women. For good measure, the Hangman also threw in 2,000 Jews to be delivered to Switzerland.

In a letter to Himmler, dated December 21, 1944, Kersten wrote: "... I would like to refresh your memory, very respectable Herr Reichsfuehrer, of our talk about the Jews. My request was for the release of 20,000 Jews from Theresienstadt [a concentration camp in Czechoslovakia] for Switzerland. On your part you told me, to my regret, that you could not do this under any circumstances but agreed to release between 2,000 to 3,000, as a first installment ... I am leaving for Sweden tomorrow with an easier heart in the knowledge that your promise will certainly be fulfilled."

In Kersten's opinion, Himmler, who earlier would have shot anyone interceding on behalf of Jews, was of a mellower mood in view of the desperate military and political situation in which the Third Reich found itself in 1944. Kersten was not unaware that Himmler, determined to save himself even as the Hitlerian edifice was slowly crumbling, was jockeying for a favorable position in the event the Allies agreed to negotiate. But even though Himmler appeared willing, the release of a large number of Jews from the Nazi dungeons was no simple matter, not even for a man so powerful as the Chief of the German Security Police. It had to be done without Hitler's knowledge. Moreover, opposition was immediately encountered from Himmler's closest collaborators in the administration of Jewish Affairs, Ernst Kaltenbrunner and Adolf Eichmann. To further complicate the situation, Hitler's obsessive determination to exterminate all his captive victims was implemented by a new order, an order to blow up all concentration camps before the Allies' surging armies reached them and freed the prisoners.

Hillel Storch, head of the Swedish office of the World Jewish Congress, met with Kersten in February, 1945. He suggested that Himmler be petitioned not to carry out Hitler's order to destroy the camps and their inmates, whose numbers ran into the hundreds of thousands. He further suggested that Himmler be asked to permit parcels of food and medicine to be sent to Jewish inmates of the camps (non-Jews enjoyed such privilege); that all Jewish prisoners be concentrated in special Jewish camps under the supervision of the International Red Cross; that several thousand Jewish prisoners be released to Sweden and Switzerland, and 3,000 Jews with South American passports be freed from the Bergen-Belsen concentration camp.

As Storch conferred with Kersten in Stockholm, two other representatives of the World Jewish Congress, Dr. Leo Kubowitzki and Dr. Gerhardt Riegner, met in Geneva with the president of the International Red Cross, Max Huber. The Red Cross was subjected to considerable criticism during the war because of its policy of aiding prisoners of war exclusively, failing to intervene on behalf of those who were being exterminated by the enemy or to aid other persecuted groups of noncombatants. Critics accused the Red Cross of timidity and complacency, and demanded that the organization obtain the status of civilian prisoners of war for the Jews held in the ghettos and camps. Such status would entitle the Jews to the care and protection of the Red Cross. In October, 1944, the International Red Cross finally sent a note to the German Ministry of Foreign Affairs requesting that all foreigners held in Germany and German-occupied areas be recognized as civilian prisoners of war.

The two representatives of the World Jewish Congress discussed with Max Huber the imminent danger of a wholesale massacre of prisoners in German camps and prisons. The problem was again considered by a meeting of various national Red Cross delegations on February 26 in Geneva. Subsequently, Huber left for Germany to negotiate with the German authorities. But even prior to the Geneva meeting, a distinguished officer of the International Red Cross took it upon himself to confer directly with Himmler. This was the vice-president of the Swedish Red Cross, Count Folke Bernadotte. A seasoned diplomat and member of the royal family of Sweden, Bernadotte had no difficulty arranging to see Himmler. Prior to his meeting with the Hangman, who appeared more accessible now than at any time in the past, Bernadotte was briefed on matters pertaining to Jews by representatives of the World Jewish Congress, who had met him in London in November, 1944, and by the Congress' Swedish members, with whom he was in constant touch. He met with Himmler on February 19, 1945. This is how Bernadotte recorded the conversation in his memoirs: "He [Himmler] failed to make any mention of the millions of Jews murdered ... I asked him if he would deny that there were decent people among the Jews, just as there were among all races. I told him that I had many Jewish friends. To my surprise, he took no issue with me but said that we in Sweden did not have a Jewish problem and therefore could not understand the German point of view. An indication that Himmler had lately undergone a change so far as the Jews are concerned can be found in his agreement with Musy [a Swiss diplomat who negotiated with the Germans the transfer of a number of Jewish prisoners to Switzerland]. Later on, Himmler agreed that if necessity should arise, he would permit the interned Jews to be handed over to the Allied military authorities instead of removing them from the camps where they were held."

While Bernadotte was negotiating with Himmler, representatives of the Jewish Rescue Committee were meeting in Budapest with Adolf Eichmann. The question arises: Were all these actions co-ordinated? The answer is in the negative, although it should be stated that the time was propitious. Moreover, co-ordination was eventually achieved between Bernadotte and Kersten, after initial differences of opinion. The nature of their differences and disagreements is not clear. Himmler, experienced at intrigue, once remarked to Kersten: "Bernadotte understands the Jewish peril. He refuses to take any Jews to Sweden. Now you speak for them and claim that Sweden will take them! Which of you am I to believe?" Unquestionably the unscrupulous Himmler distorted Bernadotte's words, but the fact remains that there were divergences of opinion between Bernadotte and Kersten. Bernadotte, the skilled diplomat, apparently saw no advantage in dwelling on the Jewish issue and wanted Kersten to refrain from mentioning the Jews, particularly to Himmler. The logic of his argument was that direct references to Jews irritated the Nazis and made Himmler's position as negotiator more difficult. Bernadotte assumed that once an agreement had been reached to release prisoners in general, as many Jews as possible could be included in the rescue action. On his part, Kersten feared that unless the Jews were specifically mentioned in an agreement, they would be left out of the rescue plans. Eventually, the demand for the release of Jews was explicitly entered into the agreement with Himmler. It appears that both men, Kersten and Bernadotte, successfully negotiated with Himmler.

Kersten and Himmler signed their first important agreement on March 12, 1945. The agreement included the following points: Himmler pledged to ignore Hitler's orders to destroy the concentration camps and kill all the prisoners; the concentration camps would not be evacuated as the Allied armies continued their advance, but would be surrendered to the Allies in good order, with white banners; the killing of Jews would cease forthwith. Himmler signed the agreement as "Reichsfuhrer SS," and Kersten, officially representing no one, put down, "In the name of humanity."

According to Kersten, negotiations continued between them. On March 15 he again suggested to Himmler the transfer of certain categories of Jewish prisoners to Switzerland and Sweden, a matter discussed several months before. Himmler agreed to give the matter his prompt attention and to discuss it with Bernadotte.

Several days later, on March 21, Himmler notified Kersten that two trainloads of Jewish prisoners had left for Switzerland. However, no mention was made in his letter of any comparable release to Sweden. "You will be glad to learn," Himmler wrote Kersten, "that I have taken action, thus realizing what was once a mere idea discussed by both of us. Two thousand, seven hundred Jewish men, women, and children have been taken to Switzerland by train. This achievement is in line with a policy I and my co-workers have been pursuing for years and which the war made it impossible to continue." Distorting history at will, Himmler went on: "You must surely know that in the years 1936, 1937, 1938, 1939, and 1940, I founded an organization in conjunction with Jewish-American societies, which did excellent work. The transportation of Jews to Switzerland is a continuation of this work."

Thus the Grand Inquisitor of the Thousand-Year Reich, the man who projected, sponsored, and developed the SS, Gestapo, and Special Police with their arsenal of torture instruments, the creator and sponsor of gas ovens and crematoria, the man who in his speech of October, 1943, in Posen, to top officers of the SS posed as the modern Genghis Khan and recommended the extermination of all Jews, thereby to write a "page of glory in our history"—this man who now saw unmistakably the handwriting on the wall sought to exorcise the orgy of blood which was his past. The rotten edifice of Nazism was crumbling and Himmler was desperately attempting to save his own skin.

The news of the release of Jewish prisoners elicited a characteristic outburst of rage from Hitler, but for the moment this was the only reaction. He did not propose to shoot Himmler, as the latter had feared.

On March 17, Kersten made a new move. He startled Himmler by suggesting he meet with a representative of the World Jewish Congress. At first Himmler rejected the notion of meeting with a Jew as utterly fantastic. Quite apart from moral scruples, with which Himmler was never encumbered, he doubted the soundness of the idea. "I cannot receive a Jewish visitor," he complained to Kersten. "If the Fuehrer learns of my having a Jewish visitor, he will have me shot." Kersten asserts that he attempted to mollify his boss, assuring him that such a meeting, if it came off, would be held in strict secrecy. Himmler finally relented. Kersten left for Stockholm and presented to Minister Guenther a list of 20,000 to 25,000 concentration camp inmates to be released to Sweden. Among the prisoners, who included Dutch, Norwegian, Belgian, French, and Polish nationals, were between 5,000 and 6,000 Jews. Guenther was pleased and assured Kersten that all the refugees would be "heartily welcomed in Sweden." Kersten then saw Hillel Storch of the World Jewish Congress and suggested a meeting with Himmler on his, Kersten's, estate, near Berlin. Storch readily agreed to submit the suggestion to an emergency meeting of the Congress. The Swedish section of the Congress accepted the suggestion after a wrangle, some members of the organization expressing shock at the very idea of negotiating with Hitler's Chief Executioner. However, the prospect that a substantial number of Jewish survivors might be saved by such action won over the opposition. It was agreed that one of those present should volunteer for this dangerous and unpleasant mission, but not as a representative of the World Jewish Congress; he was to go as a private citizen, representing himself. Several volunteered, and Norbert Masur was chosen.

But Masur had no German entry permit, Himmler having insisted that, for the sake of secrecy, the Jew not apply for a visa at the German Embassy in Stockholm. Masur was to travel armed with no more than a letter of safe-conduct, without his name being inscribed on it. The document, signed by an SS *Brigadefuehrer*, was to be handed to Masur upon his arrival at

Templehof Airport in Berlin. In Stockholm on April 19, at 2:00 P.M., Masur, accompanied by Kersten, boarded a plane carrying Red Cross packages to Germany. They arrived at Tempelhof four hours later and drove through the bomb-scarred capital to Kersten's villa in Hartzwalde. Himmler put in an appearance well past midnight, accompanied by two SS advisers. "I wish to bury the hatchet between us and the Jews," he declared to Kersten before the meeting with Masur began.

Prior to the introductions, Masur had asked himself: "Will this *de facto* master of Germany behave like the despot he is or will he show signs of contrition? Soon, I said to myself, you will be facing the man who put to death millions of Jews. Understandably, I was agitated."

Himmler's manner was proper. He launched into a dissertation on his past attitude toward the Jews, which in his opinion always had been guided by fairness and objectivity. After he had finished his long apologia, that impressed no one, he proceeded to the point. He estimated that 65,000 to 70,000 Jews were held in three large concentration camps still in German hands: Theresienstadt, Ravensbrueck, and Mauthausen. After protracted and miserly bickering on his part, Himmler finally agreed to release 1,000 Jewish women from Ravensbrueck, to be transported to Sweden by the Red Cross. But he insisted those released were to be designated as Polish and their arrival in Sweden be held in strict secrecy. He dangled before Masur the hope of releasing a number of Jews from Theresienstadt.

Several hours after the Masur visit, Himmler saw Bernadotte and discussed with him the problem of transportation by the Red Cross. Himmler, it appears, began to vacillate, and was on the point of withdrawing his consent. Bernadotte prevailed upon him to release a number of "French" women from Ravensbrueck, and further to promise that the Red Cross bus convoy be allowed to take not a thousand women, but as many as it could carry.

Himmler was loath to concede even one Jew more than was necessary at a time when the Nazi edifice, built on the skulls of so many peoples, was falling apart in chaos and confusion. Hitler committed suicide on April 30; Himmler, who had snuffed out the lives of 6,000,000 Jews, clung to his own for another three weeks. While the Nazi *Götterdämmerung* was being enacted against the backdrop of Allied siege guns, 3,500 Jewish women were transported from Ravensbrueck to Sweden. In addition, 60,000 Jewish prisoners who would have been destroyed by Hitler's order before he died were saved from annihilation.

Jews throughout the world have praised both Bernadotte and Kersten. Bernadotte was hailed as a savior of the Jews and presented with a scroll by the Chief Rabbi of Stockholm. Kersten's deeds were no less celebrated. The World Jewish Congress paid tribute to Himmler's doctor in many official statements, and Christians have been no less generous in their praise of him. He was decorated by the Dutch, and nominated by them in 1952 as their candidate for the Nobel Peace Prize. The Finnish government awarded him the Cross of the Count of the White Rose, and he was also appointed Finnish Medical Counsellor.

As in the case of Bernadotte, whose decisive role in rescuing the Jews is disputed by the distinguished English historian, H. R. Trevor-Roper, Kersten has been challenged by various sources, among them a Swedish "White Paper" which states that while he was helpful in rescuing Jews and others, the role he arrogates to himself is out of all proportion to the deeds he performed.

We shall not try to evaluate the deeds performed by either Bernadotte or Kersten. We are willing to call them heroes if they saved even one human life.

*   *   *   *   *

CONCLUSION

For over a decade, in our time, in full view of all our senses, a great evil manifested itself in the guise of a dictator. Deranged, sadistic, he gained power, and during his regime perverted the very nature and essence of man.

All men were his victims: the innocent, those who helped him, those who opposed him, those who closed their eyes and minds and hearts. All men were his victims, and yet in the end he was destroyed. And he was destroyed by bombs; destroyed by artillery. But the greater truth is that he was doomed to destruction as long as there was one man who persisted in his God-given right to say nay when the bayonet in his back prodded him to say aye. He was doomed to destruction as long as there was one Christian who unflinchingly obeyed the fundamental precept of his religion and helped a fellow man. One word epitomizes the evil that engulfed us—Hitler; one word evokes the redemption allowed to man—love.

The records, incomplete as they are, reveal the deeds of men and women who said nay heroically. Why were these people heroes? Were they simply brave? Brave men could be found in the ranks of the oppressors. Were they profound believers in truth and justice, which they converted to action? Were they idealists, basically religious people, humanitarians? They were all of these—and more. Our surviving civilization owes these people the grateful recognition they so richly deserve.

NOTES AND REFERENCES

Ten years of research on the Jewish catastrophe under the Nazi regime have accumulated immense material in the hands of this writer. One of the most fascinating aspects of this material is the documentation of relations between Jews and non-Jews in the Nazi-occupied or dominated countries. Especially noteworthy were the behavior and actions of those courageous men and women who dared defy the Nazi terror and who, in spite of all the dangers involved, managed to preserve their human stature and their human feelings toward their persecuted fellow men. A great wealth of facts and episodes of this kind has been recorded in innumerable books, articles and documents. As a matter of fact, this writer is engaged at the present time in preparing a bibliography of the European-Jewish catastrophe under the Nazis and was able to assemble to date about 60,000 pertinent bibliographical entries. The author could, therefore, draw upon this remarkably large amount of bibliographical information in order to select the material necessary for this book. Of course, only an infinitesimal portion, only the most relevant, is quoted in the following notes and references.

Besides the published material, the author also has had the chance to utilize some unpublished sources from the archives of the following institutions to which he is indebted: YIVO Institute for Jewish Research in New York, the Centre de Documentation Juive Contemporaine in Paris, the Central Jewish Historical Commission in Poland (now the Jewish Historical Institute in Warsaw). Another source of important information was provided by interviews and exchanges of letters with persons who willingly volunteered to supply the author with their personal materials, recollections, documents, letters, pictures, new bibliographic clues, etc. Such interviews and correspondence extended over the course of several years to numerous towns in many countries, including Poland, France, Germany, Belgium, the Netherlands, Great Britain, Israel and the U.S.A. For those materials I am particularly indebted to the following persons: Dina Abramovich, New York; Mrs. Pauline Albala, Montreal, Canada; Dr. and Mrs. Aage Bertelsen, Denmark; Mrs. Nusia Dlugi, New York; Dr. A. G. Duker, Chicago; Dr. John Fried, New York; Mrs. Sophie Fryde, New York; Dr. Samuel Gringauz, New York; N. Kantorovich, New York; Dr. David Kahane, Israel; Mary Klachko, New York; Dr. and Mrs. John Lanzkron, Middletown, New York; David Lehrer, New York; Dr. Kurt Levin, New York; Erick Lüth, Hamburg, Germany; Robert Major, New York; Dr.

Maurice Moch, Paris; Theodor T. Pianoff, Paris; Sophia Pilenko, Paris; Willy Prins, Brussels; Joseph Schwarz, Brooklyn, N. Y.; Pinkhas Schwartz, New York; I. Shmulevich, New York; R. Scola, Boston, Mass.; Dr. Vincent Shandor, New York; D. E. Skobtzoff, Paris; Anna Šimaite, Petakh Tikva, Israel; Inge Scholl, Ulm, Germany; Father Eron Marko, Woodstock, N. Y.; Waclaw Smólski, Warsaw; Dr. Michael Temchyn, Florida, N. Y.; Col. Adolfo Massimo Vitale, Rome; Dr. Leo Wels, New York.

In the bibliographical references several publications frequently quoted have been replaced by symbols (see list of abbreviations). The other titles are quoted in full only once, and thereafter referred to as *op. cit.* (*opere citato*). Where more than one publication by the same author is quoted, instead of *op. cit.*, an abbreviated title is used for identification of the particular book. Titles of articles have been omitted since the author's name and the name of the periodical (with the date of publication) are sufficient for identification of the article.

Diacritical signs and accents in foreign language texts and names have been omitted in the text except for the few which are essential to the understanding or the identification of a name.

LIST OF ABBREVIATED BIBLIOGRAPHICAL REFERENCES

AOJ — *Activités d'organizations juives en France*, Paris, 1947

AW — *Akcje i Wysiedlenia* (Actions and Deportations, *Pol.*), ed. by Jozef Kermisz, Warsaw-Lodz, 1946

BB — Jenö (Eugene) Levai, *Black Book on the Martyrdom of Hungarian Jewry*, Zürich, 1948

BFG — *Bleter far geshikhte* (Quarterly of Jewish Historical Institute in Poland, *Yid.*), Warsaw, 1948——

CJR — *Contemporary Jewish Record*, N. Y., 1939–1945

FLH — *Fun letstn Hurbn* (English subtitle: *From the Last Extermination, Yid.*), Munich, 1946–1948

IMT — *International Military Trial of the Major War Criminals*, Nuremberg, 1947, 42 vols.

JE — *Les Juifs en Europe (1939–1945)*. Paris, Éditions du Centre, 1949

JSS — Jewish Social Studies, N. Y., 1939——

MF — Philip Friedman (ed.), *Martyrs and Fighters*, N. Y., 1954

MJ — *Le Monde Juif*, Revue Mensuelle du Centre de Documentation Juive Contemporaine, Paris, 1946——

MZ — *Morgn-Zhurnal (Yid.)*, N. Y., 1939——

PSJ — Léon Poliakov and Jacques Sabille, *Jews under Italian Occupation*, Paris, 1955

Rundbrief — *Rundbrief zur Foerderung der Freundschaft zwischen dem alten und dem neuen Gottesvolk im Geiste der beiden Testamente*. Freiburg in Breisgau, 1949——

WLB — *Wiener Library Bulletin*, London, 1946——
YA — *YIVO Annual of Jewish Social Science*, N. Y., 1946——
YBLG — *Yediyot bet lohamey ha'getaot* (Bulletin of the Ghetto
Fighters Home, *Heb.*), Historical Institute, Haifa,
1956——

INTRODUCTION

PAGES 15-17

There are a considerable number of documents on various, sometimes very ingenious, hiding techniques used during the Nazi period (hideouts were usually known as "bunkers"). Of these, only a few of the most relevant are mentioned; a detailed description of three large bunkers in Rohatyn, Galicia, is included in the June 30, 1943, report of the German Police Chief in Galicia, SS General Fritz Katzmann (Document L 18 in *IMT*, vol. 37). A description of bunkers in Boryslaw, Galicia, and Stolpce, Belorussia, as well as a plan of a bunker were published in Betti Ajzensztajn, *Ruch podziemny w ghettach i obozach* (The Underground Movement in the Ghettos and Camps, *Pol.*), Warsaw-Lodz, 1946.

The builders of the bunkers used various devices to camouflage them. Sometimes the entrance was hidden in a kitchen stove, a toilet (outhouse), a well, etc., *e.g.*, see the photo of a bunker entrance camouflaged in a well, in B. Mark, *Der oyfshtand in Bialystoker gheto* (The Uprising in the Ghetto of Bialystok, *Yid.*), Warsaw, 1950. Bunkers in the sewers were sometimes inhabited by whole families; they were described in *Dzieci oskarzaja* (Children Accuse, *Pol.*), Cracow-Lodz, 1947; Tovie Borzykowski, *Tsvishn falndike vent* (Among Falling Walls, *Yid.*), Warsaw, 1949. The life of a whole "underground city" was depicted in Abraham Sutzkever's poem *Di geheimshtot* (The Secret City, *Yid.*), Tel Aviv, 1948. Another "underground ghetto" was recorded in *Sefer Baranovich (Yid. & Heb.)*, Tel Aviv, 1953. Bunkers were built even in cemeteries, beneath the tombs; Jacob Pat, *Ashes and Fire*, N. Y., 1947; in camouflaged double walls, Leib Rochman, *Un in dayn blut zolstu lebn* (And in Thy Blood Thou Shalt Live, *Yid.*), Paris, 1949, and the article of Pinkhas Schwartz in *Der Veker (Yid.)*, New York, May 1, 1946. A hiding place in a camouflaged annex to an office building in Amsterdam is described in Anne Frank, *Diary of a Young Girl*, New York, 1952. About children hidden in dust bins and baking stoves see the article of I. M. Kersht in *Forward (Yid.)*, Nov. 24, 1945. A Jew who used a cave in the mountains as a hiding place was called "Robinson Crusoe" by the peasants in the neighborhood, *Pinkas Kremenetz (Heb.)*, Tel Aviv, 1954. A great wealth of information about various types of bunkers and the life therein is to be found in the following books: M. J. Fajgenbaum, *Podlasie in umkum* (The Destruction of Podlasie, *Yid.*), Munich, 1948 (in Yiddish the bunker dwellers were called *tsadikim, i.e.,* saints); Aaron Peretz, *Dem goyrl antkegn* (Facing Fate, *Yid.*), Haifa, 1952; Gershon Taffet, *Zaglada Zydow zolkiewskich* (Extermination of the Jews of Zolkiew, *Pol.*), Lodz, 1947; Abraham Weissbrod, *Es shtarbt a shtetl* (A Town Dies, Skalat Destroyed, *Yid.*), Munich, 1948; Pawel Wiederman, *Plowa Bestia* (The Blond Beast, *Pol.*), Munich, 1948; Benjamin Orenstein, *Hurbn Chenstochov* (The Destruction of Czestochowa, *Yid.*), n.p., 1948; Mark Dworzecki, *Yerusholaim d'Lite in kamf un umkum* (The Fight and the Destruction of the Lithuanian Jerusalem, *Yid.*), Paris, 1948; *Yizkor bukh fun der Zelekhover yidisher kehile* (Memorial Volume of the Zelechow Jewish Community, *Yid.*), Chicago, 1953; *Sefer Skernievits (Yid.)*, Tel Aviv, 1955; *Hurbn un gvure fun shtetl Markuszow* (Destruction and Heroism of the Town of Markuszow, *Yid.*), Tel Aviv, 1955; Jonas Turkow, *Azoy iz es geven* (The Way It Was, *Yid.*), Buenos Aires, 1948; the same, *In kamf farn lebn* (Fighting for Survival, *Yid.*), Buenos Aires, 1949; *Dzieci oskarzaja.*

PAGE 16

Gusia Obler's story is based upon her own account to this writer immediately after her liberation.

Meir Stein's story inspired a Jewish poet in Brazil, Moshe Shkliar, to write a Yiddish poem "The Eagle" published in *Der Poylisher Yid*, No. 4, Rio de Janeiro, Feb. 1953.

The story of Dr. Lachowicz was told by Jacob Kenner, in *Bafrayung (Yid.)*, Munich, May 7, 1948.

PAGE 17

The rewards for denouncing a Jew were subject to variations, at different places and times. Thus, *e.g.*, the original price in the Netherlands was 50 to 75 florin but later, in some places, dropped to only 7½ gulden (about 2 U.S. dollars); in France, 100 to 500 francs; in the Gouvernment General of Poland, a bottle of vodka, five pounds of sugar and two cartons of cigarettes; in Vilna and its environs about 120 pounds of sugar; in Eastern Galicia a quart of brandy, two pounds of sugar and 300 zloty, and so on. *WLB*, X, 3-4 (1956); Sz. Kaczerginski, *Hurbn Vilna* (The Destruction of Vilna, *Yid.*), N. Y., 1947; A. Weissbrod, *op. cit.; Le droit à la patrie*, ed. by Miriam Bath-Ami [Novich], Paris, 1946.

PAGES 17-18

The Tarnopol story was told by survivors to Jacob Kenner and published by him in *MZ*, May 13, 1948.

PAGES 18-19

The story of the cattle dealer Jozefek in the suburb Klepariv of Lwow was widely discussed in Lwow at the time of his execution. This writer, who incidentally was in Lwow at that time, was also able to talk to several survivors who, during the Nazi occupation, were temporarily sheltered or supported by Jozefek. The death penalty for hiding or helping a Jew took effect in 1942. The new law was announced to local Nazi authorities simply by interoffice communications such as the circular letter of Sept. 21, 1942 sent out by Dr. Boettcher, governor of the district of Radom. The photostat copy of the circular is in L. Brenner's *Vidershtand un umkum in Chenstokhover Ghetto* (Resistance and Extermination in the Ghetto of Czestochowa, *Yid.*), Warsaw, n.d. People found guilty of sheltering or helping a Jew were usually executed on the spot without a trial, beaten to death in jail, or hanged publicly. For the many cases of such executions a few examples may be quoted: *Skierniewice*; *Markuszow*; *Yizkor bukh Chelm* (ed. by M. Bakalchuk-Fellin, *Yid.*), Johannesburg, S.A., 1954 (a Christian baker executed for bringing food to some hiding Jews); Elimelekh Feinzilber, *Oyf di hurves fun mayn haym* (On the Ruins of My Home, *Yid.*), Tel Aviv, 1952; Renia Kukielko, *Escape from the Pit*, N. Y., 1947 (a Polish woman, 25 years old, mother of two small children, hanged for sheltering a Jew, her former employer); *Zelechów*; M. Dworzecki, *Yerusholaim*; *Aynikeyt*, June 1, 1944 (twelve Greeks hanged in Athens).

Sometimes whole families were ruthlessly exterminated for sheltering Jews: see Ludwik Hirszfeld, *Historia jednego zycia* (The History of a Life, *Pol.*) Warsaw, 1946; Feinzilber, *op. cit.* (a Polish peasant who permitted two Jewish workers in the village to sleep in his home was hanged and his wife sent to a concentration camp). A Polish underground report sent to New York in July, 1944 by the HICEM office (a Jewish emigration organization) in Lisbon quotes many instances where people were executed for sheltering a Jew or even for selling bread to a Jew (a baker, his wife and son shot). The document is available in YIVO archives in New York (the HIAS-HICEM Collection, XII, Poland, 10). Another collection of interviews made with several survivors by Mr. Joseph Schwarz of New York lists a number of Ukrainians who risked their lives for saving Jews (MSS. in the YIVO archives and in my private archive).

Sometimes the Germans happened to forego the death penalty for another form of punishment. Thus, Antoni Jakubowski in Bialystok was "proselytized"; the Germans gave him a Jewish passport with the name Abraham Lewin, a Jewish armband with the Star of David and sent him to the ghetto (B. Mark, *Bialystok*). In spite of the heavy penalties the helpers did not stop their rescue work. According to a secret report of the German Chief of the Police in the Gouvernment General to the Reich Chief Security office, Dept. VII, Berlin, dated Cracow, October 7, 1943 the number of cases against those guilty of helping Jews in Special Courts *(Sondergerichte)* of the District of Galicia was ever increasing. The report advocates the death penalty as the only kind of punishment and recommends that all these cases should be immediately handled by the police, without the necessary delay of court hearings. The original document is in the archives of the *Instytut Zachodni* (Research Institute for the Western Area) in Poznań; an authorized copy is in my archive.

The moving letter of Francisca Rubinlicht, an artist, painter and decorator of the Warsaw theatres, addressed to her relatives in the U.S., Israel and Canada, was published in *AW*. Francisca Rubinlicht did not survive the Nazi holocaust.

PAGE 19

The Kowalski story has been recorded by the Israeli correspondent Simon Samet, who visited Poland in 1946, in *B'voi l'mohorat* (When I Came the Following Day, *Heb.*), Tel Aviv, 1946.

Karol Kiciński's story has been recorded in Feinzilber's *Siedlce*. The Bialystok story was reported in the meeting of the Jewish Regional Committee in Bialystok and taken down by J. Pat, an American-Jewish writer who attended the meeting, J. Pat, *Ashes* . . . Other records about Poles who were threatened with severe penalties or were killed by anti-Semitic underground groups for helping Jews: *Zelechów*; *Israelitisches Wochenblatt*, No. 59, Zürich, June 9, 1950; *Tog*, Feb. 1, 1945; *Dzieci oskarżaja*.

CHAPTER ONE
The Heart of Woman

PAGE 21

The late archivist of the Warsaw ghetto, the historian Emanuel Ringelblum, devoted in his diaries an inspired eulogy to the Jewish women in the ghettos, their courage, endurance and self sacrifice. The diaries were published in the Yiddish original, *Notitsn fun Varshever Ghetto* (Notes from the Warsaw Ghetto), Warsaw, 1952. For English translation see *MF*.

PAGES 21-25

About Anna Šimaite much had been published in the Jewish press and in memoirs of Jewish survivors, as in M. Dworzecki, *op. cit.*; I. Shmulevich, in *Forward*, June 2, 1953 and August 14, 1955; Hirsh Abramovich, in *Litvisher Yid (Yid.)*, Nos. 7-8, Apr.–May 1946; Itzhak Rimon in *Kanader Odler (Yid.)*, Montreal, March 30, 1953. These materials were supplemented by an exchange of letters with Mrs. Anna Šimaite and by interviews with a survivor of the Vilna ghetto, Dina Abramovich, now librarian at the YIVO Institute in New York. From Šimaite's articles about the Nazi period these are particularly relevant: her letter to the editors of *Litvisher Yid* in Nos. 6-7, Apr.–May 1946, discussing the attitude of the Catholic clergy in Lithuania toward the Jews, and the article, "Lithuanians and Jews during the Nazi occupation" in the volume *Lite (Yid.)*, N. Y., 1951, vol. I.

PAGES 26-27

The information on Mother Superior is based on Abraham Sutzkever, *Vilner Ghetto, 1941–1944 (Yid.)*, Paris, 1946; Cf. also Joseph Tenenbaum, *Underground*, N. Y., 1952.

On the activities of Janina Bukolska, see the memoirs of Rachel Auerbach, *Be'hutsot Varsha* (In the Streets of Warsaw, *Heb.*), Tel Aviv,

1954, and Bathia Temkin-Berman, *Yoman ba'mahteret* (An Underground Diary, *Heb.*), Tel Aviv, 1956. This writer met Mrs. Bukolska after liberation in Lodz where she worked for the Central Jewish Historical Commission in Poland, and thus was able to supplement the published information by personal observation and interviews. See also the two articles on Bukolska by Rachel Auerbach in *Nowe Widnokręgi (Pol.)*, No. 13 (1945) and in *Arbeter-Vort (Yid.)*, Paris, Sept. 29, 1945.

PAGES 29-30
About Duniec and Adamowicz see A. Sutzkever, *op. cit.*; M. Dworzecki, *op. cit.*, also Melekh Neustadt (ed.), *Hurbn un oyfshtand fun di Yidn in Varshe* (The Destruction and the Uprising of the Jews in Warsaw, *Yid.*), Tel Aviv, 1948, vol. 1.

About Dębicka, Laterner, Plawczyńska, see J. Pat in *Forward*, May 20, 1946.

About Stephania Sempołowska and other members of the socialist underground who helped Jews see the notes to Chapter 8.

PAGES 30-31
There is a great deal of material published on Mother Maria, *Mat Maria, Stikhotvorenia, poemy, vospominanya* (Mother Maria, verses, poems, memoirs, *Russ.*), Paris, 1947; Tatiana Manukhina, in *Novy Zhurnal (Russ.)*, N. Y., vol. 41 (June, 1955). Mother Maria's poem on the Jewish Star was published in her collection of poems. Documentary material on Mother Maria and her group is also available in the Archive of Russian and East European History and Culture in Columbia University (Butler Library) in N. Y. Of the many articles published in Jewish periodicals these should be mentioned: Marc Vishniak in *Yidisher Kemfer (Yid.)*, N. Y., Oct. 12, 1945; I. Shmulevich, in *Forward*, Apr. 17, 1948; J. Tulin, in *Forward*, Sept. 19, 1945. Mother Maria's arrest and death in the concentration camp were also described by Simone Saint-Clair, *Ravensbrück: L'Enfer de femmes*, Paris, 1945. The story about Mother Maria's self-sacrifice was told by Israel Efroykin, *Kedushe un gvure bay yidn amol un haynt* (Holiness and Bravery in Jewish Life in the Past and in the Present, *Yid.*), N. Y., 1949.

However, the most important and valuable sources were placed at my disposal by the closest friends and relatives of Mother Maria: by her mother, 95-year-old Sophia Borysovna Pilenko, by one of Maria's closest collaborators in her Paris rescue work, Theodor Timofeyevich Pianoff; by Maria's divorced husband, the writer D. Skobtzoff; and, last but not least, by Anna Šimaite.

Particularly great was the part played by women in saving Jewish children. The plight of the orphaned or abandoned Jewish child, helpless and often unaware of the terrible danger ahead, brought a special response from women. There are innumerable accounts of this rescue work from almost every European country.

There is the story of the young sister Josephine of the Convent of *Notre Dame de Sion* in Grénoble who helped to smuggle many Jewish children and women to Switzerland. See Simon Gurvich, in *Dos Vort* *(Yid.)*, Paris, Jan. 24, 1945.

A moving story is that of 23-year-old Marianne Colin, who was arrested by the Nazis while escorting a group of Jewish children from France to Switzerland. She was offered her freedom for the price of abandoning the children to their own fate, but she refused to leave them and was executed by a German firing squad on July 8, 1944, only a few weeks before the liberation. Helmut Gollwitzer and others, (eds.), *Du hast mich heimgesucht bei Nacht (Ger.)*, Munich, 1954.

Many Jewish children were saved by their former teachers, housemaids, servants, nurses. Several instances are recorded by M. Dworzecki, *op. cit.*, and Berl Kahan, *A Yid in vald* (A Jew in the Woods, *Yid.*), N. Y., 1955. An extraordinary act of courage was reported from the small town of Mordy, near Siedlce in Poland. There, during a deportation action, a Polish lady, Elizabeth Przewłocka, grabbed a Jewish child from the death transport, right under the nose of the Nazi convoy guards and succeeded in hiding him. Of course it was too dangerous for her to keep the child, who was consequently removed to Warsaw and placed in a Polish orphanage. Maria Czapska, in *Tygodnik Polski (Pol.)*, Apr. 27, 1947. In Warsaw, a group of Polish women, members of the underground headed by the "wonderful Irena Sandler," saved a number of Jewish children, risking their own lives. J. Turkow, *Azoy...*

CHAPTER TWO
Battle of the Badge

PAGE 33
For a more detailed and documented account of the problems discussed in this chapter and for a fuller bibliography see Philip Friedman: "The Jewish Badge and the Yellow Star in the Nazi Era," *Historia Judaica*, vol. XVII, No. 1, (1955); Bruno Blau, "Der Judenstern der Nazis" *(Ger.)*, *Judaica*, vol. IX, No. 1, Zürich, 1953; "The Yellow Star. A Shibboleth in Nazi Europe," *WLB*, vol. VIII, Nos. 5-6, (1954).

The strange story of Ozorków was recorded by a survivor, Shlomo Lipman, in *Bleter fun payn un umkum* (Pages of Agony and Extermination, *Yid.*), Melbourne, 1949.

PAGES 34-35
The diary of the Jewish teacher Mr. Wortman of Berlin was published in the Ph.D. thesis of Hans Lamm, *Ueber die innere und aeussere Entwicklung des deutschen Judentums im Dritten Reich (Ger.)*, University of Erlangen, 1951; Siegmund Weltlinger published his reminiscences of the Nazi period in a small pamphlet, *Hast Du es schon vergessen? (Ger.)*, Frankfurt a/M, 1954. The selected letters of Major-

General Helmuth Stieff, later executed by the Nazis, were published in *Vierteljahreshefte fuer Zeitgeschichte (Ger.)*, vol. II, No. 3, 1954. Ringelblum's anecdotal story is recorded in his *Notitsn*.

PAGE 35

Joseph Radermacher, *Ketzergedanken im Dritten Reich (Ger.)*, Krefeld, 1946.

PAGES 35-36

Else R. Behrend-Rosenthal, *Ich stand nicht allein: Erlebnisse einer Juedin in Deutschland 1943–1944 (Ger.)*, Hamburg, 1945.

PAGE 36

The Goebbels Diaries 1942–1943, ed. by Louis Lochner, N. Y., 1948.

The full text of Ripka's BBC broadcast was published in *The Governments in Exile and Their Attitude toward the Jews*, ed. by Z. H. Wachsman, N. Y., 1944.

PAGE 37

The Hebrew paper of the Jewish underground in Lodz was produced in full in *Dapim* (historical journal in Hebrew devoted to the research of the Jewish catastrophe and resistance during the Nazi regime), No. 1, Haifa, 1950.

E. Ringelblum, *op. cit.*; Bernard Goldstein, *The Stars Bear Witness*, N. Y., 1949 and Władysław Szpilman, *Smierć miasta* (The Death of the City, *Pol.*), Warsaw, 1946.

PAGES 37-38

About the travel restrictions against Jews and Negroes see Léon Poliakov, *L'Étoile jaune (French)*, Paris, 1949; Gerhard Reitlinger, *The Final Solution*, N. Y., 1953.

PAGE 39

One of the French girls deported to camp Drancy for demonstrating against the Jewish badge, Alice Couroble, later published a book about this experience under the title: *Amie des Juifs*, Paris, 1945.

PAGES 39-40

The strong reaction of the French population against the Jewish badge is described by several Jewish writers in the *Yizkorbukh tsum andenk fun 14 umgekumene Parizer yidishe shrayber* (Memorial Volume to Commemorate Fourteen Murdered Jewish Writers of Paris, *Yid.*), Paris, 1946; L. Poliakov, *Étoile* ...John M. Oesterreicher, *Racisme-Antisemitisme-Antichristianisme*, N. Y., 1943.

The story of Monsignor Chaptal was recorded in John M. Oesterreicher, *op. cit.*; *WLB*, vol. VIII, Nos. 5-6, and Hugh Martin and others, *Christian Counter-Attack*, N. Y., 1944.

PAGE 40

Concerning Belgian reaction to the Jewish badge see Joseph L. Baron, *Stars and Sand*, Philadelphia, 1943; *Hitler's Ten-Year War on the Jews*, N. Y., 1943.

PAGES 40-41

About the attitude of King Christian X see Poliakov, *Étoile* ...; Aage Bertelsen, *Oct. '43*, N. Y., 1954.

PAGE 41

About Archbishop Stepinac's statement see Helen Walker Homan, *Letters to the Martyrs*, N. Y., 1951.

PAGES 41-42

About Bulgaria: Poliakov, *Étoile* . . . ; G. Reitlinger, *op. cit.;* Peter Meyer, "Bulgaria" in *The Jews in the Soviet Satellites*, Syracuse, 1953; Jacques Sabille, in *MJ*, No. 30 (1950) (documents).

About Romania: Matatias Carp (ed.), *Transnistria (Yid.)*, Buenos Aires, 1950; Joseph Schechtman, *The Jews in Romania During World War II* (typescript in the archives of YIVO, N. Y.).

CHAPTER THREE

France

PAGE 42

For the attitude of the French population see: Léon Poliakov, *Harvest of Hate*, Syracuse, 1951; the same in *JSS*, vol. XV, No. 2, (1953); G. Reitlinger, *op. cit.;* E. H. Zerner, in *Public Opinion Quarterly*, vol. XII (1948-1949), *La Persécution raciale en France*, Paris, 1947; George Wellers, in *MJ*, No. 16, (1946); *AOJ*; Victor M. Bienstock, in *Menorah Journal*, vol. XXXIII, No. 1, (1945). An interesting personal narrative of a French-Catholic doctor who volunteered for medical service in concentration camps in order to help the Jewish victims was published by Charles Odic *(pseud.)*, *Stepchildren of France*, N. Y., 1945; a personal narrative of a French woman imprisoned by the Nazis for helping Jews was published by Madeleine du Fresne, *De l'enfer des hommes à la cité de Dieu*, Paris, 1947.

PAGE 46

The incident in Lyons is recorded in Michal Borwicz, *Arishe papirn* (Aryan Documents, *Yid.*), Buenos Aires, 1955, vol. III.

PAGES 46-47

The sympathetic attitude of the French police and administration towards the Jews was recorded in many of the above mentioned sources. See also J. M. Oesterreicher, *op. cit.* About the statement of André Chaigneau, prefect of Nice, see: Léon Poliakov and Jacques Sabille, *Jews under the Italian Occupation*, Paris, 1955; Zanvel Diamant, in *YA*, vol. VIII, 1953.

PAGE 47

Léon Poliakov's quotation is from his book *Harvest* . . .

The French philosopher and ambassador to the U.S., Jacques Maritain, strongly condemned anti-Semitism and racialism in his public addresses, articles and books, such as *Anti-Semitism*, London, 1939; *A Christian Looks at the Jewish Problem*, N. Y., 1941; "On Anti-Semitism," in *Commonweal*, vol. XXXVI, 1942; Paul Claudel, the French poet and playwright, former ambassador to the U.S. (1927–1933), published his *Catholic Essays against Anti-Semitism* at the beginning of the German occupation of France but the book was soon suppressed by the Nazis. See Kopel S. Pinson, in *JSS*, vol. VII, No. 2, (1945). See also P. Claudel's *Une Voix sur Israél*, Paris, 1950. The Catholic writer François Mauriac expressed his indignation against anti-Semitism and against indifference to Jewish sufferings on many occasions. See his preface to Léon Poliakov's, *Bréviaire de la haine*, Paris, 1951, and his passionate attacks against anti-Semites in his address at the Congress of the International League against Racialism and Anti-Semitism in Paris (*Jewish Chronicle*, London, Dec. 10, 1954). The poet Paul Elouard is particularly to be remembered for his moving poem "On the Ruins of the Warsaw Ghetto," in his *Poèmes politiques*, Paris, 1949. Some of Louis Aragon's powerful short stories, *Servitude et grandeur de France*, Paris, 1945, deal with the Jewish tragedy in France. Vercors gave a strong expression to his sympathy for persecuted Jews in his *Lettres aux Américains*, Paris, 1946; Romain Rolland's friendship with a Jewish underground fighter during the Nazi occupation was described in *Lettres de Romain Rolland à un combatant de la résistance*, Paris, 1947; Jean-Paul Sartre's most poignant work on the Jewish question was his *Réflexions sur la question juive*, Paris, 1946; David Rousset's bulky diary concerning his experience in the Nazi concentration camp, *Les Jours de notre mort*, Paris, 1947, devotes much attention to the sufferings of his Jewish fellow-prisoners and their narratives.

PAGES 48-49

About the Jewish participation in the French resistance movement see: *AOJ*; David Knout, *Contribution à l'histoire de la résistance juive en France, 1940–1944*, Paris, 1947; Denise Mitrani, *Réseau d'évasion*, Paris, 1946; Jacques Lazarus (Capitaine Jacquel), *Juifs au combat*, Paris, 1947; Léon Poliakov, in *YA*, vol. VIII. A personal narrative of Léon Blum's experience during the years 1940–1945 including his arraignment before a Vichy Tribunal at Riom and his deportation to German concentration camps, is to be found in *L'œuvre de Léon Blum: Mémoires: La prison et le procès. A l'Échelle humaine, 1940–1945*, Paris, 1955; Daniel Mayer published his memoirs from the period of his resistance activities in the French-Jewish magazine *Évidences*, Paris, Nos. 6, 9, 10, 12, 13 (1949–1950); Pierre Mendès-France published a book about his experiences during the Nazi period under the title, *The Pursuit of Freedom*, London, 1956; the story of the duke "Levy" has been recorded by L. Poliakov, in *YA*, vol. VIII.

The appeal published in the French underground paper *Le Combat* was published in English translation in *CJR*, Oct. 1943.

About the attitude of the French church, Catholic and Protestant, see: Dante Lattes, in *JE;* about Cardinal Jules Saliège see, in particular: Lattes, *op. cit.*; J. M. Oesterreicher, *op. cit.*; L. Poliakov, in *La Terre retrouvée*, June 15, 1951. Saliège's addresses were published in *Un Évêque français sous l'occupation: Extraits de messages de S. Ex. Mgr. Saliège, Archevêque de Toulouse*, Paris, 1945.

PAGE 50

The pastoral letter of Bishop Théas was reproduced in Oesterreicher, *op. cit.* and in English translation by K. Pinson, in *JSS*, vol. VII, No. 2. About Cardinal Gérlier see: Oesterreicher, *op. cit.*; Martin Hugh, *op. cit.*; D. Lattes, *op. cit.*; F. Shrager, in *Forward*, Aug. 4, 1946.

PAGE 51

The venomous attack by Marcy is reproduced in Oesterreicher, *op. cit.*

The attitude of the Protestant church is discussed in Lattes, *op. cit.*

The help given to persecuted Jews and to Protestants of Jewish origin is described in Henri Cadier, *La Calvaire d'Israel*, Paris, 1945.

PAGES 51-52

French police reports on the activities of the clergy emphasize the great impact of the pastoral letters and messages on the French population, particularly on the peasants: G. Wellers, in *MJ*, No. 16; see also the personal narratives of the Jewish writer I. Kornhendler, *Briv fun Lectoure* (Letters from Lectoure, *Yid.*), Paris, 1947, and of the French priest Frère Birin, *16 Mois de bagne Buchenwald-Dora*, Epernay, 1947, who was deported for helping Jews.

PAGES 52-53

About Father Chaillet see Oesterreicher, *op. cit.*; Lattes, *op. cit.* In the monthly of the B'nai B'rith of France, *Agir*, No. 4 (Nov.–Dec. 1949), are interesting new details about Abbé Chaillet's rescue activities. Six issues of his *Cahiers clandestines d'témoignage chrétien* were published in Paris, in 1946, in a separate volume.

PAGE 54

About Abbé Glasberg much information besides the above mentioned books can be found in the articles of I. Shmulevich, *Forward*, Feb. 17, 1948 and of A. S. Lirik, *Forward*, Feb. 9, 1952. See also Glasberg's articles about the displaced persons in *Chemins de monde: Personnes déplacées*, Paris, 1948.

PAGES 53-54

About Father Devaux see in *Agir*, No. 4; Oesterreicher, *op. cit.*; I. Lichtenstein, in *Arbeter Vort (Yid.)*, Paris, Nov. 24, 1945. For more information about Fathers Chaillet and Devaux, I am indebted to Dr. Maurice Moch, secretary of the Anti-Defamation League of B'nai B'rith in Paris.

PAGES 54-55

About Pastor Vergara, see the above mentioned books and articles, particularly *Agir*.

PAGES 55-59

A great many official German reports about Father Marie Bénoit, Gen. Lospinoso and Angelo Donati are assembled in *PSJ*; much important information is to be found in J. Rorty's article in *Commentary*, N. Y., Dec. 1946; see also D. Knout, *op. cit.*; J. Tenenbaum, *Race and Reich*, N. Y., 1955; I. Wilner, in *Forward*, Oct. 8, 1944, and *La tragedia degli Ebrei sotto il terrore tedesco*, Rome, 1945; also the article by one of Father Bénoit's chief assistants, a Jewish lieutenant of the French underground, Joseph-André Bass, in *Droit et liberté,* Paris, Sept. 15, 1949.

CHAPTER FOUR
The Low Countries

PAGE 60

About the general attitude of the Dutch population, see Jacques Sabille, in *MJ*, No. 29, 1950; *Dagboek fragmenten 1940–1945*, s'Gravenhage, 1954; L. Poliakov, *Bréviaire* . . .; G. Reitlinger, *op. cit.*; Sam de Wolff, *Geschiedenis der Joden in Nederland*, Amsterdam, 1946; J. Tenenbaum, *op. cit.*; R. Mahler, in *Yidishe Kultur*, N. Y., Apr. 1949; S. Niger, in *Tog-MZ*, N. Y., May 17, 1953; "Ein Denkmal in Holland" in *Allgemeine Wochenzeitung der Juden in Deutschland*, Oct. 3, 1950, and the article by the former prime minister of the Netherlands, P. S. Gerbrandy, in *Aufbau*, N. Y., Feb. 13, 1942; B. A. Sijes, *De Februari Staking 25–26 Februari 1941*, s'Gravenhage, 1954.

About the protests of the Dutch intelligentsia, particularly the university students and professors, the teachers and physicians against the Jewish persecutions see in *CJR*, vol. VI, No. 1, Feb. 1943; Sijes, *op. cit.*; *The United Nations Review*, vol. III, No. 8, Aug. 15, 1943.

PAGES 60-63

The February strike has been extensively described in the well documented book of B. A. Sijes, *op. cit.*; see also F. Grewel, in *Nieuwe Stem*, No. 10, 1955 and "Herdenking von de Staking von 25 Februari 1941" in *Nieuwe Israelitisch Weekblad*, Amsterdam, March 1, 1946.

PAGE 63

Anne Frank, *op. cit.*

PAGES 63-64

The Hordijk story was told in many newspaper articles, such as that by H. von Disen, in *MJ*, July 27, 1952. After the Hordijk family arrived in the U.S., articles appeared in almost all large newspapers including the *New York Times*. A picture of the Hordijk family was reproduced in the Polish paper *Nowy Swiat*, N. Y., Apr. 18, 1955. Stories of other individual efforts to help Jews were recorded in the following books: Ernestine Th. von Heemstra, *In hun greep, Dagboek . . . (Dutch)*, Leyden, 1945; Braha Habas, *Drakhim Aveluth* (The Sad Ways, *Heb.*), Tel Aviv, 1946; Carrie van Boom, *A Prisoner and Yet*, Toronto, 1947; Henrietta Haas, *Orange on Top*, N. Y., 1945; B. de Joode, *Aalten in besettingstijd (Dutch)*, Aalten, 1946. The story of a Dutch woman, Mrs. Weissmueller, who in 1940 helped many Jews to escape from Vilna to Palestine was told in Braha Habas (ed.) *Sepher Aliyat Hanoar* (The Book of the Youth Immigration, *Heb.*), Jerusalem, 1951, and Benzion Ben-Shalom, *Be'saar be'yom sufa* (In the Stormy Days, *Heb.*), Tel Aviv, 1944.

PAGE 64

A complete text of the appeal of the Dutch underground to help Jews was reproduced in the *Inter-Allied Review*, vol. II, No. 12, Dec. 15, 1942. The story of how the Dutch underground helped the Jews to establish and maintain a clandestine synagogue was recorded by J. F. Krop, in *Nieuwe Israelitisch Weekblad*, May 10, 1946.

PAGES 65-67

The story of Shushu and Westerville was recorded in Marie Syrkin's *Blessed is the Match*, Philadelphia, 1947. In recent years many documents about this remarkable episode accumulated in the archives of the Historical Institute in the *Kibbutz* of the Ghetto Fighters in Galilee, Israel. Part of this material was published in the Bulletin of the Institute *YBLG* with a picture of Shushu, No. 7, No. 8 (Westerville's letter from concentration camp Vught), Nos. 9-10 and No. 13, 1954–1955.

PAGE 67

The Reformed and the Catholic churches vigorously protested against the anti-Jewish Nazi policies. Much documentary material about these activities is included in H. C. Touw, *Het Verzet der Hervormde Kerk (Dutch)*, s'Gravenhage, 1946; W. A. Visser t'Hooft, *Hollaendische Kirchendokumente*, Zürich, 1944; Hendrikus Berkhof, in *Bekennende Kirche*, Munich, 1952; H. J. Boas, *Religious Resistance in Holland*, London, 1945; Martin Hugh, *op. cit.*; Oesterreicher, *op. cit.*; *CJR*, Feb. 1943; *Aufbau*, N. Y., Sept. 25, 1942; Mark Dworzecki, in *Folk un Land (Yid.)*, N. Y., May 1956.

PAGE 68

Much important first-hand information about the Belgian attitude toward Jews during the Nazi occupation was assembled by Mr. Willy E. Prins, Antwerpen, and forwarded to me through the courtesy of Dr. Joseph Lichten, N. Y., to both of whom the author is indebted for this valuable assistance. Also, interviews with Dr. and Mrs. John Lanzkron, formerly of Bruxelles, now of Middletown, N. Y., were helpful in checking various data. See also the following books and articles: P. Struye, *L'Evolution du sentiment public en Belgique sous l'occupation allemande*, Bruxelles, 1945; Anna Sommerhausen, *Written in Darkness: A Belgian Woman's Record on the Occupation 1940–1945*, N. Y., 1946; Alfred Errera, *La Belgique devant l'allemagne antisemite*, Bruxelles, 1934; Maurice Jamine, *Sous le coup de 5 condamnations à mort et toujours vivant*, Bruxelles, 1945; H. Singer, *Four Years Under German Occupation in Belgium, an Eyewitness Report*, Montreal, 1945; G. Reitlinger, *op. cit.*; J. Tenenbaum, *Race and Reich*; E. Weinstock, *Beyond the Last Path*, N. Y., 1947; D. Lehrer, in *Tog*, July 2, 1933; J. Pat, in *Forward*, Nov. 13, 1949; M. Dworzecki, in *Undzer Vort (Yid.)*, Paris, May 17, 1946; the bulletin *News from Belgium*, N. Y. (since 1941); and the article of the former prime minister of Belgium, Hubert Pierlot, in the *Jewish Bulletin*, London, Apr. 1942.

PAGES 68-69

About Jeanne Damman and Jeanne de Mulienaere see the articles in *Aufbau*, N. Y., May 17, 1946; in *Forward*, May 27, 1946 and by Jeanne Jaffe in *Tog*, Feb. 3, 1946.

PAGES 69-70

The appeal of the Belgian Socialist Party was reproduced in *Unzer Tsayt*, Aug. 1943. About the activities of the Belgian underground on behalf of the Jews and the attack on the deportation train from Malines see in the above mentioned books, in the materials of Willy Prins and in Fernand Demany, *Mourir débout: Souvenirs du maquis*, Bruxelles, 1946.

PAGES 70-71

About Father André see: I. Midrash, in *Kanader Odler*, Apr. 13, 1948; Rabbi Harold Saperstein, in *Forward*, Dec. 29, 1945; Ernst Landau, in *Juedische Rundschau*, Marburg an der Lahn, No. 6, 1946; *European Jewry after Ten Years*, N. Y., 1956.

PAGE 71

About Abbé Louis Célis see *Israelitisches Wochenblatt fuer die Schweiz*, Feb. 24, 1950; July 10 and 17, 1953; also *Rundbrief* No. 7 and Nos. 21-24, (1954).

About Cardinal van Roey and Queen Elizabeth: *Le Cardinal van Roey et l'occupation allemande en Belgique, actes et documents publiés par le chanoine Leclef*, Bruxelles, 1945; H. Gaag, *Rien ne vaut l'honneur: L'Église belge de 1940 a 1945*, Bruxelles, 1946; *European Jewry . . .* ; G. Reitlinger, *op. cit.*; Oesterreicher, *op. cit.*; the *Inter-Allied Review*, vol. II, No. 10, Oct. 1942 and No. 12, Dec. 1942.

About Father Froidure see: E. Weinstock, *op. cit.*; *New York Times*, Apr. 3, 1946. Froidure also published a book about his experience as a prisoner in the Nazi concentration camps under the title, *Le Calvaire des malades au bagne d'Esterwegen*, Liege, 1945.

CHAPTER FIVE

Italy, the Reluctant Ally

PAGE 72

For the attitude of the Italians in general see Poliakov's *Harvest...*; G. Reitlinger, *op. cit.*; *La tragedia degli Ebrei*. I am indebted to Col. Max Adolfo Vitale, Rome, for his detailed descriptions of the Jewish sufferings in Italy under the Fascist and Nazi regimes, as recorded in his two manuscripts in my archives (partly published in *JE* and *YIVO Bleter (Yid.)*, vol. XXXVII).

About Mussolini's attitude toward the Jews and the vacillations in his policy see: Joshua Starr, in *JSS*, vol. I, No. 1, (1939); Israel Cohen, in *The Contemporary Review*, London, Dec. 1938; Luigi Villari, *Italian Foreign Policy under Mussolini*, N. Y., 1956; Abraham L. Sachar, *Suffering Is the Badge*, N. Y., 1939; Hugo M. Valentin, *Anti-Semitism*, N. Y., 1936; Louis I. Newman, *A Chief Rabbi of Rome Becomes a Catholic*, N. Y., 1945; Eugenio Zolli, *Before the Dawn*, N. Y., 1954; William Phillips, *Ventures in Diplomacy*, Boston, 1952; Bernard D. Weincyb, *Jewish Emancipation under Attack*, N. Y., 1942; *CJR*, Jan. 1939; [Count Galeazzo] *Ciano's Hidden Diary 1937-1938*, N. Y., 1953; Sozius *(pseud.*, Eli Rubin)*, The Jews in the World*, Vienna, 1936; the same, *Mussolini, raciste et antisemite*, Paris, 1938.

PAGE 73

In a savage German retaliation for an act of sabotage of the resistance movement, 340 inhabitants of Rome were dragged on March 24 and 25, 1944 to the *Fosse Ardeatine* (Ardeatine caves) and executed without trial. Among the victims were many Jews. Attilio Ascarelli, *Le Fosse Ardeatine*, Rome, 1945. About Nazi anti-Jewish terror see: The diaries of M. de Wyss, *Rome under the Terror*, London, 1945, and of Jane Scrivener, *Inside Rome with the Germans*, N. Y., 1945; Giacomo Debenedetti, *Otto Ebrei (Ital.)*, Rome, 1944; Armando Troisio, *Roma sotto il terrore Nazi-Fascista*, Rome, 1944. About the Jews in the Italian resistance see: M. A. Vitale, *YIVO Bleter (Yid.)*, vol. XXXVII, 1953; Mario Bellini, in *Forward*, Sept. 24, 1944; Benvenuta Treves, *Tre vite del ultimo '800 alla metá del '900: Studie memorie de Emilio-Emanuele-Ennio Artom (Ital.)*, Firenze, 1954.

Signor Mario di Marco, popular among the Jews as the "good Mariesciallo" of Rome, was a police officer who cooperated with Father Benedetti (Marie-Bénoit) in saving many hundreds of Jewish lives. Eventually he was arrested and tortured by the Gestapo but did not yield his secrets. In summer 1952 and March 1954 di Marco visited New York and was enthusiastically welcomed by Jewish organizations and the Jewish press. See: Richard Dyck, in *Aufbau*, Sept. 5, 1952; "The Good Policeman" in *Jewish Newsletter*, vol. VIII, No. 15, July 1952; I. N. Kersht, in *Forward*, July 11, 1952; "An Italian Police Chief," in *Forward*, March 23, 1954; D. Kranz, in *Tog-MZ*, March 18, 1954.

Dr. Giovanni Palatucci, police chief of Fiume, who helped many Jews, was deported to Dachau and killed. In order to commemorate his noble deeds, the community of Ramat-Gan in Israel named a street in his honor. His uncle, Bishop Giuseppe Mario Palatucci, was guest of honor and speaker at that ceremony. See articles in *Aufbau*, Aug. 14, 1953; *WLB*, vol. X, Nos. 1-2, 1956, and A. L. Jamini, in *Movimento liberazione Italia*, No. 37, July 1955.

About Signor Mario di Nardis see the letter of a group of Jewish survivors from Italy whom he rescued, in *Forward*, July 17, 1947.

On the tenth anniversary of the Liberation, in Apr. 1955, a celebration took place in Milan, where 23 Italians were awarded gold medals by the Union of the Jewish Communities in Italy for their outstanding rescue work during the Nazi terror. See: "La Riconoscenza degli Ebrei Italiani . . . ," in *Corriere della sera*, Milan *(Ital.)*, Apr. 14, 1955; Percy Eckstein, in *Aufbau*, July 8, 1955; "Italian Jews Honor Four Priests," Boston, Mass., *Pilot*, Apr. 23, 1955. Similar ceremonies took place in other cities: The Jewish community of Genoa honored 50 Italians, *Forward*, Feb. 25, 1956. The Jews of Florence gratefully remembered their Italian saviors, W. W. Bienstock, in *Forward*, Aug. 16, 1954. A Jewish poet, Jacob Stahl, wrote a poem dedicated to the "Italians who sacrificed their lives for rescuing Jews," in *Undzers (Yid.)*, Tel Aviv,

1949; the Jews in London arranged a hearty reception for a simple man of San Remo, the porter Mario Masselino who helped smuggle many hundreds of Jews across the Italian-French border. (For the material I am indebted to Mr. Pinkhas Schwartz of the YIVO, N. Y., and Mr. M. Zylberberg, London.)

PAGE 74

For the help of the Italian clergy see: Oesterreicher, *op. cit.*, L. Newman, *op. cit.*; Bernard Berenson, *Rumor and Reflection 1941–1944*, London-N. Y., 1952; M. Borwicz, *op. cit.*, vol. III. The material about Giuseppe Sala was supplied from Italian-Jewish sources through the courtesy of the B'nai B'rith in Italy and Dr. Joseph Lichten in New York.

An Italian-Jewish sculptor, Arrigo Minerbi, saved by the Fathers of Divine Providence, created a statue of the Madonna as a symbol of brotherhood and charity. See: *Don Orione's Messenger*, vol. I, No. 3, Oct. 1954, Boston, Mass.; *The Italian News*, Boston, Mass., May 7, 1954. For the material I am indebted to Mr. R. Scola, editor of *The Italian News*.

PAGES 74-76

About the help given to Jews by the Italian army and administration in Yugoslavia see: *PSJ*; J. Sabille, in *MJ*, Nos. 46-47 and 48, 1951; *European Jewry after* . . . ; J. Tenenbaum, *Race and Reich*. For the sympathetic attitude of the Foreign Office see the official publication, *Relazione sull' opera svolta del Ministero degli Affari Esteri par la tutela della communitá ebraiche (1938–1943)*, Rome.

PAGE 76

The help given to Jews in Greece by the Italian occupation forces has been extensively described in *In Memoriam*, 2 vols., Salonika, 1948 and 1949, ed. by Michael Molho; *PSJ*; *MJ*, No. 49. French and Italian help to the Jews of Tunisia was described in J. Sabille, *Les Juifs de Tunisie sous Vichy et l'occupation*, Paris, 1954; Robert Bergel, *Étoile jaune et croix gammée*, Tunis, 1944.

PAGE 77

After the Badoglio armistice the Germans occupied the Italian Zone in France and started to hunt down the Jews. Many Jews managed to find refuge in the neutral principality of Monaco and from there escaped to Spain, Switzerland or to the French resistance units (Maquis). Probably several thousand were thus saved. See: *PSJ*; Z. Diamant in *YA*, vol. VIII.

CHAPTER SIX

Hungary, the Unwilling Satellite

PAGE 78

For the general background see: Jenö (Eugene) Levai, *Black Book on the Martyrdom of Hungarian Jewry*, Zürich, 1948, and his *Szürke Könyv* (Gray Book, *Hung.*), Budapest, 1946; Bernhard Klein, *Hungarian Jewry in the Nazi Period* (M. A. Thesis, Columbia University, N. Y., 1955); Eugene Duschinsky, "Hungary," in *Jews in Soviet Satellites*;

John H. Montgomery, *Hungary, the Unwilling Ally*, N. Y., 1947; Ernest (Ernö) Munkácsi, *Hogyan történt?* (How it Happened, *Hung.*), Budapest, 1947; G. Reitlinger, *op. cit.*; the annotated bibliography of Leslie C. Tihany, in the *American Slavic and East European Review*, N. Y., vol. VI, Nos. 16-17, 1947.

PAGE 80

The Jewish Rescue Committee of Budapest tried through its chairman Dr. R. Kasztner and others to negotiate with Dieter Visliczeny and Adolf Eichmann in order to ransom the Jews of Hungary. These negotiations, filled with dramatic and unexpected turns, led to no tangible results and were later bitterly criticized, particularly during the Gruenwald–Kasztner trial in Israel. For the pertinent literature see: Rezso Kasztner, *Der Bericht des juedischen Rettungskomitees aus Budapest, 1942–1945*, Basel, 1946; R. Kasztner's affidavit in *IMT*, vol. XXXI, Interrogation of Dieter Visliczeny, *IMT*, vol. IV; Walter Laqueur, in *Der Monat*, Berlin, vol. VII, No. 84, 1955, and in *Commentary*, vol. XX, No. 6, 1955; Emanuel Prat, *Hamishpat hagadol: parshat-Kasztner* (The Great Trial; The Kasztner Case, *Heb.*), Tel Aviv, 1955; Shalom Rosenfeld, *Tik Pelili 124: Mishpat Gruenwald-Kasztner* (Criminal File 124: The Gruenwald-Kasztner Trial. *Heb.*), Tel Aviv, 1955; Alex Weissberg, *Die Geschichte von Joel Brand*, Koeln-Berlin, 1956; and a series of articles in leading Hebrew periodicals and in the Yiddish press in the U.S. and in other countries during the trials (1954–1955 and 1957).

Premier Nicholas Kállay tried to explain his attitude and that of his government colleagues about the Jewish question in his memoirs, *Hungarian Premier: A Personal Account of a Nation's Struggle in the Second World War*, N. Y., 1954.

A verbatim report on the Hitler-Horthy meetings, *IMT*, vol. XXXV. About the Nazi campaign against Admiral Horthy and his son as Jewish friends see: *The Goebbels Diaries*, and Nicholas Horthy's memoirs, *Ein Leben fuer Ungarn (Ger.)*, Bonn, 1953. About Admiral Horthy see: G. Reitlinger, *op. cit.*; J. Tenenbaum, *Race and Reich*; R. Kasztner, *op. cit.*; E. Duschinsky, *op. cit.*; about Horthy's son, see Kasztner, *op. cit.*

PAGE 81

For the help of the foreign legations, and the Apostolic Nunciature see J. Levai, *Fehér Könyv* (White Book, *Hung.*), Budapest, 1946; *Unity in Dispersion: A History of the World Jewish Congress*, N. Y., 1948; H. Monneray, *op. cit.*; *BB*; E. Munkácsi, *op. cit.*; R. Kasztner, *op. cit.*; M. Syrkin, *op. cit.* The daily life in a Swiss protected house was described in Teri Gacs, *A Mélységböl kiáltunk Hozzád* (We cry to you from the Depths, *Hung.*), Budapest, 1945; Hillel Seidman, in *MZ*, Dec. 1, 14 and 28, 1947 and Jan. 4, 1948. For the intercessions of the U.S. Government see also Cyrus Adler and Aaron M. Margolith, *With Firmness in the Right: American Diplomatic Action Affecting Jews 1940–1945*, N. Y., 1946. For the appeals of the International Red Cross see G. Reitlinger, *op. cit.*; for the Swedish intervention and the rescue efforts of Raoul Wallenberg see notes for Chapter Thirteen.

PAGE 82

The full extent of the crimes committed by the Szálasi regime was revealed when he and his accomplices were tried: Ferenc Abraham and Endre Kuszinsky, *A Szálasi Per* (The Szálasi Trial, *Hung.*), Budapest, 1946; also: István Gyenes and Károly Kiss, *A Tizhónapos Tragedia* (The Ten-Month Tragedy, *Hung.*), Budapest, 1945; David M. Gasparne, *A Sárga Csillag* (The Yellow Star, *Hung.*), Budapest, 1945.

PAGE 83

About the contradictory statistical reports concerning the number of Jews saved in the International Ghetto see BB.

István (Stephan) Bibo, in *Válasz (Hung.)*, vol. VIII, Budapest, Oct.–Nov. 1948; Mr. Robert Major—personal affidavit and statements.

PAGES 83-84

The attitude of the Hungarians in the crucial period of 1944–1945 is discussed at length in the diary of Miksa Fenyo, *Az Elsodort Ország* (The Country that Was Swept Away, *Hung.*), Budapest, 1946, in which he records many instances of Hungarians who risked their lives and made many sacrifices to save Jews. The story of General Hegyessi is told in his memoirs.

PAGE 84

There are many autobiographical narratives of survivors of the Jewish forced labor battalions such as György Bencze, *Szabaditó Börtön* (Liberating Prison, *Hung.*), Budapest; Hillel Danzig, *Im Schatten der Pferde (Ger.)*, (typescript in the archives of the World Jewish Congress, N. Y.); István György, *Fegyvertelenül a Tüzvonalban* (Unarmed in the Front Line, *Hung.*), Budapest, 1945; László Szüts, *Bori Garnizon* (Garrison in Bor, *Hung.*), Budapest, 1945; Zoltán G. Vajda, *A Lapátos Hadsereg* (The Army with Shovels, *Hung.*), Budapest, 1945; Oszkar Zsadanyi, *Mindenki Szolgája* (Everybody's Servant, *Hung.*), Budapest, 1945. Also important is the book by the former Minister of Defense in Kállay's cabinet, Vilmos Nagy, *Végzetes Esztendök* (Fatal Years, *Hung.*) Budapest, 1946.

PAGES 84-85

The help of some individuals in the Hungarian army and administration has been extensively recorded in BB and in *Szürke Könyv*.

PAGE 85

In a letter to Joseph Cardinal Mindszenty of Feb. 28, 1946 Father Marie-Bénoit tells about the great help given to him by the consul of the Hungarian Legation in Rome, Mr. Szász, who issued hundreds of identity papers to Father Bénoit's Jewish protégés and thus saved them from the Nazis. J. Levai, *Szürke Könyv*, tells of another Hungarian diplomat in Paris, Dr. Anthony Uhl, who issued letters of baptism and other documents protecting many Jews from deportation.

The Miller story was told by I. B. Gal in *Forward,* Sept. 4, 1949.

PAGES 85-90

About the attitude of the Protestant and Catholic churches in Hungary see: *Szürke Könyv; BB;* Albert Bereczky, *Hungarian Protestanism and the Persecution of the Jews,* Budapest; Emerich Kadar, in *Judaica (Ger.),* vol. V, No. 2, Zürich, 1949; Antal Meszlényi, *A Magyar katolikus Egyház és az Emberi Jogok Védelme* (The Hungarian Catholic Church and the Protection of Human Rights, *Hung.*), Budapest, 1947; László Palásti, in *Képes Figyelö (Hung.),* vol. III, Apr. 5, 1947 (about Father Koehler who saved many Jews.)

PAGE 86

Intervention on behalf of baptized Jews see: E. Munkácsi, *op. cit.*

PAGE 87

About the Ujváry episode and the interventions of the Papal Nuncio see *BB.*

PAGE 89

About the Calvinist rescue work: *Szürke Könyv;* M. Fenyö, *op cit.*

PAGES 86-88

About the opposition in Christian circles to merely formal baptism see M. Fenyö, *op. cit.*

PAGE 89

About the Scottish mission see *BB; Szürke Könyv.*

The statement of William Juhász, in *Church and Society,* N. Y., 1953, about the rescue work of Cardinal Mindszenty on behalf of the Jews is not corroborated by other sources, except in Helen W. Homan, *op. cit.*

PAGES 89-90

The work of the Jewish rescue organizations and their underground railroad from Turkey through Romania and Hungary to Slovakia and Poland and vice versa has been described in Ira A. Hirschman, *Lifeline to a Promised Land,* N. Y., 1946; Marie Syrkin, *op. cit.;* Oskar J. Newman, *Im Schatten des Todes (Ger.),* Tel Aviv, 1955; P. E. Singer, *They Did Not Fear,* N. Y., 1952. The plan to arm the Jewish labor battallions for self-defense is recorded in E. Munkácsi, *op. cit.*

PAGE 90

About the negotiations with the Hungarian opposition parties and with government officials see R. Kasztner, *op. cit.*

About the cooperation between the Jewish and Hungarian resistance movement see: R. Kasztner, *op. cit.;* László Dömöter and István Szilagyi, *Pártunk harca a demokráciáért* (Our Party's Fight for Democracy, *Hung.*), Budapest, 1946.

PAGE 91

About the last weeks of the ghetto in Budapest and its liberation see, in addition to the above: L.P., *MJ,* Nov. 1948; J. Levai, *A Pesti getto* (The Ghetto of Pest, *Hung.*), Budapest, 1946.

CHAPTER SEVEN
"We Let God Wait Ten Years"

PAGE 92

For the general background see: Philip Auerbach, *Wesen und Formen des Widerstandes im Dritten Reich*, Ph.D. Thesis, University of Erlangen, 1949; *Die evangelische Kirche Deutschlands und die Judenfrage*, Geneva, 1945; Heinz Schmidt, *Die Judenfrage und die christliche Kirche in Deutschland*, Stuttgart, 1947; *Deutsche Kirchendokumente*, Zürich, 1946; Mary Alice Gallin, *Ethical and Religious Factors in the German Resistance to Hitler*, Washington, D. C., 1955; J. Neuhaeusler, *Kreuz and Hakenkreuz*, Munich, 1946, 2 vols. For more detailed information and bibliography see: Philip Friedman, in *YA*, vol. X, 1955.

About Bonhoeffer see: Dietrich Bonhoeffer's *Letters and Papers from Prison*, London, 1953; W. A. Visser 'tHooft, in *Das Zeugnis eines Boten. Zum Gedaechtnis von Dietrich Bonhoeffer*, Geneva, 1945; Hans Rothfels, *The German Opposition to Hitler*, Hinsdale, Ill., 1948.

PAGES 92-93

About the statistics of Jewish converts in Germany and Austria see: Friedrich Burgdoerfer, in *Forschungen zur Judenfrage*, vol. III, Hamburg, 1938; Oskar Karbach, in *JSS*, vol. II, No. 3, 1940; Bruno Blau, in *JSS*, vol. XII, No. 2, 1950.

PAGE 93

The story of the demonstration in Berlin is told by Bruno Blau, in *YA*, vol. VIII. A moving personal narrative of a Christian-German woman in Munich who married a Jew, adopted Judaism, remained faithful to the Jewish faith and, after the death of her husband, raised her daughter in the same spirit in spite of constant pressures and threat of the Gestapo, is recorded by Anna Holzman, in *FLH*, No. 7, Munich, 1948; other stories of devotion in mixed marriages were recorded by R. Behrend-Rosenfeld, *op. cit.*; Lotte Paepke, *Unter einem fremden Stern*, Frankfurt am Main, 1952; Ruth Hoffman, *Meine Freunde aus Davids Geschlecht*, Berlin, 1947; David Rodnick, *Postwar Germans*, New Haven, 1948.

Cardinal Michael Faulhaber's sermons were published also in English as *Judaism, Christianity and Germany*, N. Y., 1935. About the Cardinal's attitude to Jews see also: Friedrich Stummer, in *Rundbrief*, Nos. 21-24; *WLB*, vol. VI, Nos. 3-4, 1952; Joseph Weissthanner, in *Welt ohne Hass*, Berlin, 1950; Martin Hugh, *op. cit.*

PAGE 94

About Bishop von Galen see: Heinrich Portmann, *Dokumente um den Bischof von Meenster*, Muenster, 1948; the same, *Kardinal von Galen. Ein Gottesmann seiner Zeit*, Muenster, 1948; Hans Rothfels, *op. cit.*

About Cardinal von Preysing see: Bischoefliches Ordinariat Berlin, *Dokumente aus dem Kampf der Katholischen Kirche im Bistum Berlin gegen den Nationalsozialismus,* Berlin, 1946. The full text of Preysing's pastoral letter was also published in *Rundbrief,* Nos. 8-9, 1950.

PAGES 94-95

Alfons Erb, *Bernhard Lichtenberg,* Berlin, 1946; Max Jordan, *Beyond All Fronts,* Milwaukee, 1944. PAGE 95

Gertrude Luckner is the editor of the *Rundbrief.* About her visits in Israel and in England see: *Rundbrief,* vol. II, No. 7, 1950, and vols. III-IV, Nos. 12-15, 1951. PAGES 96-97

About Martin Niemoeller see: *Bekennende Kirche, Martin Niemoeller zum 60. Geburtstag,* Munich, 1952; Basil Miller, *Martin Niemoeller, Hero of the Concentration Camp,* Grand Rapids, Mich., 1942; Niemoeller's statements in the years 1933–1935 are reproduced in Kurt D. Schmidt, *Die Bekenntnisse des Jahres 1933, 1934, 1935,* vol. I. Goettingen, 1934–36; Niemoeller's trial was reported by his brother, Wilhelm Niemoeller, *Macht geht vor Recht, der Prozess Martin Niemoellers,* Munich, 1952. The most important statements by Martin Niemoeller about the problem of Jewish persecutions during the Nazi era are included in his *Of Guilt and Hope,* N. Y.

PAGE 97

Valerie Wolffenstein's account was published in Eric Boehm, (ed.), *We Survived,* New Haven, 1949.

PAGES 98-99

About Bishop Wurm see: Heinrich Fraenkel, *The German People Versus Hitler,* London, 1940; Heinrich Hermelink (ed.), *Kirche im Kampf: Dokumente des Widerstandes . . . der Evangelischen Kirche Deutschlands, 1933–1945,* Tuebingen, 1950; Theophil Wurm, *Erinnerungen aus meinem Leben,* Stuttgart, 1953.

PAGES 99-100

About the Bureau Grueber see: *An der Stechbahn. Erlebnisse und Berichte aus dem Bureau Grueber,* Berlin, 1951; *Bekennende Kirche; Die Evangelische Kirche . . .* PAGE 100

About Hermann Maas see the articles by Emil Belzner, in *Aufbau,* May 5, 1950 (also *Aufbau,* Apr. 21, 1950 and Feb. 22, 1946), by Miriam Wolman-Sieraczek, in *Yidishe Tsaytung,* Buenos Aires, Nov. 10, 1953 and by Marian Zhyd, in *Yidishe Tsaytung,* March 14, 1952. Hermann Maas's two books about Israel are: *Skizzen von einer Fahrt nach Israel,* Karlsruhe, 1950, and *-und will Rachels Kinder wieder bringen ins Land,* Heilbronn, 1955.

CHAPTER EIGHT
The Unvanquished

PAGE 101

For the general background see: P. Meyer, "Czechoslovakia" in *Jews in Soviet Satellites;* Gerhard Jacoby, *Racial State: The German Nation-*

alities Policy in the Protectorate of Bohemia-Moravia, N. Y., 1944 (with a substantial bibliography).

About the Nazis' unsuccessful attempt to incite the Czech population against Jews see: J. Hronek, *Volcano under Hitler*, also the articles in *MZ*, Jan. 2 and Apr. 13, 1939.

PAGE 102

There is a large literature on the Theresienstadt ghetto. The most important books are: Zdenek Lederer, *Ghetto Theresienstadt*, London, 1953, and the bulky and well-documented book of H. G. Adler, *Theresienstadt, 1941–1945: Das Antlitz einer Zwangsgemeinschaft (Ger.)*, Tuebingen, 1955, which contains also a comprehensive annotated bibliography.

About Czech gendarmes punished or executed for helping Jews see: Z. Lederer, *op. cit.*; H. G. Adler, *op. cit.* Hundreds of Jewish children were taken care of and sheltered in hostels and orphanages by the Czech Caritas Catholica; see Dorothy Macardle, *Children of Europe*, Boston, 1951; about the general friendly attitude of the Czech population see also Leo W. Schwarz, (ed.) *The Root and the Bough*, N. Y., 1949; J. Tenenbaum, *Race and Reich*.

PAGES 102-103

The story of the friendly Czech reception in Pilsen for the Jewish camp inmates was told by a survivor, Itzhak Nemenchik, in *Landsberger Lager Cajtung (Yid.)*, May 3, 1946.

PAGES 103-104

The Rudolf Masaryk story was recorded by several survivors of Treblinka and participants of the uprising. See: Stanislaw Kon, in *Nayvelt (Yid.)*, Tel Aviv, July 19, 1946; the same, in *Undzer Moment (Yid.)*, Regensburg, Apr. 13, 1947; *Landsberger Yidishe Cajtung (Yid.)*, July 25, 1947; Shabtai K., in *Hadoar (Heb.)*, N. Y., Dec. 22, 1946; S. Reisman, in *Odrodzenie (Pol.)*, Lublin, Nos. 4-5, 1945; also in *Sefer milhamot ha-getsot* (Book of the Fighting in the Ghettos, *Heb.*), Tel Aviv, 1954. Another staunch friend of the Jews was Jan Masaryk, vice premier and minister of foreign affairs of the Czechoslovak Government in Exile, and son of the founder and first president of the Czechoslovak Republic, Thomas Masaryk. During his stay in the U.S. and Great Britain, Jan Masaryk devoted much of his time to participation in relief activities of Jewish organizations. In his public addresses he expressed great sympathy with and concern about the plight of the Jews in Nazi-occupied Europe. See: Z. H. Wachsman, *The Governments in Exile and Their Attitude Towards Jews*, N. Y., 1944, and the reprint from it, *Jews in Czechoslovakia; Der Vidershtand (Yid.)*, vol. IV, No. 1, N. Y., 1943; *MZ*, Jan. 16 and Jan. 31, 1939; *The Jewish Bulletin*, London, Nov. 1943.

PAGE 104

Czech colonist-farmers in Poland were helpful to Jews. Several records of Jewish survivors in various towns and villages of Volhynia mention their selfless help. See: *Yalkut Volhyn (Heb.)*, Tel Aviv, 1945–1947, vol. I, No. 4 and No. 8; vol. II, No. 10 and Nos. 15-16. According to B.

Mark, *Bialystok*, some Czech soldiers (from the Sudetenland) of the German army, stationed in Bialystok, were in contact with the Jewish underground organizations there.

In Slovakia, where pro-Jewish sentiments were rare and the Nazi-dictated anti-Jewish legislation and extermination policy was relentlessly carried out, there were individual cases of sympathy and help to perse-cuted Jews, as recorded in the recently published memoirs of the Zionist and Jewish Community leader Dr. Oskar Neumann, *Im Schatten des Todes*, Neumann particularly dwells upon the helpful attitude of the Slovak Minister for Education and Culture, Dr. Joseph Sivak, and of Dr. Augustin Pozdech, a Catholic priest and underground leader of Bratislava. He also extensively describes the cooperation between the Jewish and the Slovak resistance movement and their common fight against the Nazis in the uprising of Banska Bistrica.

For the general background in Yugoslavia see: *Jevrejski Almanah 1954,* Belgrade *(Serb.* and *Croat.); Dr.* Isak Eskenazy, *Dozivijaji za wreme nacizma* . . . (Experiences during the Nazi Period, *Croat.*), N. Y., 1955 (mimeogr.); Pauline Albala, *Yugoslav Women Fight for Freedom,* N. Y., 1943.

For the attitude of Tito's partisans to the Jews and Jewish participation in the partisan movement see: David Alkalay, in *Jewish Frontier,* Jan. 1953; *European Jewry* ...; David Flinker, in *Tog,* Apr. 26, 1952; The interviews with Moshe Pijade, a former leader of the resistance move-ment and after the war vice-president of Yugoslavia, by M. K., in *Droit et Liberté,* Sept. 4, 1946; by J. Shmulevich, in *Forward,* Jan. 12, 1953, and by Raymond A. Davies, *Odyssey through Hell,* N. Y., 1944. There is a large literature about the Jewish parachutists from Israel who were dropped in Yugoslavia to work with the Yugoslav partisans and to help the Jewish communities under the Nazis. See: Dorothy and Pesah Bar-Adon, *Seven Who Fell,* Tel Aviv, 1948.

A story of selfless sacrifice and courage was that of young Cyril Kotnik, an attaché of the Yugoslav Embassy to the Vatican, who made many successful efforts to help the Jews in Rome, was eventually arrested and in spite of his diplomatic immunity brutally investigated and tortured by the Gestapo. Released thanks to the Vatican's intervention, Kotnik did not recover from his wounds and died. See: *La Tragedia degli Ebrei,* and Percy Eckstein, in *Aufbau,* July 8, 1955.

PAGES 104-105

About the friendly attitude of the Bulgarian people see: G. Reitlinger, *op. cit.*; L. Poliakov, *Harvest* ...; Nathan Grinberg, *Dokumenty (Bulg.),* Sofia, 1945; Hayim Benadov, in *JE*; Peter Meyer, "Bulgaria" in *Jews in the Soviet Satellites*; Jacques Sabille, in *MJ,* vol. V, No. 30-31, 1950; see also the testimony of the Sephardic-Jewish girl from Bulgaria, Dzhanka Avishai, in *Dos naye lebn* (*Yid.*), No. 80, Lodz, Sept. 7, 1947.

About the mass "mercy baptisms" and the mixed marriages see: P. Meyer, *op. cit.*

PAGE 106

A great wealth of material about the helpful attitude of the Greek population is contained in the work *In Memoriam.* See also: I. A. Matarasso, *Ki homos holoi tous den pethanan* ... (However not all had been killed, *Greek*), Athens, 1948; Laura Melamed, in *Cahiers de l'Alliance Israelite Universelle,* Nos. 95, 96, 97, Paris, 1956. For more bibliographical information see: Philip Friedman, in *Joshua Starr Memorial Volume,* N. Y., 1953.

PAGE 109

About the attitude of the Greek partisans and the Jewish participation in the resistance movement see also *European Jewry* ... ; Isaac Kabeli, in *YA,* vol. VIII. The escape routes from Greece to Turkey and from there to Palestine had been graphically described by Jon and David Kimche, *The Secret Roads,* London, 1954. The story of Volo had been recorded in *In Memoriam,* vol. II. The happenings in some òf the islands of the Greek archipelago were also recorded in Abraham Galanté, *Appendice à l'histoire des Juifs des Rhodes, Chio, Cos, etc.* Istanbul, 1948.

CHAPTER NINE
"For Your Freedom As Well As Ours"

PAGE 111

For the general background see: J. Tenenbaum, *In Search of a Lost People,* N. Y., 1948; *Biuletyn Komisji Głównej Badania Zbrodni Niemieckich w Polsce* (Bulletin of the Chief Committee to Investigate the German Crimes in Poland, *Polish*), Warsaw, 1946–1955, 8 vols., and *German Crimes in Poland,* 2 vols., Warsaw, 1946–1948; Simon Segal, *The New Order in Poland,* N. Y.; Abraham (Adolf) Berman, in *Pinkas Varshe (Yid.),* Buenos Aires, vol. I., and in *Warsaw,* vol. I of the *Encyclopedia shel Galuyot* (Encyclopedia of the Diaspora, *Heb.*), Jerusalem-Tel Aviv, 1953; Temkin-Berman, *op. cit.* For more bibliographic information see: Philip Friedman in *Jewish Book Annual,* N. Y., vol. IX, 1952–1953.

PAGES 111-112

E. Ringelblum, *op. cit.* Some excerpts of Ringelblum's Diary were translated into English in *MF,* and in *Midstream,* vol. II, No. 1, N. Y., 1956.

PAGES 112-113

The statement of Zelwerowicz is quoted from his article in *Opinia,* Warsaw-Lodz, Apr. 19, 1948.

PAGE 113

Maria Czapska, in *Tygodnik Polski,* vol. V, No. 8, N. Y., 1947 discusses Polish help to Jews, telling many interesting facts and episodes.

The story of the baker of Brzeziny was told in a contemporaneous record (dated May 2, 1942) found in the archives of Judenrat of Lodz and published in *AW.*

PAGE 114

In his book *The Captive Mind,* N. Y., 1953, the Polish writer Czesław Miłosz, who lived through the German occupation in Poland, thus describes the attitude of a famous Polish writer whom he identifies by the pseudonym "Alpha": "When the German authorities set out to murder systematically the 3,000,000 [there were approximately 3,500,000.—P.F.] Jews of Poland, the anti-Semites did not feel compelled to worry much; they condemned this bestiality aloud, but many of them secretly thought it was not entirely unwanted. Alpha belonged to those inhabitants of the town [Warsaw] who reacted violently against this mass-slaughter. He fought with his pen against the indifference of others, and personally helped Jews in hiding even though such aid was punishable by death."

The Mosdorf story was told by fellow-prisoners in Auschwitz; by the Jewish lawyer, Maślanka, by Wolf Glicksman and by Tadeusz Hołuj; see Itzhak Berensztein, in *Dos naye lebn*, Sept. 25, 1946; Philip Friedman, *Oświęcim*, Buenos Aires, 1950.

Wolf Glicksman, now in Philadelphia, published his article in *YA*, vol. VII, 1953. Cyrankiewicz was an executive member of the underground committee of prisoners and in this capacity wrote the appalling reports on the mass extermination of the Jews in Auschwitz. The reports were smuggled out of the camp to the free world. Some of these reports are published in Ph. Friedman, *This Was Oswiecim*, London, 1946.

About Piasecki and Nowaczyński see: M. Borwicz, *op. cit.*, vol. II; E. Ringelblum, *op. cit.*

PAGE 115

The Rudnicki story was told by Rachel Auerbach, *op. cit.* The Witaszewicz story in M. Feinzilber, *op. cit.*

The Kowalski story was told in M. Borwicz, *op. cit.*, vol. III. Other anti-Semitic leaders who under the impact of the Nazi persecutions changed their attitude toward Jews were the physician, Dr. Filipowski, of the *Armia Krajowa*, who helped the Jewish Fighters' Organization in Bialystok, after the uprising in August, 1943, giving them medical care and medicines—Mordecai Tenenbaum, the commander of the Jewish Fighters' Organization in Bialystok, entrusted to him the third box of the archives of the Jewish underground, *YBLG*, Sept. 1955; the Catholic lawyer, Józef Barski, helped and rescued many Jews, risking his life. See: A. Berman, in *Encyclopedia*. . . .

PAGE 116

Mrs. Eva Horn-Rosenthal published her memoirs in a series of articles, in *Der Tog*. This particular story was published in the issues of June 29, July 2 and 3, 1946.

Quoted from Rachel Auerbach, in *Nowe Widnokręgi*, No. 13 (1945).

PAGES 116-117

Other stories about helpful Poles, in J. Pat, *Ashes and Fire* and his articles in *Forward*, May 20, 1946 and Jan. 12, 1947; J. Kurtz, *Sefer Eduth* (Book of Testimony, *Heb.*), Tel Aviv, 1949; *Markuszow*; *Skernievits*. Sometimes even a simple manifestation of sympathy to the persecuted could cost the person involved his life. Thus in Mława the Gestapo staged a cruel public execution of fifty Jews in April 1942. The Nazis forced the entire population to witness this spectacle for the sake of "racial education." One of the Poles who could no longer control himself started to shout: "Down with Hitler! Innocent blood is being shed." He was instantly caught and killed by the Germans, *Pinkas Mławe*.

PAGE 117

Szpilman, *op. cit.* tells of his Polish friends who saved his life.

Hirszfeld, *op. cit.* Another story of help given to the theatre director Arnold Szyfman is narrated in his diary written in 1943. A fragment of it was published in *Twórczość*, vol. 2, No. 4, Warsaw, 1946.

Jonas Turkow in his memoirs, *op. cit.*, particularly in vol. II, describes many instances of help given to him and to other Jews by Poles, individuals and organizations.

The Grabski story, in M. Borwicz, *op. cit.*, vol. III.

The Humnicki story in M. Feinzilber, *op. cit.*

PAGES 117-118

The Maślak story was told by Tadeusz Zaderecki, Prof. of the University of Lodz, in *Opinia*, No. 2, July, 1946.

The story would not be complete if we did not mention the numerous simple people who helped Jews. There were Polish housemaids who helped former employers. The distinguished painter, Arthur Szyk, told in the introduction to his Bible drawings, N. Y., 1946, the story of his seventy-year-old mother, Eugenie Szyk, deported in March, 1943, from Lodz to a concentration camp. Her housemaid Josepha, a Polish peasant girl, voluntarily joined the old lady in the journey to death, *Der Tog*, Aug. 18, 1946. Abraham Sutzkever tells the story of a housemaid who voluntarily accompanied her Jewish employers to the Vilna ghetto and perished there together with them, A. Sutzkever, *op. cit.*

Sometimes Polish working people showed sympathy and offered help, as did workers of the Warsaw trolley-bus service. E. Ringelblum, *op. cit.*, and N. Gross, in *Nasze Słowo*, Warsaw, Apr. 19, 1947. A group of twenty-odd Jews found shelter during a Nazi extermination operation in the sewers of Lwow under the most unsanitary and dangerous conditions. They were discovered by a group of Polish workers of the Sanitation Department. The men not only did not report them to the German authorities but organized secret help for them. They provided the Jews with food and were very kind to them, M. Borwicz, *op. cit.*, vol. II.

PAGE 118

Quoted from Jerzy Zawiejski's article, in *Martwa Fala* (The Dead Wave, *Pol.*), Warsaw, 1947, and from J. Andrzejewski's article, *ibidem*. Andrzejewski published a short story: "Wielki tydzień" (The Holy Week, *Pol.*), Warsaw, 1945, where he impressively described the sufferings of a Jewish family remaining in Warsaw with Aryan papers. S. Otwinowski, *ibidem;* Otwinowski was one of the first Polish writers to publish, after the war, a dramatic work in which he glorified the Warsaw uprising, *Wielkanoc* (Easter, *Pol.*), Cracow, 1946. The uprising of the Warsaw ghetto became a central topic for many Polish writers, see, e.g. the poems by Władysław Broniewski and Tadeusz Sarnecki (in English translation in *MF*). About the reaction of Polish writers to the Jewish catastrophe see: *Almanakh fun der poylisher literatur vegn der tragedye fun di yidn be'eys der Hitler okupatsie* (Almanac of the Polish Literature on the Jewish Tragedy during the Hitler Occupation, *Yid.*), Warsaw, 1950; B. Mark, *Di yidishe tragedye in der poylisher literatur* (The Jewish Tragedy in Polish Literature, *Yid.*), Warsaw, 1950; M. Borwicz, (ed.) *Pieśń ujdzie cało* (The Song Will Survive, *Pol.*), an anthology, Warsaw-Lodz, 1947; Victor Shulman, in *Zukunft*, Sept. 1947; Rachel Auerbach, in *Kiyoum* (*Yid.*), vol. III, Nos. 9-10, 1948; Joseph Wulf, in *Yidishe Shriftn*, vol. I, Lodz, 1946; Mendel Man, in *Bafrayung*, Munich, No. 53, 1947.

PAGE 119

Stefan Korboński, *Fighting Warsaw: The Story of the Polish Underground State*, 1939-1945. N. Y., 1956. See also *MF*.

S. Kossak-Szczucka was eventually deported to Auschwitz. After various interventions she was released and resumed her underground work in Warsaw. She published a clandestine pamphlet about Auschwitz and after the war published a book about her recollections of Auschwitz. One chapter is devoted to the sufferings of Jewish women.

PAGE 120

The story of the Council for Aid to Jews, its foundation and activities, was recorded by many authors: A. Berman, *Encyclopedia*, vol. I; M. Neustadt, *op. cit.*; T. Borzykowski, *op. cit.*; J. Turkow, *op. cit.*, vol. I; M. Borwicz, *op. cit.*, vol. II; *In di yorn fun yidishn umkum* (In the Years of the Jewish Catastrophe, *Yid.*), N. Y., 1948; Władka (Feigele Peltel-Miedzyrzecki), *Fun bayde zaytn geto moyer* (From Both Sides of the Ghetto Wall, *Yid.*), N. Y., 1948, in English translation in *M.F.* See also the article of T. Seweryn, in *"W trzecią rocznicę zagłady ghetta krakowskiego* (On the Third Anniversay of the Extermination of the Ghetto in Cracow, *Pol.*), Cracow, 1946; Marek Arczyński in *Prawo człowieka* (*Pol.*), No. 1, Warsaw, 1945; Witold Bieńkowski in *Dziś i Jutro* (*Pol*), No. 19, Warsaw, 1946; about J. Grobelny see in *Głos Bundu* (*Pol.*), Lodz-Warsaw, Apr. 15, 1947.

PAGE 122

The relations between the Polish and the Jewish underground movement have been dealt with in many publications: *MF*; Marek Edelman, *The Ghetto Fights*, N. Y., 1946; M. Neustadt, *op. cit.*, vol. I; Władka, *op. cit.*,; A. Berman, *Encyclopedia . . .*; J. Kermisz, *Powstanie w getcie warszawskim* (The Uprising in the Warsaw Ghetto, *Pol.*), Lodz, 1946; B. Mark, *Powstanie w getcie warszawskim* (The Uprising in the Warsaw Ghetto,

Pol.), Warsaw, 1953; T. Bor-Komorowski, *The Secret Army*, London, 1951; Marek Celt, *By Parachute to Warsaw*, London, 1945. About the negotiations in Vilna and Bialystok see: R. Korchak, *Lehavot ba'efer* (Ashes in the Fire, *Heb.*), Merhavia, 1946; B. Mark, in *BFG*, vol. V, No. 3; the same, in *Bialystok;* M. Tenenbaum-Tamaroff, *Dapim min ha'dleyka* (Leaves from the Fire, *Heb.*), Tel Aviv, 1947.

PAGES 122-123

The appeal of the Jewish Fighters' Organization to the Poles: "For Your Freedom as Well as Ours," published in English translation in M. Edelman, *op. cit.*; in *MF*; Bernard Goldstein, *op. cit.*

PAGE 123

The smuggling of weapons was graphically described by Władka, *op.' cit.*, the passage through the sewers by T. Borzykowski, *op. cit.*; Bernard Goldstein, *op. cit.*; Zivia Lubetkin, in *Commentary*, May, 1947; M. Edelman, *op. cit.*; *MF*. See also the diary of Witold Dobrzański who, together with other Polish Socialists, smuggled food and arms through the sewers into the ghetto. Once they were ambushed by the Germans and three were killed. See *AW*.

PAGES 123-124

About the attitude of the *AK* (Home Army) and the *NSZ* (National Armed Forces) to the Jews see: S. Żochowski, in *Kultura* (*Pol.*), vol. 31, Paris, 1950; the same, *ibidem*, No. 36, May, 1950; W. Żbik-Kaniewski and Jan Lednicki, *ibidem*. Instances where the lower echelons of the *AK*, *NSZ*, and other formations murdered Jews in hiding or in the woods, were reported by many survivors. Just to quote some of these accounts: *Żelechów; Skernievits; Briansk (Yid.)*, N. Y., 1948; J. Tenenbaum, *Underground; Markuszów*; J. Turkow, *op. cit.*, vol. II; *A yid fun Klementow dertsaylt* (A Jew from Klementów Narrates, *Yid.*), Warsaw; S. L. Shneiderman, *Between Fear and Hope*, N. Y., 1947; A. Berman, *Encyclopedia*, vol. I; M. Borwicz, *op. cit.*, vol. II; A. Szyfman, *op. cit.* On the other hand, there are records of protection given to Jews by some of the commanding officers of the Home Army such as those recorded in M. Borwicz, *op. cit.*, vol. II. A more friendly attitude was found among the liberal and leftist groups of the Polish underground. See: *Markuszów*; J. Turkow, *op. cit.*, vol. II; *AW*; A. Berman, *Encyclopedia* . . . ; Stanisław Nienałkowski, in *Głos Bundu*, Apr. 19, 1948; *BFG*, vol. I; *Tsum tsentn yortog fun oyfshtand in Varshever geto. Dokumentn un materialn* (On the Tenth Anniversary of the Warsaw Ghetto Uprising. Documents and Materials, *Yid.*), ed. by B. Mark, Warsaw, 1953.   PAGES 122-124

About the experiences of Jews living on "Aryan" papers and exposed to constant blackmail by shady characters and to a relentless manhunt by the Nazi police see: B. Goldstein, *op. cit.*; *AW;* Władka, *op. cit.*; L. W. Schwarz, *op. cit.*; *MF*; Wincenty Rzymowski, *Epoka Hitlera* (*Pol.*), Lublin, 1945; Nathan Gross, in *YBLG*, Apr. 1956. About the efforts of the Polish and Jewish underground to fight the plague of blackmailers

and informers see: S. Korbonski, *op. cit.*; A. Berman, *Encyclopedia* . . . ;
J. Hirszhaut, in *YIVO Bleter*, vol. XXXVII, 1953, and in *Kiyoum*, vol.
III, No. 3, 1951; Aaron Brandes, *Kets ha'yehudim b'maarav Polin* (The
End of the Jews in Western Poland, *Heb.*), Merhavia, 1945.

PAGE 124

For the attitude of the Polish higher clergy to the Jews in the last prewar years and during the Nazi occupation see: G. Reitlinger, *op. cit.*;
L. Poliakov, *Bréviaire* . . . ; J. Tenenbaun, *In Search.*; the same, *Underground*; S. L. Shneiderman, *op. cit.* On the other hand see the Catholic
view on Cardinal Kakowski in J. Oesterreicher, *op. cit.*; on Cardinal
Sapieha in S. Korbonski, *op. cit.*; S. Piotrowski, *Dziennik Hansa Franka*
(The Diary of Hans Frank, *Pol.*), Warsaw, 1956. Some Polish and Jewish writers claim that the Polish church authorities were equivocal to
the Jewish ordeal under the Nazis and did not do enough to fight anti-
Semitism. See: Julian Przybos, in *Martwa Fala (Pol.)*; Jehoshua Shiloni,
Ehad shenimlat (One Who Escaped, *Heb.*), Tel Aviv, 1956. The rescue
work of various Catholic organizations, priests and converts was described by many Polish and Jewish writers: *Dzieci oskarzaja*; M. Czapska,
op. cit.; W. Smolski, *op. cit.*; R. Auerbach, *op. cit.*; *Grayeve yizkorbukh* (Grajewo Memorial Volume, *Yid.*), N. Y., 1950; A. Šimaite, in
Der Litvisher Yid, Nos. 7-8, Apr.-May 1946; M. Borwicz, *op. cit.*, vol.
II and III; E. Ringelblum, *op. cit.*; A. Sutzkever, *op. cit.*

PAGES 124-125

Gazeta Lwowska, Sept. 8, 9 and 11, 1941.

PAGE 125

About the converts in ghetto see *MF*.

The Szczebrzeszyn story was told in the diary of the Polish physician
Zygmunt Klukowski, in *BFG*, vol. IV, No. 4.

The Siedlce story in M. Feinzilber, *op. cit.*

PAGES 125-126

The Gdowski story was narrated by Herman Adler in his poetical works
Ostra Brama (Ger.), Zürich, 1945, and *Gesaenge aus der Stadt des Todes*
(Ger.), Zürich–N. Y., 1945. The Szczucin story was recorded in the
Inter-Allied Review, No. 3, March 1941.

PAGE 126

The Catholic rescue offer to the three rabbis of Warsaw was reported
by Hillel Seidman, in *MZ*, Feb. 2, and 4, 1947; Marian Zhyd, in *Forward*,
March 1, 1947; *MF*.

PAGES 126-127

The help and sympathy of Polish labor was recorded at some length in
B. Goldstein, *op. cit.*; Pinkhas Schwartz, in *Der Veker*, May 1, 1946
(particularly the help given to two leaders of the Jewish Socialist Bund
by the Polish lawyer Joseph Stopnicki and the actress Lena Zelwerowicz); see also the same writer's article about Tomasz Arciszewski (a
leader of the PPS, and later Prime Minister of the Polish Government
in Exile), in *Unzer Tsayt*, Dec. 1955. About other Socialist leaders see:

M. Neustadt, *op. cit.*, vol. I; S. Korbonski, *op. cit.* About the help of the Socialist Fighting Organization and Jewish participation in its units see: R. Gerber, in *BFG*, vol. I, No. 2, 1948; S. Korbonski, *op. cit.*

PAGES 127-128

The Pluskowski story was told by I. Shmulevich, in *Forward*, Sept. 21, 1951. About the alleged Communist help to Jews and particularly to the Jewish Fighters' Organization in Warsaw see: *Tsum tsentn yortog....*; R. Gerber, in *BFG*, vol. I, No. 2, 1948; Sz. Zachariasz, *Jozef Lewartowski* (*Yid.*), Warsaw, 1953; Sz. Zachariasz and B. Mark, (ed.) *PPR in kamf un boy* (The Polish Workers Party in Fight and in Construction, *Yid.*), Warsaw, 1952; also *BFG*, vol. IV, No. 3, 1951; M. Tenenbaum-Tamaroff, *op. cit.* (about the promised Communist help to the Jewish youth movement *Dror* which proved to be a failure and ended in disaster).

PAGE 128

About the Kazimierz Kot group see B. Mark, in *BFG*, vol. IV, No. 1, 1951.

PAGES 128-129

The story of Szymek, of "Grab" Widerkowski, Hil Grynszpan and Dr. Skotnicki is recorded in J. Turkow, *op. cit.*, vol. II, and is also based on my interview with Dr. Michael Temczyn (Temchin), now in Florida, N. Y. Dr. Temczyn organized a partisan unit in the woods near Lublin. When the partisan movement gained strength and reorganized into the Polish People's Army, Dr. Temczyn was appointed chief physician and organized its sanitary and medical services. He was very popular with the Polish and Jewish partisans as well as with the peasants under the nickname Major "Znakhor" (the Witch-Doctor).

CHAPTER TEN
Eastern Europe

PAGE 130

About the *Einsatzgruppen* and their activities in Eastern Europe at large see *Trials of War Criminals before the Nuremberg Military Tribunals Under Control Council Law No. 10*, Washington, D. C., 1945–1949, vol. IV (The Einsatzgruppen Case). Also J. Tenenbaum, *Race and Reich*; G. Reitlinger, *op. cit.*; Ph. Friedman, in *Vitebsk amol* (*Yid.*), N. Y., 1956.

PAGE 131

For statistics of Jews in the Soviet areas in the years 1939-1945 see: Solomon Schwarz, *Jews in the Soviet Union*, Syracuse, 1951.

PAGE 132

About Ukrainian-German relations during World War II see: Ihor Kamenetzky, *Hitler's Occupation of Ukraine*, 1941–1945, Milwaukee, Wis., 1956, with an extensive bibliography on this subject. About the S.S. Division *Halychyna* see: Basil Dmytryshyn, in *The American Slavic and East European Review*, vol. XV, 1956; "The Galician S.S. Division" in *WLB*, vol. IV, Nos. 5-6, 1950. For the Ukrainian viewpoint on Ukrainian-Jewish relations see: Lev Dobriansky, in *The Ukrainian Quarterly*, vol. V, No. 2, 1949 and Volodymir Doroshenko, in *Ohnishche ukrainskoy nauki* (The Center of Ukrainian Scholarship, *Ukr.*), Philadelphia, 1951; Ivan Kedryn, in *Svoboda*, New Jersey, Oct. 4, 1951. From the Jewish viewpoint see: Joseph L. Lichten, in *The Annals of the Ukrainian Academy of Arts and Sciences in the U. S.*, vol. V, Nos. 2-3, 1956.

PAGES 133-136

About Metropolitan Sheptytsky see: I. B[uchko]., *Velykyy chernets i narodolubets* (A Great Churchman and Patriot, *Ukr.*), Prudentopol, Brazil, 1949 (?); Stepan Baran, *Mytropolyt Andrey Sheptytsky* (*Ukr.*), Munich, 1947; Gregor Prokoptschuck, *Der Metropolit* (*Ger.*), Munich, 1955. Kurt Levin, now in the U. S., told the story of his own rescue and that of about 150 other Jews by the Metropolitan in his book, *Aliti mi 'Spezzia* (I Left from Spezzia for Israel, *Heb.*), Tel Aviv, 1946 and later elaborated upon it in more detail in his article in the English section of *Svoboda*, Jan., 1954. The story of Rabbi D. Kahane, now army chaplain in Israel, was told in his memoirs (non-published) and interviews with this writer, as well as in his article in *Undzer Veg (Yid.)*, Paris, Sept. 17, 1948; also in S. Samet, *op. cit.*; L. Leneman, in *Kanader Odler*, Oct. 12, 1949.

An interesting sidelight on the attitude of Metropolitan Sheptytsky is given by a German Foreign Office agent, Dr. Frederic, who was sent by his superiors on a tour through various Nazi-occupied and satellite countries to get the reaction of the population and of leading personalities toward the Germans. In his confidential report, Berlin, Sept. 19, 1943, to the German Foreign Office he discusses his meetings in Lwow with the Ukrainian leaders and Metropolitan Sheptytsky. The Metropolitan frankly told him of his disapproval of the inhuman treatment of the Jews by the Nazis and blamed them for killing 100,000 Jews in Lwow and several millions in the Ukraine. One Ukrainian boy, said the Metropolitan, told him at confession that he killed 75 Jews during one night. Dr. Frederic tried to counter Sheptytsky's charges with the usual Nazi arguments against Jews. Sheptytsky remained adamant in his statement that the killing of the Jews was an inadmissible act. To this description Frederic adds his own comment: "In this issue the Metropolitan made the same statements and even used the same phrasing as the French, Belgian and Dutch bishops, as if all of them were receiving the same instructions from the Vatican." (Document No. CXLV, a-60, in the Archives of the Centre de Documentation Juive in Paris). There are many records about simple Ukrainian people, peasants, housemaids, workmen, who saved or helped Jews. See: *Sefer Ratne (Yid.)*, Buenos Aires, 1954; Ada Eber-Friedman, in *Nasza Trybuna*, Nos. 109-118, N. Y., 1949-1950; *Yalkut Volhyn*, *op. cit.*, vol. II, 11; *Brody*, Jerusalem, 1956; S. Szende, *The Promise Hitler Kept*, N. Y., 1945; G. Taffet, *op. cit.*; Ilya Ehrenburg, *Merder fun felker* (Murderers of Nations, *Yid.*), 1944; *Pinkas Byten;* Vasyl Mudriy, in *Svoboda*, March 3, 1955 notes many instances of Ukrainian rescue activities. Petro Pik-Piasetskiy, in *Svoboda*, Apr. 9, 1953, notes the following interesting figures: In the Peremyslany county in Eastern Galicia, comprised of four small townships and thirty-six villages and surrounded by big forests, many Jews escaped to the woods and formed several armed groups. They were supported by the forest supervisors, seven of them Ukrainians and one Pole, and the forest superintendents, among them twenty-eight Ukrainians and four Poles. In one of the forest regions, particularly suitable for hiding, 1,500 Jews found shelter. In three other regions less suitable for hiding, about 200 Jews lived. The foresters kept the Jews informed of raids and movements of the Gestapo and the German police, and provided them with food and weapons. Accounts of Jewish survivors corroborate the fact that large Jewish groups hid in the "Black Forest" of Peremyslany, particularly in the forest of Jaktoriv. The German administration was aware that a number of Jews was sheltered by Ukrainian peasants. In a confidential report sent to Berlin by the S.S. and *Polizeifuehrer* in the Gouvernement General, dated Oct. 7, 1943, it was stated that "in the district of Galicia the number of trial proceedings against non-Jews guilty of hiding Jews recently increased." In the Ukrainian resistance movement, both of the nationalist and leftist brands, were few Jews. Close cooperation existed between the Jewish youth underground organization in Brody and a Leftist Ukrainian underground group in Lwow, which helped organize a unit of about 120 Jewish partisans in a forest near Brody and supplied them with weapons. The story of the Brody group and its fighting encounters with the Germans is told in B. Eisenstein, *op. cit.*; T. Brustin-Berenstein, in *BFG*, vol. IV, No. 3, 1953, and in the official report of the police and S.S. Chief for the District of Galicia, General Fritz Katzman, *IMT*, vol. 37. Another interesting account of co-operation with a Nationalist Ukrainian resistance group was published in *Nasha meta (Ukr.)*, Nos. 44, 45, 48, Toronto, Nov. 27, Dec. 4, 24, 1954, by Dr. Stella Krenzbach, now in Israel, who was invited to enter the ranks of the UPA (Ukrainian Insurgent Army) as a physician and accepted the offer.

PAGE 136

About the Lithuanian pro-German partisans and their attitude toward Jews see: *IMT*, vol. 37 (Dr. Stahlecker's Report); the clandestine Polish report, not dated (probably early 1942), "The Extermination of Jews by Lithuanians," in the archives of Instytut Historji Najnowszej (Institute of Contemporary History) in Warsaw (copy in my archive). Also see: S. Kaczerginski, *op. cit.*

PAGES 137-138

The Lithuanian underground sources are quoted in S. Schwarz, *op. cit.* The Lithuanian help to Jews was discussed in a series of articles by L. Szalna, in *Nojienos*, a Lithuanian periodical in the U. S. The theses of Szalna's articles were challenged by a memo of *ADL* (The Anti-Defamation League of B'nai Brith, N. Y.) also published in *Nojienos*, Cf. A. Šimaite, in *Lite*, vol. I. About Lithuanian help to Jews see also

H. Abramovich, in *Yidishe Tsaytung*, Buenos Aires, Dec. 14, 1953.
PAGE 138
The Stokauskas story was told by P. Schwarz, in *Veker*, May 1, 1956;
also in the above mentioned article of Abramovich.
PAGE 139
The Rutkauskas story, in M. Dworzecki, *op. cit.*

PAGES 138-139
About the help of Lithuanian intellectuals see: M. Dworzecki, *op. cit.*;
A. Šimaite, in *Goldene Kayt* (*Yid.*), vol. VIII, 1951; the same, in *Dorem
Afrike* (*Yid.*), Feb., 1954 and in *Lite*, vol. I, also her letter of Aug. 30,
1955 to Dina Abramovich, N. Y. (in my archive). On the other hand,
Dr. S. Gringauz, in *JSS*, vol. XI, No. 1, 1949, tells of a different experience in Kaunas ghetto where attempts were made to establish relations with the Lithuanian clergy and intellectuals but with no success.
As for a Lithuanian appraisal of the situation, an article of R. Mironas,
professor of Kaunas University, published in the Lithuanian periodical *Taribu Lietuova*, Feb., 1945, reflects the feelings of frustration,
repentance and self-incrimination.

About Jankauskas see: Rachel Pupko-Krynski, in *YIVO Bleter*, vol.
XXX, No. 2, 1947. Prof. Movslovitch's story was told by A. Šimaite, in
Goldene Kayt.

Zelig Kalmanovitch's Diary, written originally in Hebrew, was published
in English in *YA*, vol. XIII, 1953, in Yiddish in *YIVO Bleter*, vol. XXXV,
1951.

The story of the peasant Thaddäus and his wife was recorded by Berl
Kahan, *op. cit.*
PAGE 140
About Bishop Rainis and the attitude of the Lithuanian clergy in Vilna
see: A. Šimaite's articles in *Goldene Kayt*, and in *Lite*, vol. I, and in
Litvisher Yid, Nos. 7-8, 1946; also H. Abramovich, *op. cit.*
PAGES 140-141
The Vidukle story in H. Abramovich, *op. cit.*; A. Sutzkever, *op. cit.*
About Vaitchkus and the priest Dambrauskas see: A. Šimaite, in *Lite*,
vol. I.
PAGE 141
About Latvia and Estonia see: The Stahlecker report in *IMT*, vol. 37;
also L. Poliakov, *Bréviaire* . . .

PAGE 141-142
About the attitude of the Belorussian population see: S. Schwarz,
op. cit.; L. Poliakov, *Bréviaire* . . . ; Ph. Friedman, in *Vitebsk*; Malka
Kelrich, *Tsurik tsum lebn* (Back to Life, *Yid.*), Munich, 1948; Shmuel
Borenstein, *Plugat Dr. Atlas* (The Unit of Dr. Atlas, *Heb.*), Tel Aviv,
1948; Hersh Smoliar, in *Minsker ghetto* (*Yid.*), Moscow, 1946; *Sepher
Baranovitch.* The friendly attitude of Lukashenia to his Jewish col-
leagues was recorded by Dr. Z. Levenbuk, in *Sepher Baranovitch.* The
Bulletin of the Borysov Relief Organization (*Yid.*), vol. I, No. 2, N. Y.,

Dec., 1945 mentions the priest Grigori Klebanow who saved sixty Jewish children. The testimony of S.S. officer Machol is quoted in Simon Datner's report on the trial of Machol, in *BFG*, vol. III, Nos. 3-4, 1950 and in B. Mark, *Bialystok*.

CHAPTER ELEVEN
"We Will Not Surrender the Jews"

PAGE 143
The situation of the Jews in Finland during World War II was dealt with by Joseph Wulf in *Kiyoum* (*Yid.*), Nos. 6-8, Paris, 1952; L. Poliakov and J. Wulf, *Das Dritte Reich und die Juden*, Berlin, 1955; Jacques Sabille, in *MJ*, Nos. 39, 40, 41, 1951.

This statement is quoted from Wipert von Bluecher, *Gesandter zwischen Diktatur und Demokratie*, Wiesbaden, 1951.

PAGE 144
About the anti-Jewish motions of the pro-Nazi groups see: J. Wulf in *Kiyoum*.

PAGES 145-148
Himmler's visit to Helsinki and his negotiations with the Finnish Government are described at length in Felix Kersten, *Totenkopf und Treue*, Hamburg, 1953; J. Sabille, in *MJ*, No. 39.

PAGE 145
A general profile and biography of Kersten, in J. Sabille, *MJ*, No. 39, and H. R. Trevor-Roper, in *Commentary*, April, 1957.

The problem of the German-Jewish refugees in Finland was discussed by I. Kovalski, in *Undzer Vort*, Paris, March 23, 1947; J. Tenenbaum, *Race and Reich*.

About Kivimaeki, see: J. Sabille, in *MJ*, No. 39.

PAGE 146
The story of how the Finnish Intelligence Service got hold of Himmler's file was disclosed by the chief of the wartime Finnish censorship, Prof. Kustaa Vilkuna, and told by a correspondent of the *Christian Science Monitor*, Dec. 24, 1954.

Witting's statement: "We will not surrender the Jews," is quoted by Kersten, *op. cit.*

PAGE 147
How the vessels for the eventual escape of Finland's Jews to Sweden were prepared by the Finnish government is told by D. Kula, in *Undzer Veg*, Paris, Dec. 17, 1948.

PAGES 147-148
About the few deportations and the Finnish opposition to it, see: I. A. Fisher, in *Zionistische Stimme* (*Yid.*), Paris, Nov. 18, 1948; "Keiner sollte ausgeliefert werden," in *Duesseldorfer Allgemeine Juedische Wochenzeitung* (*Ger.*), Jan. 14, 1955.

CHAPTER TWELVE
Miracle of the Exodus

PAGE 149

For the story of Denmark's Jews during World War II, see: Julius Moritzen, in *CJR*, May, 1940; interview with Dr. Max Weinreich, in *Forward*, March 27, 1940; Henrik de Kaufman, in *Jewish Ledger*, Springfield, Mass., Nov. 12, 1943; A. Russ, in *Mibafnim* (*Heb.*), vol. VII, Eyn Harod, 1941; B. Habas, in *Sepher Aliyat Hanoar*; H. G. Adler, in *WLB*, vol. IX, Nos. 1-2, 1955; J. Sabille, in *MJ*, No. 25, 1949; Per Moller, in *Un Peuple se reveille*, Lausanne, 1946 (?); *Fun noentn over*, vol. I.; Nella Rost, in *JE*; Francis Hacket, in *Milhamtenu* (*Heb.*), vol. III, No. 34, 1945; "Danish Red Sea" in *Newsweek*, Oct. 18, 1943; Hugo Valentin, in *YA*, vol. VIII, 1953; Aage Bertelsen, *October '43*, N. Y., 1954; Pinches Welner, *I nine Dage* (In Those Days, *Dan.*), Copenhagen, 1949.

PAGES 149-150

About King Christian X see: A. Bertelsen, *op. cit.* S. Berson, in *MJ*, May 30, 1946; *Eynikayt* (*Yid.*), Moscow, Oct. 28, 1943; J. Zylberberg, in *Tog*, Sept. 15, 1953. After King Christian's death a Jewish writer in Finland published a eulogy devoted to his memory, *Lo nishkakhekho, ha'melekh* (We will not forget you, o King, *Heb.* and *Yid.*), Helsinki, 1947. A photostat copy of King Christian's letter to the rabbi of Copenhagen is published in *Fun noentn over*, vol. I.

PAGES 150-151

Dr. W. Best's reports on the strong Danish opposition to any anti-Jewish action were published by J. Sabille, in *MJ*, No. 24, 1949. Dr. Best was sentenced to death in Oct. 1948 by a Danish court. An appeal court commuted the sentence to five years' imprisonment (*N. Y. Times*, July 19, 1949).

PAGES 151-152

About Moltke and Duckwitz see: E. Boehm, *op. cit.*; H. Rothfels, *op. cit.*; A. Bertelsen, *op. cit.* Ph. Friedman, in *YA*, vol. X; *A German of the Resistance, Last Letters of Count H. J. Moltke*, London, 1946.

PAGE 152

For a detailed account of the Henriques story see: A. Bertelsen, *op. cit.*; On Hans Hedtoft see: A. J. Fischer, in *Duesseldorfer Allgemeine Juedische Wochenzeitung*, March 4, 1955 and J. Zylberberg, in *MZ*, Feb. 8, 1955.

About Swedish interventions on behalf of the Jews see: J. Sabille, in *MJ*, No. 26, 1949; H. Valentin, in *YA*, vol. X, and in *MJ*, No. 37; S. Nathan, in *Tog*, Feb. 20, 1950.

PAGES 153-154

The Gildeby story was told by I. Trotzky, in *Tog*, May 13, 1950.

A. Bertelsen, *op. cit.*; S. Nathan, in *Tog*, Feb. 20, 1950.

PAGE 153

About the saving of the Torah scrolls see: A. Bertelsen, *op. cit.*; Hayim Ehrenreich, in *Forward*, Feb. 7, 1954.

PAGE 154

The activities of the Lyngby group were described by its leader A. Bertelsen, *op. cit.* We supplemented this report by personal interviews with Mr. and Mrs. A. Bertelsen. Besides this, during their visit in New York, in 1954, the Bertelsens were interviewed by various newsmen. See: Leon Krystol, in *Forward*, May 15, 1954; Hayim Ehrenreich, in *Forward*, March 4, 1954; B. Shefner, in *Forward*, Dec. 11, 1954.

PAGES 154-155

The B. Aaudze story was told by Hayim Ehrenreich, in *Forward*, Apr. 11, 1954.

PAGES 155-156

Peter Freuchen, *Vagrant Viking*, N. Y., 1953. See also S. L. Shneiderman, in *Tog-MZ*, Jan. 17, 25 and Feb. 6, 1954.

PAGE 156

About Boxenius see: I. Levanon, in *Davar* (*Heb.*), May 5, 1950, and Aaron Zeitlin, in *Tog-MZ*, Feb. 17, 1956.

PAGE 157

The V. J. Rasmussen story was recorded by Monty Jacobs, in *The Jerusalem Post*, May 3, 1950.

PAGE 158

From the several hundred deported Jews, 466 arrived in Theresienstadt, where they were given preferential treatment and received many parcels from Danish families of all rank beginning with the royal family. Fifty-two of the Danish Jews died in Theresienstadt while the rest, thanks to Danish diplomatic efforts, were released to Sweden before the end of the war. The number of Danish Jews in Sweden totalled 5,919 "full Jews," 1,301 "half-Jews," and 686 non-Jews married to Jews. After the war the Danish-Jewish refugees in Sweden returned to their country. The welcome these Jewish repatriates received was very moving. This warm reception was described, *inter alia*, by P. Berman, in *Forward*, May 26, 1953 and H. Valentin, in *YA*, vol. VIII.

The famous Danish writer Karin Michaelis, in the U. S. since 1939, continued her varied rescue activities for Nazi refugees, especially Jewish, which she had begun in Europe. She also wrote a dramatic play about Jewish suffering under the Nazi regime in Denmark and about their escape to Sweden. See: J. Zylberberg, in *Tog*, Dec. 9, 1950.

CHAPTER THIRTEEN

Raoul Wallenberg: Hero of Budapest

PAGES 159-167

Although the fascinating story of Raoul Wallenberg has been recorded in many books and articles, there is still a great amount of mystery about various aspects of his daring venture. The reader will find additional details about Wallenberg's life and activities in the following books and articles: Rudolf Philipp, *Raoul Wallenberg, Diplomat, Kaempe, Samarit (Swed.)*, Stockholm, 1946; Jenö Levai, *R. Wallenberg (Hung.)*, Budapest, 1948; the same, *BB*; Lars G. Berg, *Vad hande i Budapest* (What Occurred in Budapest, *Swed.*), Stockholm, 1949; R. Wallace, in *Reader's Digest*, July, 1947; J. Sabille, in *MJ*, Nos. 26 and 27, 1950, and in *Figaro Litteraire*, Sept. 27, 1951; H. Valentin, in *YA*, vol. VIII; Frederic von Dardel, in *Aufbau*, Jan. 24, 1947; Kurt Juster, in *Aufbau*, Jan. 11, 1952; Alexandre Grossman, in *Évidences*, vol. VI, No. 45, Paris, 1955; I. Shmulevich, in *Forward*, Feb. 16, 19 and 21, 1952, and in June 26, 1955; H. Vital, in *Forward*, Jan. 19, 29, 1947; Joseph Galay, in *Kanader Odler*, Sept. 26, 1954; J. Sabille, *Lueurs dans la tourmente*, Paris, 1956.

CHAPTER FOURTEEN

Felix Kersten and Folke Bernadotte

Pages 168-170

About the Swedish and Norwegian assistance to Jews in general see: H. Valentin, on *YA*, vol. I, VIII; Nella Rost, in *JE*; Per Moeller and Knud Secher, *Danske flyktlinge i Sverige (Dan.)*, Copenhagen, 1945. About the activities of Gustav V of Sweden on behalf of the Jews, see H. Valentin, in *MJ*, No. 37, 1950; I. Trotzky, in *Tog*, Nov. 2, 1950. About the attitude of the Swedish government and population see: Kurt Wilhelm, Chief Rabbi of Stockholm, in *Reconstructionist*, Jan. 26, 1951; J. Sabille, in *MJ*, No. 26, 1949 and No. 27, 1950; Joseph Goebbels in his memoirs, *op. cit.*, deplores the vigorous Swedish protests against the persecution of the Jews. See also: H. Vital, in *Forward*, Feb. 20, 1947; A. Zeitlin, *MZ*, Aug. 8, 1950.

Pages 169-170

The Fight of the Norwegian Church Against Nazism, N. Y., 1943; the full text of the letter of protest of the Norwegian Church organizations against the persecution of Jews was published in the *Inter-Allied Review*, vol. II, No. 12, Dec., 1942.

About the deportations of Norwegian Jews to Auschwitz and about the rescue activities in Norway, see: J. Sabille, in *MJ*, No. 27; N. Rost, in *JE*; H. Valentin, in *YA*, vol. VIII; Helen Astrup and B. L. Jacot, *Oslo Intrigue: A Woman's Memoir of the Norwegian Resistance*, N. Y., 1954.

Odd Nansen published his diary first in Norwegian and then in an abbreviated English version, *From Day to Day*, N. Y., 1949. Norway's hospitality for the sick Jewish survivors of the Nazi holocaust was described in many articles, such as Marian Zhyd, in *Forward*, May 25, 1953.

Felix Kersten wrote two books about his dealings with Himmler in which he devoted much space to the Jewish problem: *The Memoirs of*

Dr. Felix Kersten, Garden City, 1947, and *Totenkopf und Treue*. In the second book are many photostatic copies of his letters to Himmler and other Nazi personalities, Himmler's letters to him, letters of the Swedish section of the World Jewish Congress corroborating Kersten's story, etc. See also the documents published in *MJ*, Nos. 39 and 40, 1951.

PAGES 172-173

See: F. Kersten, *Totenkopf und Treue; Unity in Dispersion*, N. Y., 1948; H. Valentin, in *YA*, vol. VIII; the interview with Hillel Storch, in *Dos Vort* (*Yid.*), Munich, Nov. 17, 1947.

PAGE 174

Folke Bernadotte recorded his negotiations with Himmler, in *Slutet*, Stockholm, 1945, published in English translation under the title *The Curtain Falls*, N. Y., 1945. Biographies of Bernadotte were published by Ralph Hewins, *Count Folke Bernadotte: His Life and Work*, Minneapolis, 1950 and by Sven Svenson, *Graf Bernadotte* (*Ger.*), Basel, 1953.

About the negotiations in Budapest between Rudolf Kasztner and Adolf Eichmann see notes to Chapter Six.

PAGE 175

Quoted from Bernadotte's, *The Curtain Falls*.

Norbert Masur published his account of these negotiations in a small pamphlet in Swedish, *En jude talar med Himmler*, Stockholm, 1945, available also in Yiddish translation in *Fun Joentn over*, vol I. See also the interview with Masur by Abraham Shulman, in *Forward*, March 8, 1956; also in *MJ*, No. 41, 1951, and Nora Finzi, in *Il Mondo*, Feb. 8, 1955.

PAGES 170-179

In his article in *The Atlantic Monthly*, vol. CXCI, No. 2, Feb., 1953, the English historian, H. R. Trevor-Roper, challenged the evaluation of Bernadotte's outstanding role in rescuing the Jews and emphasized Kersten's part in the rescue scheme. See the comments of David Flinker, in his article, in *Tog-MZ*, March 15, 1953. Against Trevor-Roper's thesis the Archives Department of the Swedish Foreign Office published a kind of a "White Paper": Kungl. Utrikesdepartementet, *1945 ars Svenska Hjälpexpedition till Tyskland*, Stockholm, 1956, based on an investigation of a great number of documents in the Swedish Foreign Office, the Swedish Embassy in Berlin, the archives of the Swedish Red Cross, the private archives of Count Bernadotte, interviews with the former Swedish ambassador to Berlin, the former Swedish foreign minister, Mr. Guenther and others. The Swedish "White Paper" gives a detailed historical background of the Swedish interventions in Germany on behalf of the deported Scandinavians and Jews, and attributes to Count Bernadotte the central role in the rescue activities. The Swedish paper is in general critical of Trevor-Roper's article and of Kersten's memoirs, asserting that he was useful but the role he attributes to himself in the negotiations with Himmler is exaggerated.

INDEX

POSTSCRIPT

A tribute was paid in New York to Christians who aided Jews in the dark days of Hitler's Europe on November 6, 1957. The Anti-Defamation League of B'nai B'rith dedicated a bronze plaque in memory of "the Christian heroes who helped their Jewish brethren escape the Nazi terror," in a ceremony attended by top diplomats from eight European countries and by American religious and secular leaders.

The plaque designed by the famous sculptor Domenico Facci was unveiled by Madame Marie-Helene Lefaucheux, a member of the French delegation to the General Assembly of the United Nations, a Chevalier of the Legion of Honor, who was awarded the Croix de Guerre and the Rosette of the Resistance. During the German occupation of France, she was assistant to Father Chaillet, a Jesuit priest who saved hundreds of Jewish children from the Nazis. Many other heroes of the resistance, as well as Jewish survivors and their rescuers, were among the two hundred persons participating in the celebration.

At the ceremony, Dr. Philip Friedman presented his book, *Their Brothers' Keepers*, to the guests of honor. The volume is the first documented and permanent record of Christian aid to Jews during the Hitler era. It is based on meticulously researched material, eyewitness accounts of individual deeds of mercy and sacrifice, first-hand reports, personal letters, official documents, diaries and memoirs. The author spent ten years unearthing this important information, from many languages. The numerous pages of "Notes and References," appended to the text, show he relied only on established and corroborated, factual material.

The memory of the brave and noble deeds of those Christian humanitarians, who risked their lives and personal safety to help Jews during the tragic years of the Hitler era, deserve to be recorded in the annals of the Jewish people.

The existence of that small army of valorous Christians, who opened their hearts and homes to the people marked for extinction by the Nazis, has helped to restore our faith in human decency and justice.

A very special way to commemorate the rescuers of Jews was initiated by the Yad Vashem, the official Martyrs' and Heroes' Remembrance Authority, in Jerusalem. The Martyrs' and Heroes' Remembrance Law (Yad Vashem 5713-1953) provides that "We shall remember and honor the Righteous Gentiles, who risked their lives for the rescue of Jews."

The "Avenue of the Righteous" (*Sderot Hassidei Umot Ha'olam*) was established on the Mount of Remembrance in Jerusalem to implement this portion of the Law. In an inspiring ceremony, on May 1, 1962, the first ten trees were planted by Ten Just Persons who had helped Jews during the Holocaust. Each tree has a plaque bearing the name of the rescuer and his country. The trees serve as a symbol of the gratitude of the Jewish people to their non-Jewish saviors.

A Public Committee for the Commemoration of the "Righteous Gentiles" was organized in 1963. A special department was created to collect material on Gentiles active in the rescue of Jews during the years of annihilation.

The Commission for the Designation of the Righteous

has established criteria for the granting of the honored title, "Righteous Among the Nations." Those chosen are also awarded Yad Vashem's highest distinction, the Medal of Honor, inscribed with the Talmudic saying: "Whoever saves one life is as though he has saved the whole world."

The Avenue of the Righteous counted 120 trees planted up to the year 1966, and over 900 by the year 1974. Hundreds of cases are still waiting for approval by the Commission for the Just.

It is our moral duty to recognize with gratitude those fearless men and women who dared to defy the Nazi terror and rushed to the aid of the condemned Jews. Their inspiring tales of rescue should be brought to light as long as there are still living survivors who can verify them.

Philip Friedman was the first historian of the Holocaust to realize the urgency of such an undertaking. His book, *Their Brothers' Keepers,* is the result of the enormous task of gathering and organizing accounts of individual acts of heroism.

At the book dedication ceremony on November 6, 1957, Dr. Friedman made the following remarks: ". . . After the Nazi Holocaust many of us were plagued by doubts and anxiety about the direction which, as it seemed, mankind was taking. We wondered if all the enlightened centuries spent in the development of humanism and the fundamentals of religion had been in vain — all erased from human hearts and mind. For me, therefore, it was a great consolation to be able to bring to light hundreds of facts and episodes testifying to the contrary . . . The individual tales presented in the book emphasize that, in spite of the horror of that period, the ideals of humanity have not been forgotten nor were they eliminated from the human heart. . . ."

Eleanor Roosevelt, in a letter to Dr. Friedman dated October 1, 1957, wrote about *Their Brothers' Keepers*: "... I would just like to tell you that I found it inspiring reading ... I have come through with a feeling that if all of us had the courage to protest immediately when we felt something was wrong, we could perhaps prevent the tragedies as Hitler brought about ... I am glad you wrote this book and I congratulate you."

Twenty years have passed since *Their Brothers' Keepers* was published. Dr. Friedman was preparing a new and enlarged edition when he died in February 1960. Since then, a great number of books, memoirs, articles and studies on the Holocaust have been published. Most touch upon the relations between Jews and non-Jews in countries the Nazis occupied or dominated. New information about aid rendered to Jews by Gentiles, individuals or groups, can be found in many of them. Numerous documents are still scattered in private letters, diaries, unpublished memoirs and archives of research institutes.

It would be futile to attempt supplementing the appended "Notes and References" of *Their Brothers' Keepers* with new and relevant material. The interested reader can resort to the available bibliographies and specialized periodicals for guidance and information on the current state of documentation of the Holocaust period.

Especially useful are the *Bibliographical Series*, issued jointly by the Yad Vashem Martyrs' and Heroes' Memorial Authority in Jerusalem and the YIVO Institute for Jewish Research in New York. Since the publication, in 1960, of the first volume, *Guide to Jewish History Under the Nazi Impact*, edited by Jacob Robinson and Philip Friedman, eleven volumes have been published. The latest volume is *The Holocaust and After: Sources and Literature in English*, edited by Jacob Robinson, with the assistance of Mrs. Philip

Friedman, 1973. Part Five of this book, "The Non-Jewish World and the Holocaust," lists over 500 bibliographical sources, including a chapter on help and rescue by non-Jews.

Among the vast number of books on the Holocaust, there is a dearth of documented accounts of Christian aid to Jews, especially in the English language. It is of the utmost importance to fill the gap by assembling and publishing all the records of courage and compassion, as a lasting tribute to those selfless humanitarians who were willing to sacrifice their lives for justice and a belief in the dignity of man.

Dr. Ada Eber-Friedman

UPDATED BIBLIOGRAPHY

Bartoszewski, Wladyslaw and Zofia Lewin, eds. *Righteous Among Nations. How Poles Helped the Jews 1939-1945*. London: Earlscourt, 1969, 834 p. American edition: *The Samaritans. Heroes of the Holocaust*. New York: Twayne Publishers, 1970.

An expanded version of the Polish original: *Ten jest z ojczyzny mojej* (He Is My Fellow Countryman), Krakow: Znak, 1967. Thorough documentation. Introductory treatise by Wladyslaw Bartoszewski, titled: *On Both Sides of the Wall* (published also separately).

The Polish original reviewed by Alexander Donat: "Their Brothers' Polish Keepers," *Midstream*, April 1968, pp. 69-74.

Bartoszewski, Wladyslaw. *The Blood Shed United Us. Pages from the History of Help to Jews in Occupied Poland*. Warsaw: Interpress Publ., 1970, 243 p., illus.

Bauminger, Arieh L. *The Roll of Honour*. Jerusalem: Yad Vashem (auspices), 1970, 95 p., illus.

Sketches of 24 case histories of "Righteous People" from various countries. List of about 350 names, arranged alphabetically by countries of origin of those, who up to 1969 have been awarded the Yad Vashem Medal of Honor. Photographs of rescuers, survivors, presentations of awards.

Berenstein, Tatiana and Adam Rutkowski. *Assistance to the Jews in Poland 1939-1945*. Translated from the Polish. Warsaw: Polonia, 1963, 82 p., illus.

Boom, Corrie. *A Prisoner and Yet*. New York: Pyramid Books (by arrangement with Christian Literature Crusade Inc.), 1971, 176 p.

(Rescue in Netherlands)

Chary, Frederick B. *The Bulgarian Jews and the Final Solution, 1940-1944*. U. of Pittsburgh Press, 1972, 246 p.

Flender, Harold. *Rescue in Denmark*. New York: Simon and Schuster, 1963, 281 p. Also in paperback, 1968.

Friedman, Philip. Was there An "Other Germany" During the Nazi Period?

Reprinted from *YIVO Annual of Jewish Sciences*, X, 1955: 52-127.

Grossman, Kurt D. *Die unbesungenen Helden. Menschen in Deutschlands dunklen Tagen/ (The Unsung Heroes. People in Germany's Dark Days).* Berlin, Arani Verlag, 1958, 388 p.
  A most valuable account of aid to Jews under the Nazis. (The book appeared only in German). Reviewed by Gerhard Jacoby in *Congress Weekly*, Oct. 27, 1958: 13-14.

Hirschmann, Ira A. *Caution to the Winds.* New York: McKay, 1962, 312 p.
  (Rescue of Jews during World War II.)

Horbach, Michael. *Out of the Night.* Translated from the German. London: Vallentine, Mitchell, 1968, xi, 261 p.
  (Eleven true episodes of help rendered by Germans. Interviews with survivors.)

Iranek-Osmecki, Kazimierz. *He Who Saves One Life. A Documented Story of the Poles Who Struggled to Save the Jews During World War II.* Preface by Joseph L. Lichten New York: Crown, 1972, 329 p.

Kessel, Joseph. *The Man with the Miraculous Hands.* Translated from the French. New York: Farrar, Strauss and Cudahy, 1961, xiii, 235 p.
  (Felix Kersten)

Lazar, Albert P. *Innocents Condemned to Death. Chronicles of Survival.* New York: William Frederick Press, 1961, 97 p.
  (Hungary. Persecution of Jews. Help by a group of people.)

Leber, Annedore, et al. *Conscience in Revolt. Sixty Four Stories of Resistance in Germany 1939-1945.* Translated from the German. Westport, Conn.: Associated Book Sellers, 1957, xxvi, 270 p., illus.

Leboucher, Fernande. *Incredible Mission.* Translated from the French. Garden City, New York: Doubleday, 1969, 165 p.
  (Père Marie-Bénoit, the rescuer of Jews)

Leuner, Heinz David. *When Compassion was a Crime. German Silent Heroes 1933-1945.* Translated from the German. London: Oswald Wolff, 1966, 164 p.

Melchior, Marcus. *A Rabbi Remembers.* Translated from the Danish. New York: Lyle Stuart, 1968, 256 p.

Papanek, Ernst and Edward Linn. *Out of the Fire.* New York: Morrow, 1975, 299 p.
  (The role of OSE in saving Jewish children)

Snoek, Johan M. *The Gray Book*. A Collection of Protests against Anti-Semitism and the Persecution of Jews Issued by Non-Roman Catholic Churches and Church Leaders during Hitler's Rule. Introduction by Uriel Tal. Assen: Van Gorcum, 1969, 315 p., bibliogr.

Yahil, Leni. *The Rescue of Danish Jewry. Test of a Democracy.* Translated from the Hebrew. Philadelphia: Jewish Publication Society, 1969, 536 p.

Saving of the Jews In Bulgaria 1941-1944. Photo-Album. State Publishing House, Sept. 1977, Bulgaria.

Hallie, Philip P. *Lest Innocent Blood Be Shed*. The Story of the Village of Le Chambon and How Goodness Happened There. (Harper & Row. 1977. $12.95.)

How a tiny Protestant town in southeastern France harbored Jews successfully during World War II.